Shackleton W9-CFQ-535

SHACKLETON

His Antarctic writings selected
and introduced by

Christopher Ralling

ARIEL BOOKS
BRITISH BROADCASTING CORPORATION

The BBC Television series *Shackleton* was written by Christopher Ralling, produced by John Harris and directed by Martyn Friend. Maggie Stevens was Production Assistant, Mark Williams Assistant Floor Manager, Michael Treen Production Manager, and Nicholas Mallett Production Associate. The main characters were played as follows:

Sir Ernest Shackleton David Schofield; *Frank Wild* David Rodigan; *Cmnd. Frank Worsley* John Watts; *Frank Hurley* Peter Dahlsen; *Thomas Crean* John Flanagan; *Harry McNeish* Leonard Maguire; *Percy Blackborrow* John Wheatley; *Captain R. F. Scott* Neil Stacy; *Dr Edward Wilson* Paul Hastings; *Emily Shackleton* Victoria Fairbrother

Published by the British Broadcasting Corporation
35 Marylebone High Street,
London W1M 4AA

First published 1983
First paperback edition 1985

ISBN 0 563 20438 9

Set in 10 on 11 Linotron Ehrhardt
by Phoenix Photosetting, Chatham and printed
in England by Mackays of Chatham Limited

CONTENTS

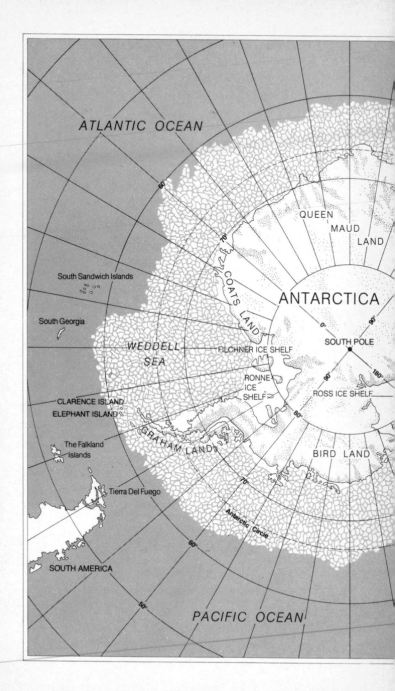

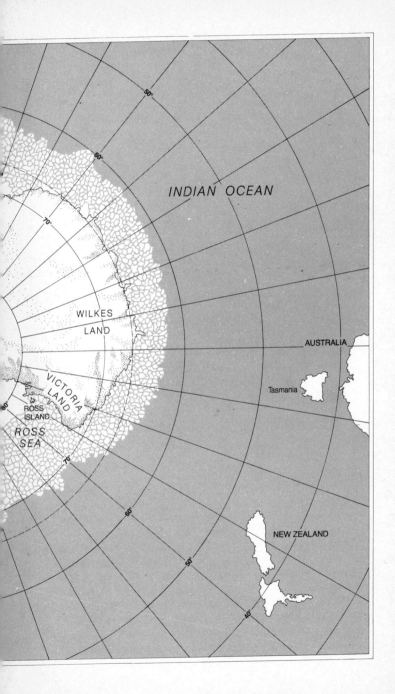

For Jo

INTRODUCTION

by Christopher Ralling

This book is neither a biography nor an autobiography. For the former the reader should turn to James and Margery Fisher's excellent and very full account of Shackleton's life, published in 1957. The latter, unfortunately, does not exist. Had he lived to a mellow old age, Shackleton might one day have turned to the task of writing his own reminiscences. As it was, he died of a heart attack at the age of forty-seven, on the point of setting out once more for the icy wastes of the Antarctic that were his passion and his life.

What remains of his writing are letters, diaries, newspaper articles, some poetry and of course the published volumes which tell the story of his two famous expeditions: *Heart of the Antarctic*, and *South*. This book is a selection from all these sources, which have never previously been collected together in a single volume. The linking passages that I have added are designed to serve two purposes; to fill in the gaps, so that the reader will have a clearer idea of the overall pattern of his life; and also to throw light on some events in the story where he does himself less than justice, or avoids an issue altogether, rather than ruffle the feathers of his contemporaries.

Official accounts of expeditions, while they have their own fascination, also suffer from limitations. In the first place they are designed to be handbooks for the benefit of others who might later tread similar paths. In consequence, they are packed with information about diet, clothing, the design of sledges and tents, the merits of single sleeping bags as compared with the 'three-in-a-bed' variety, and so on. For the purposes of the present volume, enough has been retained to catch the flavour of all this, but much has been omitted, since it tends to clog the narrative, and was never really intended for the general reader.

Another of the shortcomings of 'official' accounts of expeditions, written in Shackleton's day, was the practice of playing down personal relationships. He writes endlessly about the quirks and habits, most of them thoroughly annoying and disagreeable, which made the little Manchurian ponies such individual characters, but very little in similar vein about his human companions. It seems to me that the 'authorised version' of an expedition sometimes resembles the end of a Christmas party for the very young. All those tears and tantrums never really happened; and everyone gets sent home with a present of roughly equal value. Though not a great respecter of tradition in other ways, Shackleton had too generous a nature to break this particular taboo. But at this distance in time, I think we are entitled to break it for him. Now that the protagonists have left the stage, it seems to me important that we should know rather more than Shackleton himself was prepared to put into words about his likes and dislikes, foibles and frustrations. With a little extra knowledge on the part of the reader, his own writings immediately take on a new vividness.

Times have changed. Many of today's expedition leaders, most notably perhaps Chris Bonington, recognise the fact that the borderline between discretion and distortion can be a very narrow one. Today, not only do they write in a much more uninhibited fashion about their adventures, but they also invite reporters and film crews to accompany them.

I had the good fortune to be a member of the BBC film team which accompanied the British Everest Expedition in 1975. On that occasion we persuaded Chris Bonington to carry a miniaturised personal tape recorder of very high quality, which he used every evening to record his private thoughts and feelings. As a result, his very words spoken at the time, sometimes at moments of crisis and stress, at others in more contemplative vein, formed part of the commentary to the film, giving it an immediacy and honesty probably unobtainable in any other way.

Shackleton and his contemporaries had no such electronic luxuries. For them it was the painful chore of the daily diary and the pencil gripped in icy fingers. Considering the conditions under which they wrote, suffering at intervals from frostbite, snow blindness and starvation, one can only marvel at the dogged perseverance of these wilderness diarists. And marvel too at the beauty and power of some of the writing. On 13 November 1908, after many miles of sledging on half rations, and at sub-zero temperatures, Shackleton described the day in his diary like this:

> The whole place and conditions seem so strange and so unlike anything in the world in our experience, that one cannot describe them in fitting words. At one moment one thinks of Coleridge's 'Ancient Mariner': 'Alone, alone, all all alone, alone on a wide wide sea', and then when the mazy clouds spring silently from either hand and drift quickly across our zenith, not followed by any wind it seems uncanny. There comes a puff of wind from the north, another from the south, and anon one from the east or west, seeming to obey no law, acting on erratic impulses. It is as though we were truly at the world's end, and were bursting in on the birthplace of the clouds and the nesting home of the four winds, and one has a feeling that we mortals are being watched with a jealous eye by the forces of nature.

Great leader of men and man of action that he was, at heart Shackleton was a romantic.

It remains for me to record my indebtedness to The Scott Polar Institute for their help, particularly with the selection of the pictures: to Lord Shackleton, who, with typical open-handed generosity, made papers in his possession available to me for as long as I wished; to Toby Roxburgh and Stephen Davies who steered the book towards completion with wisdom, precision and kindness; and above all to Margery Fisher, without whose pioneer work the present undertaking would have been impossible.

NOTE

Shackleton's spelling
This tended to be rather eccentric, especially in his personal correspondence. I have tidied it up occasionally, but only where it might otherwise be difficult to follow his meaning.

Technical terms
Shackleton uses very few words which are not in general use.

However the following short list of terms may not be familiar to the general reader.

Finnesko	Boots made from the skin of a reindeer, usually the head, with the fur on the outside.
Pemmican	A preparation of dried and pounded meat; usually of the best beef, with sixty per cent extra fat added.
Sastrugi	Wavelike irregularities on hard polar ice, caused by the action of the wind.
Sennegrass	Dried grass of long fibre with a special moisture-absorbing quality.

FOREWORD

by Christopher Ralling

What sort of an explorer was Ernest Shackleton? The task of pushing back the frontiers of geographical knowledge attracts very different kinds of men. At one end of the spectrum are those who, while far from mad, seem driven by some inner force or daemon, which sets them apart from their fellow men. In their very different ways, Richard Burton and David Livingstone were two of this sort. Each of them made solitary journeys deep into the heartland of Africa, often at the expense of their nearest and dearest, driven on by some inner compulsion which, for them, made the ordinary world a place of frustration.

At the other end of the spectrum one might place the modern astronaut. To go to the stars, it seems it is necessary to be as normal, indeed conformist as possible, preferably with one loving wife, two happy children and a house in some leafy suburb. (I am speaking of course of the American variety.) It is very hard to believe that either Burton or Livingstone would ever have survived the physical or mental selection process which sifts out today's astronauts.

As for Shackleton, I would place him somewhere in the middle of this imaginary spectrum. The son of a south London doctor, his training ground was the Merchant Navy. He was a staunch patriot, but not what we would now call an Establishment man. Indeed he thoroughly disliked, and succesfully rebelled against, the class-conscious clubbishness of the Royal Geographical Society as it was in his day. In this respect he was undoubtedly ahead of his time; and much more concerned than Scott to break down the social barriers between men engaged on identical tasks in the wilderness. Scott, with his Royal Navy background, ran his expeditions, as no doubt he ran his ships, with strict naval discipline and a clear division between officers and ratings.

Shackleton was not looking for respect. The one quality he demanded, and usually got, was loyalty. Either you were his man through and through; or you were not. And if ever that loyalty was withdrawn, for however short a period, he could be quite unforgiving. The carpenter Harry McNeish was to discover this on the long haul back to civilisation after the *Endurance* went down. For a few brief hours, under the strain of their plight, he succumbed to near-mutinous behaviour. Shackleton never forgot it; and even after the work he did modifying the *James Caird* for the perilous boat journey to South Georgia, which undoubtedly contributed to their salvation, and then acting as a member of the crew on that heroic voyage, McNeish was to find himself one of a handful from whom the Polar Medal was withheld.

Although he could, and did, drive himself very hard, Shackleton was not the fittest of men. His rugged physique concealed a heart murmur, which may well have been the cause of his physical breakdown while sledging with Scott and Wilson in 1903. It led eventually to his early death from a coronary thrombosis in 1922. But whatever he may have known about his own condition, he successfully concealed it from his men. They responded to his warmth and energy, his boyish good humour, and a buccaneering quality which characterised all his ventures. He was forever dreaming up new schemes to make his own fortune, and theirs.

But above all, it was a quality of leadership to which they all responded. Frank Wild, who had been on more Antarctic expeditions than anyone else living, called him 'the greatest leader of them all, bar none'. Nowadays leadership is rather out of favour, and the word itself somewhat devalued, suggesting the sort of thing you would expect to find on the curriculum at a military academy. The secret of Shackleton's leadership clearly sprang from his personality, and consequently died with him. Some of those who served with him have tried to define it, but somehow all their phrases, 'concern for his men', 'total confidence in his judgment', fall short of the quality itself, which all the men who came into contact with him experienced, and very few were prepared to denigrate. Whatever it was, it made him into a great man.

Shackleton himself came to regard his first venture to the Antarctic as a disaster. It proved to be a disaster which shaped his life.

The National Antarctic Expedition, more widely known today as the *Discovery* Expedition, was the brain child of Sir

Clements Markham, at that time President of the Royal Geographical Society. He was one of those imposing Victorian figures who commanded great respect and dispensed patronage like an eastern potentate. Markham was determined that the Expedition would be as much a Royal Naval one as he could make it, with his one protégé, a young naval officer called Robert Falcon Scott, as leader. When Shackleton applied to join he found that his Merchant Navy background was against him, but his experience with sailing ships finally won him a place.

In the first weeks of 1902, at the age of twenty-seven, he found himself heading south through the pack-ice for the first time. The course of his life was set. Almost from the first there seems to have been a feeling of strain between him and his leader. Scott was a reserved man who tended to keep aloof from his fellows. Shackleton, on the other hand, with his open nature and forceful personality, quickly became one of the most popular members of the team, as they shared a hut through the long dark months of winter.

The only man with whom Scott himself had a really close relationship was Edward Wilson; and when he saw Shackleton strike up a similar friendship, sharing Wilson's enthusiasm for poetry and evening strolls round the base, he may have felt excluded.

As soon as the daylight returned, and the sledging season began, a number of scientific programmes would be carried out. But everyone knew that the most important of these would be the Southern Journey; the first attempt to reach the South Pole itself. Scott had originally envisaged a party of two men with dogs. But Wilson persuaded him that three men could travel almost as lightly as two. If anyone fell ill, or met with an accident, the whole team would then stand a much better chance of surviving. In spite of a history of tuberculosis, Wilson had already been selected to go as doctor. Now Scott needed a third man to join the party. His choice fell on Shackleton. Whether he did it to please Wilson, or out of personal conviction, we shall never know. It was a decision he lived to regret, quite possibly for the rest of his life.

So it was that the three most famous names in British Antarctic history set off with a team of reluctant and inexperienced dogs for the unknown perils of the south.

The night before, Shackleton wrote a letter to Emily, the woman he was hoping to marry on his return. It was to be opened only if he failed to do so.

November 1st 1902

Beloved I hope you may never have to read this, but darling loved one if it comes to you, you will know that your lover left this world with all his heart yours my last thoughts will be of you my own Heart, Child I am carrying your little photo with me South and so your face will be with me to the last; Child remember that I am your true lover, that you and you alone have been in my heart and mind all this time. Beloved do not grieve for me, for it has been a man's work and I have helped my little mite towards the increase of knowledge; child there are millions in this world who have not had this chance. You will always remember me my own true woman and little girl. I cannot say more my heart is so full of love and longing for you and words will not avail, they are so poor in such a case. Child we may meet again in another world, and I believe in God, that is all I can say but it covers all things; I have tried to do my best as a man the rest I leave to Him. And if there is another world and he wills it we shall find each other. I feel that there must be; this cannot be the end, but I do not know, I only believe from something in me. Yet again I cannot tell if there is, I hope. Child you will comfort those at home. Know once more that I love you truly and purely and as dearly as a woman can be loved. And now my true love goodnight.

Your lover   Ernest

This is not the place to tell the full story of the Southern Journey in all its detail. I am concerned here with those aspects of it which were to have a profound effect on Shackleton's later life, and particularly the conduct of his own expeditions.

First there was the performance of the dogs, which was so poor that both Scott and Shackleton came to the conclusion that they were not to be relied upon for long Antarctic journeys. Within ten days of starting, all the dogs became weak and dispirited, so much so that the three men had to burn up their own energies in helping to pull the sledges. Several reasons were put forward. First, and most obviously, their rations appeared to be causing them to vomit, and so lose weight and energy. Another view was that with spindrift blowing into their faces day after day on the vast featureless expanse of the Barrier, they simply lost heart. Both factors played a part. But in the light of Amundsen's spectacular success with dogs in the

Antarctic nine years later, the real reason lay in their treatment. Unlike the Norwegians, the British had no experience or training in the handling of sledge teams, and consequently no idea how to get the best out of them. After this experience, Scott never overcame his prejudice against dogs. In the end it was to cost him not only the prize of the Pole itself, but his own life. Shackleton persevered, taking dogs with him on both his subsequent expeditions, but for his own attempt to reach the Pole in 1908, he put his faith in tough little Manchurian ponies.

The performance of the dogs dashed any hopes Scott and his party may have had of reaching the Pole. On the last day of the year 1902, they turned for home.

During the next two weeks, Shackleton's physical condition deteriorated sharply. They were all suffering from exhaustion, but undoubtedly he was the weakest of the three. When Wilson examined him on 14 January, he found he was suffering from shortness of breath, coughing fits and all the symptoms of scurvy. He was also spitting blood.

It was at this time, too, that his relations with Scott apparently reached their lowest point; though it seems likely that Shackleton's real anger was directed at himself. He now found himself under orders to do no work about the camp, and to walk beside the sledge without pulling. Galling as it must have been, it was a clear measure of the alarm his companions must have been feeling. In fact we know that, for a time, Wilson doubted whether he would survive the journey at all, and communicated his fears to Scott. Years later Shackleton related having overheard this exchange, and claimed that he swore then and there that he would outlive them both. (He did. Scott and Wilson both died within a few miles of that very spot, in March 1912.)

Then came the most ignominious day of all. Shackleton was asked, or told, to sit on the back of the sledge and steer with a ski pole, while the others continued to pull. After that there was a slight improvement in his condition, and he was able to complete the journey back to the ship on foot. It had been touch and go nevertheless.

When Scott published the official account of the Southern Journey two years later, Shackleton was deeply hurt. There was no reference to steering with a ski pole, leaving the impression that he had simply been a passenger. Quoting from his diary, Scott described him as 'worn and despondent', then a few days later 'livid, speechless and in very low spirits', and finally 'painful to watch'. No doubt it was all true, but it greatly hurt his pride.

Once back on board *Discovery*, Scott had the task of deciding which members of the expedition would spend another winter in Antarctica before completing the scientific programme the following season, and which would go home on the relief ship *Morning*, now waiting in open water a few miles to the north.

There can be little doubt that Scott wanted to be rid of Shackleton for a number of reasons. He had broken down on the job; there had been at least one serious clash of temperament, falling only a little short of insubordination; and lastly he was a Merchant Navy man. Scott was firmly convinced that the Royal Navy personnel had weathered the rigours of the Antarctic much better.

But Shackleton's case was a difficult one. Once aboard *Discovery* he had recovered fast; much more quickly than Wilson, who was still confined to his bunk after two weeks. But Scott wanted Wilson. He may even have felt after the previous winter that he wanted him to himself.

The expedition medical officer, Dr Koettlitz, on Scott's instructions, gave Shackleton a thorough medical examination, which failed to reveal the evidence Scott was looking for. Back on a diet of fresh seal meat, he had made a rapid recovery from scurvy. Persistent coughing had probably caused the burst blood vessel, which would be unlikely to recur. Basically Shackleton's health was sound. At this stage, Scott is reported to have said to Koettlitz: 'Either he goes home sick, or he goes home in disgrace.' It was the second-in-command, Armitage, years later, who quoted this remark. If it is true, it must have been passed on to him by Dr Koettlitz. Armitage had his own reasons for disliking Scott. At this distance all a modern student of these events can do is judge for himself whether or not the remark rings true. In the event, Koettlitz's report went like this:

Mr Shackleton's breakdown during the Southern Sledge Journey was undoubtedly, in Dr Wilson's opinion, due in great part to scurvy taint. I certainly agree with him; he has now practically recovered from it; but referring to your memorandum as to the duties of an executive officer, I cannot say that he would be fit to undergo hardships and exposure in this climate.

It was enough for Scott. With the resounding cheers of the ship's company ringing in his ears, Shackleton was invalided home.

The entry in Shackleton's own diary, written on the evening the *Morning* sailed north, contains no bitterness or recrimination.

A beautiful day, but a sad one indeed for me; for today I have left my home and all those who are chums as much as I will have anyone for chums. I cannot write much about it, but it touched me more than I can say when the men came up on deck and gave me three parting cheers. Ah. It is hard to leave before the work is over and especially to leave those who will have to stay down here in the cold dark days for there seems to my mind but little chance of the old ship going out.

By the time he reached London, the bleakness of his immediate prospects had come home to him. He was in his late twenties, without a job, and without any real idea what he wanted to do. His one burning ambition, to become an Antarctic explorer, now seemed closed to him forever. In his first attempt, he had failed utterly.

Today we know how he overcame that failure and turned it into a springboard for his later triumphs, but at the time he must have been on the edge of despair.

It is easy, with hindsight, to read too much into one event. Nevertheless I believe that his breakdown on the Southern Journey, and Scott's decision to invalid him home, were the events which transformed his life. If nothing quite so traumatic had occurred; if he had remained as a relatively junior member of the expedition, fulfilling some rather less dramatic tasks the following season, then his growing desire to rival (one is tempted to say get even with) Scott, might never have taken root. As it was, the truth gradually came home to him during the next few unsettled years that the only way for him to get back to the Antarctic was as the leader of his own expedition.

Meanwhile more pressing matters confronted him. He wanted to get married; and he badly needed to earn his living. The truth was that almost any job involving office hours was going to prove irksome; a successful expedition to find buried treasure was more the sort of thing he had in mind. But prospective bridegrooms need prospects. He tried journalism, and for a time, became sub-editor of the *Royal Magazine*.

This was not his first venture into newspaper production. Without any prior training, working in a cramped hut through the long polar night, Shackleton had edited five editions of *The South Polar Times*, which still stand as a small landmark in the history of journalism. And if further proof were needed, this present volume provides ample evidence that he might indeed have made a career for himself with his pen. His talent for expressing himself, his ebullient nature and easy way with people of every sort were all considerable assets.

But it was not to be. Within a few months, the post of Secretary to the Royal Scottish Geographical Society became vacant. Several heavyweights of the geographical world, like Sir Clements Markham and Hugh Robert Mill, were prepared to put their sponsorship behind Shackleton; and in due course the job was offered him. He decided to take it; and so he and Emily began their married life in Edinburgh.

In spite of long separations when the sirens of the Antarctic called, Emily always remained one of the cornerstones of his life. She alone really saw and understood the emotional side of his nature, never far below the surface of the rough, tough exterior he presented to the world. Six years his senior, and from a much wealthier background, she was probably the dominant partner in the early years of the eighteen they were to share together. With striking features and a strong personality, she regularly defeated him on the golf course, was more at home than he among the rich and famous, and possessed many of the social graces that he always felt he lacked. But they had much in common, sharing particularly a love of poetry. She introduced him to her own favourite poet Robert Browning, and quickly made him a convert. The word 'Prospice' became a kind of secret talisman between them. It is worth quoting in full the poem of that title, since it throws much light on Shackleton's state of mind during those years, and Emily's instinctive understanding of it.

> Fear death? – to feel the fog in my throat,
>   The mist in my face
> When the snows begin, and the blasts denote
>   I am nearing the place,
> The power of the night, the press of the storm,
>   The post of the foe;

Where he stands, the Arch Fear in a visible form,
Yet the strong man must go;
For the journey is done and the summit attained,
And the barriers fall,
Though a battle's to fight ere the guerdon be gained,
The reward of it all.
I was ever a fighter, so – one fight more,
The best and the last!
I would hate that death bandaged my eyes, and forebore,
And bade me creep past.
No! Let me taste the whole of it, fare like my peers
The heroes of old,
Bear the brunt, in a minute pay glad life's arrears
Of pain, darkness and cold.
For sudden the worst turns the best to the brave,
The black minute's at end,
And the elements' rage, the fiend voices that rave,
Shall dwindle, shall blend,
Shall change, shall become first a peace out of pain,
Then a light, then thy breast,
O though soul of my soul! I shall clasp thee again,
And with God be the rest.

Meanwhile, Shackleton was installed in the Scottish Geographical Society. Once the novelty had worn off, the frustrations he experienced there are well caught in a letter he wrote to Hugh Robert Mill:

I am in a nice light room upstairs where you must visit me when you come up. There is a typewriter in the office and there is a telephone! You should have seen the faces of some of the old chaps when it started to ring today. They had, after a great discussion, decided that I could have it, and said 'Well, it will take six months to get in'; but that was four days ago, and by worrying, I got it in and working today. . . . You would have laughed had you seen their faces when the jangle of the telephone disturbed them in a discussion as to whether the younger of the two lads in the office should continue to spend one week a month addressing wrappers, or should be up to date and save time badly needed for looking after the library . . . and get the wrappers finished and printed at Constables. Thank goodness the progressives carried it. I wanted to see the

Society do all in its power to promote geography; and unless we have a system, and go at the thing thoroughly, not stepping aside for politics or sport, or our other little interests, we can do nothing of use.

Beneath the impatience with the Society, one begins to detect a growing impatience with himself. Shortly after this, he shattered the hushed atmosphere even more by slicing a golf ball straight through one of the library windows and out into the cold grey streets of the city. It would not be long before he would follow it.

The opportunity to sever his connection with the Society came in the form of an invitation to stand for Parliament as a Liberal-Unionist candidate in 1905.

Despite his Irish roots, there is not much evidence that Shackleton had more than a passing interest in political issues; even in the hot topic of Home Rule. But the idea of fighting an election was a challenge; it was something new, and for a man trying with some desperation to find his way in the world, it might prove to be the way forward.

In his biography of Shackleton, Hugh Robert Mill quotes from a newspaper report on one of his election meetings in Dundee. It lacks something in political depth, but it has the authentic Shackleton flavour:

VOTER: If ninety-five per cent of the Irish people want Home Rule, would you give it?

SHACKLETON: I'm an Irishman myself, and I would never give them anything that's not good for them.

SECOND VOTER: How about votes for women?

SHACKLETON: The fact is, sir, my wife is present here today, so I think my wisest course is to refuse to answer that question.

THIRD VOTER: Are you in favour of Poles working in the Lanarkshire mines?

SHACKLETON: No. I would shift all Poles.

THIRD VOTER: Even the South Pole?

SHACKLETON: The only poll I would not shift is the one I'm going to come top of at this election.

But he did not come top. His exit from the political arena was as swift as his entry. He never tried again.

The year 1906 was restless and difficult for Shackleton. He now had a son of a year old, and domestic responsibilities were crowding in. But whichever way he turned he seemed to fail. There were business ventures, most notably the transport of 40,000 Russian troops back to their homeland from the Far East. Like others of the same sort, it came to nothing. The money-making schemes that Shackleton dreamed up were always grandiose and never time-consuming. The notion of putting brick on brick was foreign to his nature. In her biography, Margery Fisher aptly describes him as 'following the dancing light of a prospective fortune across a marsh of speculation'.

But throughout his life, there were always a select handful of perceptive people, sometimes quite unconnected with the exploring world, who saw some deeper quality in this restless and apparently reckless young man. One of these was a Scottish industrialist named William Beardmore, who in due course was to give his name to the world's largest glacier.

He had met Shackleton in Edinburgh and, in spite of the differences in age, became a close friend. Shackleton knew that the offer of a job in one of Beardmore's enterprises was always open, should he need it. Now the time had come. The work itself, as secretary to a committee which was looking into the commercial possibilities of a new type of gas engine, was not particularly congenial. But the influence of William Beardmore was to prove crucial. Within a matter of months his course was set. Not only did he recover his lost faith in himself as a potential Antarctic explorer, but he believed, and was encouraged by Beardmore to believe, that he could lead his own expedition. Furthermore he now had a patron and a backer.

At last, all his energies were harnessed to a single project. On 11 February 1907, he descended on London and announced his plans at a dinner of the Royal Geographical Society. The reaction of the members was one of startled bewilderment. Many of them had thought that Shackleton's days as an Antarctic explorer were over. To have him bouncing back out of the Scottish mists, publicly announcing his intention to lead a privately funded expedition with the express purpose of attaining the geographical South Pole, and the magnetic South Pole, was more than some of them could stand. Words like 'bounder' and 'upstart' were heard in the smoking room. With its long and distinguished history in the field of exploration, the Royal Geographical Society had acquired the role of major sponsor to British expeditions, wherever they might be heading. With the Society's official backing, funds became easier to acquire, assistance from the Armed Services more readily granted, and where necessary, the cooperation of foreign governments. In return for this, the Society expected to keep its hand firmly on the tiller. Most expeditions of any size could expect to be under the control of a committee, usually dominated by senior officers of the Society itself.

Suddenly, here was Shackleton abjuring the very idea of a committee and prepared to proceed with or without the Society's backing. In the climate of those times, it must have seemed like a direct challenge to their authority and prestige.

But the situation also had its personal side. Ever since the *Discovery* expedition, Sir Clements Markham had regarded Scott as his personal protégé. He and the Society's Secretary, John Scott-Keltie, already knew in confidence that Scott himself was planning a second attempt at the Pole. If it came to a choice between the two men, there was no doubt where their sympathies would lie. At this time, Scott was serving on HMS *Albermarle* somewhere in the Atlantic. It wasn't long before the news reached him. He assumed immediately that Shackleton was trying to jump his claim. There followed one of the most bizarre episodes in the whole Antarctic story.

Scott, from his battleship on the high seas, fired the first salvo. He wrote to Shackleton on 18 February, giving his address as Atlantic Fleet.

> Your announcement cuts right across my plans . . . I don't want to hurt you, but in one way I feel I have a sort of right to my own field of work in the same way that Peary claimed Smith's Sound, and many African travellers their particular locality. I am sure you will agree with me in this, and I'm equally sure that only your entire ignorance of my plan could have made you settle on the *Discovery* route without a single word to me.

He was right about Shackleton's ignorance; wrong in expecting his erstwhile subordinate to fall so readily into line.

The reply was polite but firm.

> I want at the outset to say that your communication will have my very earnest consideration, and you must understand that this is a very serious matter for me in view of the

publicity already given and the position as affecting myself with my supporters.

Then, as the letter progresses, it becomes apparent that the old wounds were far from healed:

As regards my own plans, I tried unsuccessfully two years ago to get funds for another expedition, and practically chucked all idea of the thing, though my mind and heart ever turned towards the district that we had worked in; especially I think my desires were as great, if not greater, than anyone else's to return, seeing that I was cut off by a premature return to this country from further participating in the expedition.

This was a clear warning to Scott that he would not be ordered off the ice a second time.

Some sort of compromise seemed the only solution, with Wilson, who had remained a close friend to both men, the most obvious arbiter.

There were two distinct schools of thought in geographical circles at that time on the subject of 'prior rights'. Some took Scott's view that a territorial claim should stand, at least for a number of years. But there were those like Major Darwin, then President of the Royal Geographical Society, who thought such claims were nonsense, and that any explorer who had the enterprise to set out should be free to go wherever he wished. But the use of an established base was another matter. In a letter to Shackleton, Wilson made it quite clear where he stood:

I think that if you go to McMurdo Sound and even reach the Pole – the gilt will be off the gingerbread because of the insinuation which will almost certainly appear in the minds of a good many, that you forestalled Scott who had a prior claim to the use of that base.

Shackleton took the point. His relations with Scott were delicate enough; there were plenty of people only too eager to set them up like a pair of fighting cocks, and then sit back and enjoy the sport. But if he conceded the base, what would he be conceding as well? What artificial obstacles would he be setting for himself in that frozen land where the hazards of nature already provided obstacles enough? Shackleton felt bitter. Whichever way he turned, the shadow of Scott seemed to fall across his life. On 11 March, he wrote to Wilson:

I do not agree with you, Billy, about holding up my plans until I hear what Scott considers his rights. There is no doubt in my mind that his rights end at the base he asked for, or within reasonable distance of that base. I will not consider that he has any right to King Edward the Seventh Land, and only regard it as a direct attempt to keep me out of the Ross quarter if he should even propose such a thing. I have given way to him in the greatest thing of all, and my limit has been reached . . . You may perhaps remember that Scott, in his letter to me, said 'I do not think the foreigners will do much. The whole area is *ours* to attack.' He did not say 'The whole area is *mine* to attack.' . . . You know as well as I do I have given up a certainty almost, for a very uncertain base as regards the ultimate success of the Pole. . . . But all this is beside the question, and I cannot see that he will be upheld by anybody in this matter; but whether he is upheld or not, and if he wishes to do this, I shall fight. I consider I have reached my limit, and I go no further.

It is quite on the cards that the Belgians may publicly announce they are going to land a party at King Edward the Seventh's Land, so unless I hear from Scott within the next few days, I am going to make an announcement to protect myself . . . This is all very worrying but I do not see how I can give way any more, in justice to myself and my supporters. It is bad enough as it is.

In one respect, Shackleton was absolutely right. Whatever 'Queensberry' style rules the English might draw up amongst themselves, there was absolutely no chance of persuading other nations to adhere to them.

When HMS *Albermarle* eventually reached port, the two rivals finally met face to face.

These two ambitious young explorers now sat down and divided a vast segment of the Antarctic between them, like a pair of Caesars dividing up Gaul. It was an artificial exercise, and in the light of subsequent events, an entirely fruitless one. Both have been accused of behaving like spoilt children, but at the time perhaps there was little else they could do.

Undoubtedly Shackleton had the worst of it. He, not Scott, now had to put his signature to an agreement which limited his chances of success, and would put him firmly in the wrong if he stepped outside it. He did this to accommodate a future expedition of Scott's, which might or might not take place two years hence.

The precise implications of the agreement can be better illustrated by a map (see page 33), but the document itself still reeks of the tight-lipped atmosphere which gave it birth. Here is part of it.

I am leaving the McMurdo Sound base to you, and will land either at the place known as Barrier Inlet or at King Edward VII Land, whichever is the most suitable. If I land at either of these places I will not work to the westward of 170 meridian W. and shall not make any sledge journey going W. of that meridian unless prevented when going to the South from keeping to the East of that meridian by the physical features of the country.

If I encounter mountains and it is possible to ascend them by the glaciers I shall do so.

I do not, however, expect, and neither do you, that there will be any land or open sea that will necessitate my going to the West of 170 W.

I propose to make one journey to the South of King Edward VII Land, one journey to the East and one to the Northeast. . . .

I shall not touch the coast of Victoria Land at all. If I find it impracticable to land at King Edward VII Land or at Barrier Inlet or further to the NE, I may possibly steam north, and then to westward and try and land to the west of Kaiser Wilhelm II Land, going down to the meridian that *Challenger* made her furthest south. This meridian is about 80 E.

If I find a landing there I will travel south and also west by sledge journeys.

I think this outlines my plan, which I shall rigidly adhere to, and I hope this letter meets you on the points that you desire.

Scott's reply was brief and formal.

My dear Shackleton, I return this copy of your letter which is a very clear statement of the arrangement to which we came.

If as you say you will rigidly adhere to it, I do (not) think our plans will clash and I shall feel on sure ground in developing my own.

Yours very sincerely,
R. F. Scott

As we shall see, Shackleton did not 'rigidly adhere' to any of it. There are some who have maintained he never had the slightest intention of doing so. They miss the point. It was entirely understandable that the two main contenders for the greatest geographical prize of the day, the South Pole, should stake out their rival claims. But when the elemental forces of nature prevailing in those regions made nonsense of their piece of paper, they were the first to recognise the absurdity of it.

So at last, on 30 July 1907, the *Nimrod* left the East India Docks and headed for the open sea. To Shackleton it must have been a moment of intense relief. The last man-made hurdle was behind him. Scott was mollified. Even the Royal Geographical Society added their half-hearted blessing with a grant of £500 and the loan of some chronometers. At the Isle of Wight, the King himself would come aboard to give the intrepid little band a Royal send-off. Shackleton had dared to launch his own private expedition. Now he was on his way.

He decided to make the passage to New Zealand not on the *Nimrod*, but as a passenger on the *India*. A faster ship would give him extra time in Australia to recruit some scientists to accompany the expedition. The Australian Government had voted £5000 towards his costs; and Shackleton wanted to make a gesture in return.

By the time final preparations were made, the *India* was already steaming through the Bay of Biscay. Shackleton had to catch her up by travelling overland. On the long train journey across France, he spent the time writing to Emily, and he poured out his heart. The emotional strain of those last few weeks must have been very great. In his relationship with his wife, he found his release.

My darling wife,
Your dear brave face is before me now and I can see you just as you stand on the wharf and are smiling at me my heart was too full to speak and I felt that I wanted just to come ashore and clasp you in my arms and love and care for you; Child honestly and truly it was the worst heart aching moment in my life. If I failed to get the Pole and

was within ten miles and had to turn back it would or will not mean so much sadness as was compressed into those few minutes: I never realized till we had parted all that it was going to mean to me but above all I was proud of your dear face and the thought that you could be all that braced me up and made me really feel how wonderful you were: Child little wife I am thinking very much of you now and I want to tell you that in those last few moments you showed yourself to be a splendid glorious woman: and now for the brighter side of things darling: you have the two darlings – and they will be a great comfort and help to you whilst I am away and they are two of the sweetest and dearest in the world. You will be happy with them and will watch them during the time that I am away even more lovingly if that is possible.

And now child the time will go more quickly than you may think for you will be in touch with me till March and then again next March soon it will be 1908 and then you can say that next year I will be back: you will be just one year without hearing from me and I promise you that I will take every care and run no risks and this time there is no need to as the equipment is perfect the ship is really better than the 'Discovery' though not so big and the men are all picked with the greatest care: and we have our experience with us this time for one thing I am certain I shall not run any risk for the sake of trying to get to the 'Pole' in the face of hard odds. I have not only myself but you and the children to consider and always remember that and also that you will be with me wherever I go in storm or calm and if inclined to do anything rash I will think of my promise to you and not do it. You must think that from this hour you are with me and in the morning instead of being sad be proud that it is my chance to do a great work there are thousands who would give their eyes to go: and this Expedition owes nothing to the World at large and yet it may help the honour of the Country: if successful there will be ample money and instead of having to grind away at W.B's year in and year out and only save a few hundreds a year there will be plenty for us to live our lives as we wish: I promise you darling that I will come back to you safe and well if God wishes it and also that I will not be sharp or hasty with my men: You are a thousand times too good for me darling, and I see you know it in a hundred ways, but I can say no more than this that I will try and be worthy of the glory that is you. From early days you have been my light and my pride and in the everyday existence I may not have always realized it yet in the bottom of my heart I knew it. I will write again tomorrow the train is awfully jerky: my dear love to the children.

Your husband Ernest

At this point Shackleton's own narrative begins.

Selections from

THE HEART
OF THE ANTARCTIC

by E. H. Shackleton

THE INCEPTION AND PREPARATION OF THE EXPEDITION

Men go out into the void spaces of the world for various reasons. Some are actuated simply by a love of adventure, some have the keen thirst for scientific knowledge, and others again are drawn away from the trodden paths by the 'lure of little voices', the mysterious fascination of the unknown. I think that in my own case it was a combination of these factors that determined me to try my fortune once again in the frozen south. I had been invalided home before the conclusion of the *Discovery* expedition, and I had a very keen desire to see more of the vast continent that lies amid the Antarctic snows and glaciers. Indeed the stark polar lands grip the hearts of the men who have lived on them in a manner that can hardly be understood by the people who have never got outside the pale of civilisation.

In the *Geographical Journal* for March 1907 I outlined my plan of campaign, but this had to be changed in several respects at a later date owing to the exigencies of circumstances. My intention was that the expedition should leave New Zealand at the beginning of 1908, and proceed to winter quarters on the Antarctic continent, the ship to land the men and stores and then return. By avoiding having the ship frozen in, I would render the use of a relief ship unnecessary, as the same vessel could come south again the following summer and take us off. 'The shore-party of nine or twelve men will winter with sufficient equipment to enable three separate parties to start out in the spring', I announced. 'One party will go east, and, if possible, across the Barrier to the new land known as King Edward VII Land, follow the coast-line there south, if the coast trends south, or north if north, returning when it is considered necessary to do so. The second party will proceed south over the same route as that of the southern sledge-party of the *Discovery;* this party will keep from fifteen to twenty miles from the coast, so as to avoid any rough ice. The third party will possibly proceed westward over the mountains, and, instead of crossing in a line due west, will strike towards the magnetic pole. The main changes in equipment will be that Siberian ponies will be taken for the sledge journeys both east and south, and also a specially designed motor-car for the southern journey. . . . I do not intend to sacrifice the scientific utility of the expediton to a mere record-breaking journey, but say frankly, all the same, that one of my great efforts will be to reach the southern geographical pole.'

The programme was an ambitious one for a small expedition,

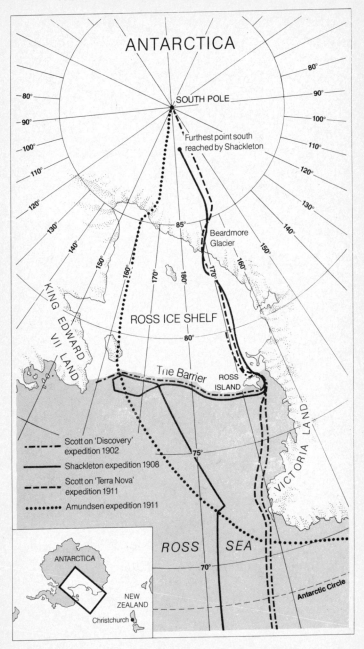

ANTARCTICA

SOUTH POLE

Furthest point south
reached by Shackleton

Beardmore
Glacier

KING EDWARD VII LAND

ROSS ICE SHELF

The Barrier

ROSS ISLAND

VICTORIA LAND

Scott on 'Discovery'
expedition 1902

Shackleton expedition 1908

Scott on 'Terra Nova'
expedition 1911

Amundsen expedition 1911

ROSS SEA

Antarctic Circle

ANTARCTICA

NEW ZEALAND

Christchurch

no doubt, but I was confident, and I think I may claim that in some measure my confidence has been justified.

THE STAFF

The *personnel* of an expedition of the character I proposed is a factor on which success depends to a very large extent. The men selected must be qualified for the work, and they must also have the special qualifications required to meet polar conditions. They must be able to live together in harmony for a long period without outside communication, and it must be remembered that the men whose desires lead them to the untrodden paths of the world have generally marked individuality. It was no easy matter for me to select the staff, although over four hundred applications arrived from persons wishing to join the expedition. I wanted to have two surgeons with the shore-party, and also to have a thoroughly capable biologist and geologist, for the study of these two branches of science in the Antarctic seemed to me to be of especial importance. After much consideration I selected eleven men for the shore-party. Three of them only, Adams, Wild and Joyce, had been known to me previously, while only Wild and Joyce had previous experience of polar work, having been members of the *Discovery* expedition. Every man, however, was highly recommended, and this was the case also with the officers whom I selected for the *Nimrod*. The names of the men appointed, with their particular branches of work, were as follows:

SHORE-PARTY

LIEUTENANT J. B. ADAMS, RNR, meteorologist.
SIR PHILIP BROCKLEHURST, Bart., assistant geologist, and in charge of current observations.
BERNARD DAY, electrician and motor expert.
ERNEST JOYCE, in charge of general stores, dogs, sledges and zoological collections.
DR A. F. MACKAY, surgeon.
DR ERIC MARSHALL, surgeon, cartographer.
G. E. MARSTON, artist.
JAMES MURRAY, biologist.
RAYMOND PRIESTLEY, geologist.
WILLIAM ROBERTS, cook.
FRANK WILD, in charge of provisions.

After the expedition had reached New Zealand and the generous assistance of the Australian and New Zealand Governments had relieved me from some financial anxiety, I was able to add to the strength of the staff. I engaged Douglas Mawson, lecturer of mineralogy and petrology at the Adelaide University, as physicist, and Bertram Armytage as a member of the expedition for general work. Professor Edgeworth David, FRS, of Sydney University, consented to accompany us as far as the winter quarters, with the idea of returning in the *Nimrod*, but I persuaded him eventually to stay in the Antarctic, and his assistance in connection with the scientific work, and particularly the geology, was invaluable. Leo Cotton, a young Australian, arranged to come south with us and help with the preliminary work before the *Nimrod* returned to New Zealand, accompanied us on the voyage south, returning in the steamer that towed the *Nimrod*.

The members of the ship's staff, at the time when the *Nimrod* left Great Britain, were as follows:

LIEUTENANT RUPERT ENGLAND, RHR, master.
JOHN K. DAVIS, first officer.
A. L. A. MACKINTOSH, second officer.
DR W. A. R. MICHELL, surgeon.
H. J. L. DUNLOP, chief engineer.
ALFRED CHEETHAM, third officer and boatswain.

Captain England, whom I placed in command of the *Nimrod*, had been first officer of the *Morning* when that vessel proceeded to the relief of the *Discovery* expedition, and had therefore had previous experience of work in the Antarctic. Immediately before joining the *Nimrod* he had been in the Government service on the west coast of Africa.

Davis, first officer and later captain, had not been in the Antarctic before, but he was a first-class seaman.

Mackintosh came from the service of the Peninsular and Oriental Steam Navigation Company. He was transferred to the shore-party at a later date, but an unfortunate accident finally prevented his remaining in the Antarctic with us. Dr Michell, the ship's surgeon, was a Canadian, and Dunlop the chief engineer, was an Irishman. Cheetham, the third officer and boatswain had served on the *Morning* and some of the men had also Antarctic experience.

After the *Nimrod* reached New Zealand, A. E. Harbord, an Englishman, joined as second officer in place of Mackintosh, whom I intended to transfer to the shore-party.

The following brief notes regarding the members of the shore-party may be of interest to readers:

ERNEST HENRY SHACKLETON, commander of the expedition. Born 1874, and educated at Dulwich College. Went to sea in the merchant service at the age of sixteen, became a lieutenant in the Royal Naval Reserve, and in 1901 joined the British National Antarctic expedition. Was a member of the party which established a 'furthest south' record, and on return to the winter quarters was invalided. Fitted out the *Discovery* relief expeditions under the Admiralty Committee, and also assisted fitting out the *Argentine* expedition that went to the relief of the Swedish Antarctic expedition. Married in 1904, and became secretary and treasurer of the Royal Scottish Geographical Society. Resigned to contest the Dundee seat as a Unionist at the election in 1906, and after being defeated became personal assistant to Mr William Beardmore, head of the Glasgow firm of battleship builders and armour plate manufacturers. Then decided to take an expedition to the Antarctic.

JAMESON BOYD ADAMS, born in 1880 at Rippingale, Lincolnshire. Went to sea in the merchant service in 1893, served three years as a lieutenant in the Royal Naval Reserve, and joined the expedition in March 1907. Appointed second in command in February 1908. Unmarried.

BERTRAM ARMYTAGE, born in Australia in 1869. Educated at Melbourne Grammar School and Jesus College, Cambridge. After serving for several years with the Victorian Militia and one year with the Victorian Permanent Artillery, he was appointed to the Carabiniers, 6th Division Guards, when on active service in South Africa (Queen's medal and three clasps, King's medal and two clasps). Joined the expedition in Australia. Married.

SIR PHILIP LEE BROCKLEHURST, Bart, born at Swythamley Park, Staffordshire, in 1887, educated at Eton and Trinity Hall, Cambridge. Holds a commission in the Derbyshire Yeomanry, represented Cambridge in the lightweight boxing competitions for 1905 and 1906. Unmarried.

THOMAS W. EDGEWORTH DAVID, FRS, Professor of Geology at the Sydney University, is a Welshman by birth, and is fifty years of age. He was educated at New College, Oxford, and afterwards studied geology at the Royal College of Science. He went to Australia to take up the post of Geological Surveyor to the New South Wales Government, and for the past eighteen years has held his present appointment. He is an authority on dynamical geology and glaciation, and has made a study of Australian coalfields. Married.

BERNARD C. DAY, born at Wymondham, Leicestershire, in August 1884; educated at Wellingborough Grammar School. He was connected with engineering from 1903 until September 1907, when he left the service of the New Arroll Johnston Motor-Car Company in order to join the expedition. Unmarried.

ERNEST JOYCE, born in 1875, entered the Navy from the Greenwich Royal Hospital School in 1891, became a first-class petty officer, and served in South Africa with the Naval Brigade (medal and clasp). Joined the *Discovery* expedition from the Cape, and served in the Antarctic (polar medal and clasp, Geographical Society's silver medal). Served in the Whale Island Gunnery School. Left the Navy in December 1905, rejoined in August 1906, and left by purchase in order to join the expedition in May 1907. Unmarried.

ALISTAIR FORBES MACKAY, born in 1878, son of the late Colonel A. Forbes Mackay, of the 92nd Gordon Highlanders. Educated in Edinburgh, and then did biological work under Professors Geddes and D'Arcy Thompson at Dundee. Served in South Africa as a trooper in the CIV (Queen's medal, and clasps), and later with Baden Powell's police, then returned to pass his final examinations in medicine, and went to the front again as a civil surgeon. Entered the Navy as a surgeon, retired after four years' service, and then joined the expedition. Unmarried.

AENEAS LIONEL ACTON MACKINTOSH, born in Tirhoot, Bengal, India, in 1881, and educated at the Bedford Modern School. Went to sea in 1894 in the merchant service, and in 1899, entered the service of the Peninsular and Oriental Steam Navigation Company. Was lent to the expedition in 1907. Received commission in the Royal Naval Reserve in July 1908. Unmarried.

ERIC STEWART MARSHALL, born in 1879, educated at Monckton Combe School and at Emmanuel College, Cambridge. Represented his college in rowing and football. Studied for the Church. Entered St Bartholomew's Hospital in 1899, and qualified as a surgeon in 1906. Was captain St Bartholomew's Hospital Rugby football team, 1903–4, and played for the Richmond Club, 1903–4–5. Joined the expedition as surgeon and cartographer. Unmarried.

GEORGE EDWARD MARSTON was born at Portsmouth in 1882, and received the greater part of his art education at the Regent Street Polytechnic. He is a qualified art teacher, and joined the expedition as artist. Unmarried.

DOUGLAS MAWSON was born in Australia in 1880, his parents coming from the Isle of Man. He was educated in Australia and is lecturer in mineralogy and petrology at the Adelaide University and honorary curator of the South Australian Museum. He joined the expedition in Australia. Unmarried.

JAMES MURRAY was born in Glasgow in 1865. In early life was occupied in various branches of art work. Was interested in natural history, especially botany, and in 1901, turned his attention to microscopic zoology. In 1902 was engaged by Sir John Murray as biologist on Scottish Lake Survey. Was still engaged in this work when he joined the expedition as biologist. Married in 1892.

RAYMOND E. PRIESTLEY, born 1886, and educated at Tewkesbury School. Matriculated in London in 1903, and held mastership at Tewkesbury until 1905. Then became a student at the Bristol University College, and passed the intermediate examination in science in 1906. He was taking the final course when appointed geologist to the expedition.

WILLIAM C. ROBERTS, born in London in 1872, and has worked as cook on sea and land. Engaged as cook for the expedition. Married.

FRANK WILD, born in Yorkshire in 1873. His mother was a direct descendant of Captain Cook, and one of his uncles was three times in the Arctic regions. Entered the merchant service in 1889, and in 1900 joined the Navy. He was a member of the National Antarctic expedition between 1901 and 1904 (polar medal and clasp, Royal Geographical Society's silver medal). Was at the Sheerness Gunnery School when the Admiralty consented to his appointment to the British Antarctic expedition.

THE FIRST STAGE

The work of preparing for the expedition made rapid progress towards completion, and as the end of July approached, the stores and equipment were stowed away in the holds of the *Nimrod* in readiness for the voyage to New Zealand.

We sailed in the night for Cowes, and on the morning of August 1 stopped for an hour off Eastbourne in order to enable some of the supporters of the expedition to pay us a farewell visit. On the Sunday we were anchored at Cowes, and their Majesties the King and Queen, their Royal Highnesses the Prince of Wales, the Princess Victoria, Prince Edward and the Duke of Connaught came on board. The King graciously conferred upon me the

Victorian Order, and the Queen entrusted me with a Union Jack, to carry on the southern sledge journey.

We drank success to the expedition at a farewell dinner that evening, and on the morning of Wednesday, August 7, the ship sailed for New Zealand, and after calling at St Vincent and Capetown, arrived at Lyttelton on November 23, the voyage having occupied three months and a half.

The people of New Zealand and Australia took a keen and sympathetic interest in the expedition from the first. The Commonwealth Government gave me £5000 and the New Zealand Government £1000, and this sum of money placed me in a position to increase the number of the shore-party, to add to the stores and equipment in certain directions and to strengthen the ship still further, which I could not afford to do earlier. The New Zealand Government also agreed to pay half the cost of towing the *Nimrod* down to the Antarctic Circle, so that coal might be saved for the heavy work amongst the ice, and in many other ways assisted us.

The ponies were enjoying their holiday on Quail Island and were becoming sleek and fat, and it was necessary that they should be broken to handling and sledge-hauling. The white ponies, which later proved the most hardy, were the least tractable, and there was one white pony in particular that was left behind, because, though a splendid specimen physically, it could not be brought to a reasonable state of docility in the time at our disposal. All the ponies had names, although I do not know from whom they received them, and we finally left New Zealand with 'Socks', 'Quan', 'Grisi', 'Chinaman', 'Billy', 'Zulu', 'Doctor', 'Sandy', 'Nimrod', and 'Mac'.

LYTTELTON TO THE ANTARCTIC CIRCLE

January 1, 1908, arrived at last! Warm, fine, and clear broke the morning of our last day in civilisation. Before sunset we were to sever all ties with the outer world and more than a year must elapse ere we could look again on the scenes familiar to ordinary daily life. For me this day brought a feeling of relief, after all the strenuous work of the previous year, though the new work I was entering upon was fraught with more anxiety and was more exacting than any that had gone before. We all looked forward eagerly to our coming venture, for the glamour of the unknown was with us and the South was calling.

My personal belongings were gathered out of the chaos of papers and odds and ends in my office at the hotel. Orders had been given to Captain England to have all in readiness for casting off at 4 p.m., and early in the afternoon most of us were on board. It was Regatta day and Lyttelton was crowded with holiday-makers, many thousands of whom had come to see the *Nimrod*.

Time was passing quickly, it was nearing four o'clock and all our party were on board save Professor David. Doubtless he was having a last skirmish round in case there was anything else that had been left, and just as I was getting anxious, for I did not want to delay the departure of the ship, he appeared. His arms were filled with delicate glass apparatus and other scientific parapher-nalia. As he was gingerly crossing the narrow gangway he was confronted by a stout female, of whom the Professor afterwards said: 'She was for the shore, let who would be for the Pole'. They met in the middle of the gangway. Hampered by the things he was carrying, the Professor could not move aside; he was simply charged down by superior weight, and clutching his precious goods, fell off the gangway on to the heads of some of our party. Wonderful to relate nothing was broken.

At one minute to four orders were given to stand by the engines, at 4 p.m. the lines were cast off from the wharf and the *Nimrod* moved slowly ahead. Cheer after cheer broke from the watching thousands as we moved towards the harbour entrance, with the Queen's flag flying at the fore and our ensign dipping farewell at the stern. With our powerful ally, the *Koonya*, steaming in front, and on each side passenger boats of the Union Company carrying some six or seven thousand persons, we passed down the Roads, receiving such a farewell and 'God-speed' from New Zealand as left no man of us unmoved.

We then came close up to the stern of the *Koonya* and hauled in the 4-in. wire cable she was to tow us with. A 4-in. wire is measured not as 4 in. diameter, but 4 in. in circumference, and is made of the finest steel. We passed a shackle through the eye at the end of this wire and shackled on to the free ends of both our chain cables. We then let out thirty fathoms of each cable, one on each side of the bow, and made the inner ends fast round the foremast in the 'tween decks. This cable acted as a 'spring', to use a nautical term; that is to say, it lessened the danger of the wire snapping if a sudden strain were put upon it, for the cable hung down in the water owing to its weight, even when the ship was being towed at seven or eight knots. This operation being com-pleted we signalled the *Koonya* to go ahead and we were soon in the open sea. There was a slight breeze and a small choppy sea. Before we had been under way for an hour water began to come in at the scupper holes and through the wash ports. This looked ominous to us, for if the *Nimrod* was going to be wet in such fine weather, what was she going to be like when we got a southerly gale! She moved through the water astern of *Koonya* like a reluctant child being dragged to school; she seemed to have no vitality of her own. This was due to her deeply loaded condition, and more especially to the seven tons of cable and the weight of the wire on her bows dragging her nose down into the sea. No Antarctic exploring ship had been towed to the ice before, but it meant the saving of coal to us for a time when the tons saved in this manner might prove the salvation of the expedition.

Bad weather was not long delayed. As the night of January 1 wore on, the wind began to freshen from the south-west, and the following morning the two vessels were pitching somewhat heavily and steering wildly.

Our chief anxiety was the care of the ponies, and looking back now to those days, it remains a matter of wonder to me how they survived the hardships that fell to their lot. That night I arranged for a two-hour watch, consisting of two members of the shore staff, to be always in attendance on the ponies. The pony shelter had five stalls on the port side and five on the starboard side of the deck, with the fore hatch between them. The watch-keepers named this place 'The Cavalry Club', and here in the bleak and bitter stormy nights, swept off their feet every now and then by the seas washing over the forehatch, the members of the shore party passed many a bad quarter of an hour. They bore all the buffeting and discomfort cheerfully, even as those men of old, who 'ever with a frolic welcome took the thunder and the sunshine'. Night in the pony-stables was a weird experience with inky blackness all round, save only where the salt-encrusted hurricane lamp, jerking to and fro, made a glimmer of light. The roar of the tempest rose into a shriek as the wind struck the rigid rigging, the creaking and swaying of the roof of the stable and the boat-skids, which partly rested their weight on it, seemed to threaten a sudden collapse with each succeeding and heavier roll, and the seas crashed dully as they fell on board. The swirling waters, foam-white in the dim rays of the lamp, rushed through the stable and over the hatch, and even from the bridge far aft, we could hear the frightened whinnies of the animals, as they desperately struggled to keep their feet in the water that flooded the rolling stables. Every now and then some wave, larger and fiercer than the one before, would sweep the decks, tear the mats from under the feet of the ponies, and wash the watch-keepers almost under the struggling beasts.

On the morning of the 5th, I told Captain England to signal the *Koonya* and ask her to pour oil on the water in the hope that it might help us. To a certain extent I think it did, but not enough to prevent the heaviest seas from breaking on board. I thought that the gale had reached its height on the previous day, but certainly this evening it was much stronger. The *Nimrod* rolled over fifty degrees from the perpendicular to each side; how much more than that I cannot say, for the indicator recording the roll of the ship was only marked up to fifty degrees, and the pointer had passed that mark. Let the reader hold a pencil on end on a table, and then incline it fifty degrees one way, and back again till it reaches fifty degrees on the other side and he will realise the length of arc through which the masts and deck of the *Nimrod* swung.

About 9 p.m. that night, during an extra heavy roll, one of the ponies slipped down in its stall, and when the ship rolled the opposite way, turned right over on its back, as it could not regain its footing. We tried everything in our power to get the poor beast up again, but there was no room to work in the narrow stall, and in the darkness and rushing water it would have been madness to have tried to shift the other ponies out of the adjacent stalls in order to take down the partition, and so give the poor animal room to get up itself. We had perforce to leave it for the night, trusting that when daylight came the weather might have moderated, and that with the light we might be able to do more. It speaks wonders for the vitality of the animal that in spite of its cramped position and the constant washing of the cold seas over it during the whole night, it greedily ate the handfuls of hay which were given it from time to time. Every now and then the pony made frantic efforts to get on to its feet again, but without avail, and before the morning its struggles gradually grew weaker and weaker. The morning of January 6 broke with the gale blowing more strongly than ever. There was a mountainous sea running, and at ten o'clock, after having made another futile attempt to get 'Doctor', as he was called, on his legs, and finding that he had no strength of his own, I had regretfully to give orders to have him shot. One bullet from a heavy service revolver ended his troubles.

This continuous bad weather was attributed by some on board to the fact that we had captured an albatross on the second day out. It is generally supposed by seamen to be unlucky to kill this bird, but as we did it for the purposes of scientific collections and not with the wantonness of the 'Ancient Mariner', the superstitious must seek for some other reason for the weather.

During the afternoon of January 11 the strength of the expedition was increased by Possum, one of our dogs, giving birth to six fine puppies. The mother and family were found a warm bed on the engine room skylight, where a number of our cases were stowed. We signalled the happy event to the *Koonya* by flags, and received Captain Evans' congratulations. Signalling by flags was necessarily a somewhat slow operation, especially as the commercial code of signals is not exactly adapted for this particular sort of information, and we could see by the length of time they took to verify each signal that they were at a loss as to the subject-matter of our communication, the incident of a birth naturally being farthest removed from their thoughts at such a time.

On January 14, we sighted our first iceberg, and passed it at a distance of about two and a half miles. It had all the usual characteristics of the Antarctic bergs, being practically tabular in form, and its sides being of a dead white colour.

During the afternoon we passed two more icebergs with their usual tails of brash ice floating out to leeward. The sea had changed colour from a leaden blue to a greenish grey. Albatrosses were not nearly so numerous, and of those following the ship the majority were the sooty species. Everything pointed to our proximity to the pack, so we signalled the *Koonya* that we were likely to sight the ice at any moment. I also asked Captain Evans to kill and skin the sheep he was carrying for our supplies, as they would be much more easily transported when the time came to cast off. The weather remained fine with light winds during the night.

Next morning it was fairly thick with occasional light squalls of snow, and about 9 a.m. we saw the ice looming up through the mist to the southward. It seemed to stretch from south-west to south-east, and was apparently the forerunner of the pack. Now had come the time for the *Koonya* to drop us, after a tow of 1510 miles – a record in towage for a vessel not built for the purpose. Before the *Koonya* finally cast off from us, she had achieved another record, by being the first steel vessel to cross the Antarctic Circle.

About 3 a.m. on the morning of January 16, we entered an area of tabular bergs, varying from eighty to one hundred and fifty feet in height, and all the morning we steamed in beautiful weather with a light northerly wind, through the lanes and streets of a wonderful snowy Venice. Tongue and pen fail in attempting to describe the magic of such a scene. As far as the eye could see from the crow's-nest of the *Nimrod*, the great, white, wall-sided bergs stretched east, west and south, making a striking contrast with the lanes of blue-black water between them. A stillness, weird and uncanny, seemed to have fallen upon everything when we entered the silent water streets of this vast unpeopled white city. Here there was no sign of life, except when one of the little snow petrels, invisible when flying across the glistening bergs, flashed for a moment into sight, as it came against the dark water, its pure white wings just skimming the surface. The threshing of our screw raised a small wave astern of the ship, and at times huge masses of ice and snow from the bergs, disturbed by the unaccustomed motion, fell thundering in our wake. Some of these bergs had been weathered into the fantastic shapes more characteristic of the Arctic regions, and from peak and spire flashed out the new caught rays of the morning sun. Beautiful as this scene was, it gave rise to some anxiety in my mind, for I knew that if we were caught in a breeze amidst this maze of floating ice, it would go hard with us. Already an ominous dark cloud was sweeping down from the north, and a few flakes of falling snow heralded the approach of the misty northerly wind. I was unfeignedly thankful, when, about three in the afternoon, I saw from the crow's-nest open water ahead. A few more turnings and twistings through the devious water lanes, and we entered the ice free Ross Sea. This was the first time that a passage had been made into the Ross Sea without the vessel having been held up by pack-ice. I think our success was due to the fact that we were away to the eastward of the pack, which had separated from the land and the Barrier, and had drifted in a north-west direction. All my experience goes to prove that the easterly route is the best.

THE ATTEMPT TO REACH KING EDWARD VII LAND

We were now revelling in the indescribable freshness of the Antarctic that seems to permeate one's being, and which must be responsible for the longing to go again which assails each returned explorer from polar regions. We were keeping a sharp look-out for the Barrier, which we expected to see at any moment. A light south-easterly wind blew cold, warning us that we could not be very far away from the ice-sheet. The thermometer registered some twelve degrees of frost, but we hardly felt the cold, for the wind was so dry. At 9.30 a.m. on the 23rd a low straight line appeared ahead of the ship. It was the Barrier. Shortly after noon we were within a quarter of a mile of the ice-face, and exclamations of wonder and astonishment at the stupendous bulk of the Barrier were drawn from the men who had not seen it before.

We slowly steamed along, noting the various structures of the ice, and were thankful that the weather promised to keep fine, for the inlet to which we were bound could not easily have been picked up in thick weather. The height of the Barrier about this point ranged from a hundred and fifty feet to two hundred feet.

In places the wall was perfectly smooth, clean cut from the top to the waterline, in other places it showed signs of vertical cracks, and sometimes deep caverns appeared, which, illuminated by the reflected light, merged from light translucent blue into the deepest sapphire. At times great black patches appeared on the sides of the Barrier in the distance, but as we neared them they were resolved into huge caverns, some of which cut the waterline. One was so large that it would have been possible to have steamed the *Nimrod* through its entrance without touching either side or its top by mast or yard.

About midnight we suddenly came to the end of a very high portion of the Barrier, and found as we followed round that we were entering a wide shallow bay. This must have been the inlet where Borchgrevink landed in 1900, but it had greatly changed since that time. He describes the bay as being a fairly narrow inlet. On our way east in the *Discovery* in 1902 we passed an inlet somewhat similar, but we did not see the western end as it was obscured by fog at the time. There seemed to be no doubt that the Barrier had broken away at the entrance of this bay or inlet, and so had made it much wider and less deep than it was in previous years. About half a mile down the bay we reached fast ice. It was now about half-past twelve at night, and the southerly sun shone in our faces. Our astonishment was great to see beyond the six or seven miles of flat bay ice, which was about five or six feet thick, high rounded icecliffs, with valleys between, running in an almost east and west direction. About four miles to the south we saw the opening of a large valley, but could not say where it led. Due south of us, and rising to a height of approximately eight hundred feet, were steep and rounded cliffs, and behind them sharp peaks. The southerly sun being low, these heights threw shadows which, for some time, had the appearance of bare rocks. Two dark patches in the face of one of the further cliffs had also this appearance, but a careful observation taken with a telescope showed them to be caverns. To the east rose a long snow slope which cut the horizon at the height of about three hundred feet. It had every appearance of ice-covered land, but we could not stop then to make certain, for the heavy ice and bergs lying to the northward of us were setting down into the bay, and I saw that if we were not to be beset it would be necessary to get away at once. All round us were numbers of great whales showing their dorsal fins as they occasionally sounded, and on the edge of the bay-ice half a dozen Emperor penguins stood lazily observing us. We named this place the Bay of Whales, for it was a veritable playground for these monsters.

We coasted eastward along the wall of ice, always on the look-out for the inlet. The lashings had been taken off the motor-car, and the tackle rigged to hoist it out directly we got alongside the ice-foot, to which the *Discovery* had been moored; for in Barrier Inlet we proposed to place our winter quarters.

I must leave the narrative for a moment at this point and refer to the reasons that made me decide on this inlet as the site for the winter quarters. I knew that Barrier Inlet was practically the beginning of King Edward VII Land, and that the actual bare land was within easy sledge journey of that place, and it had the great advantage of being some ninety miles nearer to the South Pole than any other spot that could be reached with the ship. A further point of importance was that it would be an easy matter for the ship on its return to us to reach this part of the Barrier, whereas King Edward VII Land itself might quite conceivably be unattainable if the season was adverse.

However, the best-laid schemes often prove impracticable in Polar Exploration, and within a few hours our first plan was found impossible of fulfilment. Within thirty-six hours a second arrangement had to be abandoned. We were steaming along westward close to the Barrier, and according to the chart we were due to be abreast of the inlet about 6 a.m., but not a sign was there of the opening. We had passed Borchgrevink's Bight at 1 a.m., and at 8 p.m. were well past the place where Barrier Inlet ought to have been. The Inlet had disappeared, owing to miles of the Barrier having calved away, leaving a long wide bay joining up with Borchgrevink's Inlet, and the whole was now merged into what we had called the Bay of Whales. This was a great disappointment to us, but we were thankful that the Barrier had broken away before we had made our camp on it. It was bad enough to try and make for a port that had been wiped off the face of the earth, when all the intending inhabitants were safe on board the ship, but it would have been infinitely worse if we had landed there whilst the place was still in existence, and that when the ship returned to take us off she should find the place gone. The thought of what might have been made me decide then and there that under no circumstances would I winter on the Barrier, and that wherever we did land we would secure a solid rock foundation for our winter home.

We had two strings to our bow, and I decided to use the second at once and push forward towards King Edward VII Land. About nine o'clock we cast off from the floe and headed the ship to the eastward, again keeping a few hundred yards off the Barrier, for just here the cliff overhung, and if a fall of ice had occurred while we were close in the results would certainly have been disastrous for us. I soon saw that we would not be able to make much easting in this way, for the Barrier was now trending well to the north-east, and right ahead of us lay an impenetrably close pack, set with huge icebergs. By 10 a.m. we were close to the pack and found that it was pressed hard against the Barrier edge, and, what was worse, the whole of the northern pack and bergs at this spot were drifting in towards the Barrier.

The seriousness of this situation can be well realised by the reader if he imagines for a moment that he is in a small boat right under the vertical white cliffs of Dover; that detached cliffs are moving in from seaward slowly but surely, with stupendous force and resistless power, and that it will only be a question of perhaps an hour or two before the two masses came into contact with his tiny craft between. There was nothing for it but to retrace our way and try some other route. Our position was latitude 78° 20′ South and longitude 162° 14′ West when the ship turned.

There was a peculiar light which rendered distances and the forms of objects very deceptive, and a great deal of mirage, which made things appear much higher than they actually were. This was particularly noticeable in the case of the pack-ice; the whole northern and western sea seemed crowded with huge icebergs, though in reality there was only heavy pack. The penguins that we had seen the previous night were still at the same place, and when a couple of miles away from us they loomed up as if they were about six feet high.

About 6 p.m. the pack-ice seemed to loosen somewhat, and by half-past seven, from the crow's-nest, I could see a lead of open water to the north through the belt of pack, and beyond that there appeared to be a fairly open sea. All night long we followed a zigzag course in the endeavour to penetrate to the east, at times steering due west, practically doubling on our tracks, before we could find an opening which would admit of our pursuing the direction we desired to follow.

The prospect of reaching King Edward VII Land seemed to grow more remote every ensuing hour. There was high hammocky pack interspersed with giant icebergs to the east and south of the ship, and it was obvious that the whole sea between Cape Colbeck and the Barrier at our present longitude must be full of ice. To the northward the strong ice blink on the horizon told the same tale. It seemed as if it would be impossible to reach the land, and the shortness of coal, the leaky condition of the ship, and the absolute necessity of landing all our stores and putting up the hut before the vessel left us made the situation an extremely anxious one for me.

I decided to continue to try and make a way to the east for at least another twenty-four hours. We altered the course to the north, skirting the ice as closely as possible, and taking advantage of the slightest trend to the eastward, at times running into narrow *culs-de-sac* in the main pack, only to find it necessary to retrace our way again.

The weather cleared again shortly, and we saw the western pack moving rapidly towards us under the influence of the wind; in some places it had already met the main pack. As it was most likely that we would be caught in this great mass of ice, and that days, or even weeks might elapse before we could extricate ourselves, I reluctantly gave orders to turn the ship and make full speed out of this dangerous situation. I could see nothing for it except to steer for McMurdo Sound, and there make our winter quarters.

For many reasons I would have preferred landing at King Edward VII Land, as that region was absolutely unknown. I did not give up the destined base of our expedition without a strenuous struggle, as the track of the ship given in the sketch-map shows; but the forces of these uncontrollable ice-packs are stronger than human resolution, and a change of plan was forced upon us.

At this point, perhaps more than anywhere else in Shackleton's published works, the reader is denied an account of what was really going on in his mind. The written agreement with Scott about the use of the McMurdo base is not even mentioned. It had never been public knowledge, and by the time *Heart of the Antarctic* was on the bookstalls, the two men had buried the hatchet.

At the time, though, it was very different. When Scott heard that Shackleton had not 'rigidly adhered' to the agreement, and gone for McMurdo, bad faith seemed the only explanation. His immediate reaction was to expose Shackleton by letting the document be seen by a wider audience. It was Sir Clements Markham who dissuaded him.

As for Shackleton himself, the personal anguish he suffered when he finally gave up the attempt to reach King Edward VII Land, and head west across that fateful 170 degree demarcation line, is all set out in a long letter to Emily. As the Fishers point out in their biography, it is really a letter to himself. Here are the salient passages.

26 January, 1908

What a difference a few short hours can make in one's life and work and destiny: Child o' mine I have been through a sort of Hell since the 23rd and I cannot even now realize that I am on my way back to McMurdo Sound and that all idea of wintering on the Barrier or at King Edward VII Land is at an end that I have had to break my word to Scott and go back to the old base, and that all my plans and ideas have now to be changed and changed by the overwhelming forces of Nature. I am feeling more now than I can say darling and wish that I were close to you telling it all to you instead of locking it up in my heart as I have to do to a great extent: and all the anxiety that I have been feeling coupled with the desire to really do the right thing has made me older than I can ever say. Child I must now write my heart out and it is to you alone that I can do for I never never knew what it was to make such a decision as the one I was forced to make last night. Well child you will have seen about it roughly and in bald facts in the papers and cables, so can understand what has happened but you I know can read between the lines and realize what it has been to me to stand up on the bridge in those snow squalls and decide whether to go on or turn back my whole heart crying out for me to go on and the feeling against of the lives and families of the 40 odd men on board: I swept away from my thoughts the question of the Pole or the success of the Expedition at that moment though in doing so I know now in my calmer moments that I was wrong to even to do that: that my money was given for me to reach the Pole not to just play with according to my ideas of right and wrong, that I had a great public trust which I could not betray that in all ways my one line of action should have been the one I am taking now: but that was not what weighed with me then and I feel that you will understand me in it all.

To the North close in the offing lay the heavy pack and I saw no chance of going North and trying again from the Northward of the pack away to the East. My heart was heavy within me for here was a direct check to my plans: if I had not promised Scott that I would not use 'his' place, I would then have gone on to MacMurdo Sound with a light heart but I had promised that I felt each mile that I went to the West was a horror to me I could see nothing for it but to go there for after the fact became apparent that Balloon Inlet had gone then obviously any idea of wintering on any other part or inlet of the Barrier would be suicidal and fraught with most serious danger not only to the success of the Expedition but also to the lives of all the men who I am responsible for; my private word of honour my promise given under pressure was one thing that weighed in the balance against my going back at once and I gladly saw towards 6 p.m. another loosening of the pack to the North-ward and after a long talk with England who put the seriousness of my position, frankly before me; by the attempt; the shortage of coal which even then was only sufficient to ensure the arrival of the ship at New Zealand: the strained conditions of the vessel: the fact that even if we eventually arrived at King E VII Land I might not be able to find a safe place to discharge and would probably have to abandon it in view of the enormous masses of land ice and hummocked up pack that was breaking away which would make the ship's position untenable: my duty to the country and King since I was given the flag for the Pole and lastly but not least my duty to all who entrusted themselves to my keeping: I myself recognised the weight and truth of all he said and I knew at the same time that he was heart and soul with me and had no thought of his personal safety indeed neither of us as we stood on the bridge the same morning thought of that but of the safety of the laughing careless crowd of men who little thought or dreamt what our feelings were as the ice was closing in; to them it was merely an interesting episode and gave them an oppor-tunity of a nearer view of seals and penguins just you imagine if you were in charge of a little skiff right under the white cliffs of Dover and saw bearing down on you going to crush you against those cliffs great masses like the Royal Exchange; or a piece the size of the N B R Hotel and

Prince's Hotel, great pieces twice the height of the Dean Bridge above the Waters of Leith other pieces as big and as square as all Belgrave Terrace and Buckingham Terrace coming down on to you one piece the length of West Hill from the top to Walter's corner; just imagine this and think that besides the safety of all those men who were with me I had had the success from the world's point of view and the eyes of the world on us, then it will come home to you what those hours meant to me and England.

I said to England that as regards the fuel question which was so urgent a one; that I was willing for him not only to burn all easily available woodwork on the ship but also to burn the deck-house cut away the mizzen mast burn it and the main topmast and anything at all that would further our object and gain time so that I could carry out my personal promise to Scott. This weighed with me even more than I ought to have allowed it to when I come to think of it in calmer moments now.

My conscience is clear but my heart is sore, and writing now I feel it as much but I have one comfort that I did my best; if I had gone back without risking and trying all I did and if eventually I got the Pole from MacMurdo Sound Base it would have been ever tarnished and as ashes to me but now I have done my best and if the whole world were to cry out at me which I am sure they would not even then I would not worry myself for I know in my own heart that I am right. Now going as we are to MacMurdo Sound there is only one thing to do and that is to do the best possible work there and much may be done there still: Indeed we may reach King E VII Land by the journey across the Barrier. I think that darling I have now put down all that has been on my mind and I know you will know that I have done all that any man could have done under the circumstances if you would like to send an extract of this part of my letter you can write it from one asterisk at the beginning to the one on this page and send it to anyone you like in the family Herbert etc. but not to outside people and to no enemies Not that I think there will be really any except the Scott faction: I dont want you little girl to be worried in any way over this for to my mind it is now perfectly clear and though I regret it all (re my promise to Scott) my mind is at rest and it will not weigh with me any more and will not in the slightest affect my work in the future.

But Shackleton had one critic on board the *Nimrod* who took a very different view of events. Dr Eric Marshall, later to be one of the party of four who made the bid for the South Pole, wrote this in his diary on the evening of January 24th:

> Up to the present time the ship has certainly not rubbed an ounce of paint off her sides. Shackleton is not going to make another attempt on King Edward the Seventh Land, . . . and says he will go to McMurdo Sound. If this is so he hasn't got the guts of a louse, in spite of what he may say to the world on his return. He has made no attempt to reach King Edward VII Land. In short, he and England funk it. It is useless talking about it. He got very angry when I told him I was sorry he had not made an attempt . . . tried to make me believe he had done as much as any human being could.

Two points need to be made about Marshall's opinion. He was little more than a passenger at the time, with no experience of seamanship, and he had already begun to take a dislike to Shackleton, as his diary in the following weeks makes all too clear.

Nevertheless it must be said that if Marshall's diary had ever been presented as evidence, it would have gone some way to confirm Scott's suspicion of 'bad faith'.

Before returning to Shackleton's own narrative this may be an appropriate point to raise the question of his relationship with Captain England. Although Shackleton was the overall leader of the expedition, England was the Captain of the *Nimrod*, with the responsibility of discharging his duties in a safe and efficient manner, and above all getting his ship back to the comparatively safe waters of New Zealand. His position was somewhat similar to that of a naval captain who has a flag officer on board.

It seems clear from his letter to Emily, quoted above, that throughout those difficult days off the Barrier, Shackleton was extremely grateful for Captain England's advice and support. But once the unloading began at Cape Royds, their relationship seems to have deteriorated. There were two matters of particular concern to both men. One was the dwindling supply of coal, already insufficient to provide an adequate reserve both for the ship's return journey, and for the shore base. In the end, an equable decision was reached as to how much coal could be landed without endangering the safe return of the ship, vital for the survival of them all; but not before some members of the shore party had accused Captain England of being unreasonably over-cautious in his estimates.

The second matter concerned the unloading of the expedition's equipment. If the ship could be kept in close to the ice for several days at a time, there was a much better chance of completing the unloading successfully before conditions changed for the worse. But Captain England had the safety of the ship to consider. He refused to take chances and kept his ship well back from any dangerous encounters with the ice.

There is no mention in Shackleton's memoirs of the 'incident' which ensued. But for a time the British and New Zealand press fastened like leeches on the rumours which came back with the *Nimrod*. There had been a 'fight on the bridge' with 'blows exchanged' between Shackleton and England. The truth, insofar as we shall ever know it, was less dramatic, but sufficient to convince Shackleton that when the *Nimrod* returned the following year to take the expedition back to civilisation, he did not want Captain England to return with it.

Matters came to a head over the question of unloading. With every hour gained of vital importance, Shackleton believed it was perfectly safe to take the ship to the edge of the ice. In a gesture of impatience or perhaps impetuosity, he put his hand on the ship's telegraph to signal 'full speed ahead' to the engine room. It was clearly not his job to do so: and Captain England promptly placed his own hand on Shackleton's, pulling the lever to 'full speed astern'. Both men then retired below to continue the argument out of hearing of the rest of the ship's crew.

No one who knows anything of the sort of strains that can occur when working in such conditions will be surprised at the flare-up itself. But this one did not subside as quickly as it arose. Nor did Shackleton behave with quite his usual openness. He sent a letter with another returning crew member, so that the luckless Captain England did not learn that he had been removed from his command until the *Nimrod* was safely back in Lyttelton Harbour, New Zealand. Too late, he discovered that you were either a Shackleton man – or you were not.

THE SELECTION OF THE WINTER QUARTERS

We now laid our course for Mount Erebus, and as I hoped to examine the Barrier more closely in the following year we made a direct course west, which took us some distance off the edge of the ice.

A great arch of clear sky rose in the south about noon; shortly before this a curious whitish appearance gave one the impression of land, and as the sky cleared this became more distinct, and proved to be Erebus and Terror, the two huge mountains we were approaching. By 2 p.m. they had grown much more distinct, and were evidently raised by mirage to even statelier altitudes than their own. We could plainly see the smoke from Mount Erebus, which from our point of view showed to the south of Mount Terror. We altered the course a little so as to make Cape Grozier.

As we steamed down McMurdo Sound we passed through occasional loose patches of pack-ice, on which immense numbers of penguins were congregated. To the west were the gigantic peaks of the western mountains with their huge amphitheatres and immense glaciers. About seven miles to the eastward lay a dark mass of rock, Cape Royds, named after the first lieutenant of the *Discovery*. So familiar were they that it seemed as though it were only yesterday that I had looked on the scene, and yet six years had gone by.

I decided to lie off the ice-foot for a few days at least, and give Nature a chance to do what we could not with the ship, that is, to break up the miles of ice intervening between us and our goal.

We unfastened most of the beams of the pony shelter, so that there would be no difficulty in getting the ponies out at a moment's notice, and removed a lot of the top hamper from the skids. Most of the poor beasts were in bad condition. Those which were white all over seemed, for some reason, to have stood the rough weather better than the parti-coloured ones, but all were enjoying the steadiness of the ship after the terrible rolling. The flanks of most of the horses had been skinned by the constant knocking and rubbing against the sides of their stalls, and Zulu was in such a bad condition from this cause that I decided to have him shot at once. This left us with eight ponies, and we considered ourselves fortunate in reaching winter quarters with the loss of only two animals.

So far the voyage had been without accident to any of the staff, but on the morning of the 31st, when all hands were employed getting stores out of the after hatch, preparatory to landing them, a hook on the tackle slipped and, swinging suddenly across the deck, struck Mackintosh in the right eye. He fell on the deck in great pain, but was able, in a few minutes, to walk with help to England's cabin, where Marshall examined him. It was apparent that the sight of the eye was completely destroyed, so he was put under chloroform, and Marshall removed the eye, being assisted at the operation by the other two doctors, Michell and Mackay. It was a great comfort to me to know that the expedition had the services of thoroughly good surgeons. Mackintosh felt the loss of his eye keenly; not so much because the sight was gone, but because it meant that he could not remain with us in the Antarctic. He begged to be allowed to stay, but when Marshall explained that he might lose the sight of the other eye, unless great care were taken, he accepted his ill-fortune without further demur, and thus the expedition lost, for a time, one of its most valuable members.

About four o'clock on 3 February we got under way and started towards Cape Barne on the look-out for a suitable landing-place. Steaming slowly north along the coast we saw across the bay a long, low snowslope, connected with the bare rock of Cape Royds, which appeared to be a likely place for winter quarters.

About eight o'clock, accompanied by Adams and Wild in the whale boat, and taking the hand lead with us, I left the ship and went in towards the shore. After about ten minutes' pulling, with frequent stops for soundings, we came up against fast ice. This covered the whole of the small bay from the corner of Flagstaff Point, as we afterwards named the seaward cliff at the southern end of Cape Royds, to Cape Barne to the southward. Close up to the Point the ice had broken out, leaving a little natural dock. We ran the boat into this, and Adams and I scrambled ashore, crossing a well-defined tide-crack and going up a smooth snowslope about fifteen yards wide, at the top of which was bare rock.

A very brief examination of the vicinity of the ice-foot was sufficient to show us that Cape Royds would make an excellent place on which to land our stores. We therefore shoved off in the boat again, and, skirting along the ice-foot to the south, sounded the bay, and found that the water deepened from two fathoms close in shore to about twenty fathoms four hundred yards further south. After completing these soundings we pulled out towards the ship, which had been coming in very slowly. We were pulling along at a good rate when suddenly a heavy body shot out of the water, struck the seaman who was pulling stroke, and dropped with a thud into the bottom of the boat. The arrival was an Adelie penguin. It was hard to say who was the most astonished – the penguin, at the result of its leap on to what it had doubtless thought was a rock, or we, who so suddenly took on board this curious passenger. The sailors in the boat looked upon this incident as an omen of good luck. There is a tradition amongst seamen that the souls of old sailors, after death, occupy the bodies of penguins, as well as of albatrosses; this idea, however, does not prevent the mariners from making a hearty meal off the breasts of the former when opportunity offers. We arrived on board at 9 p.m., and by 10 p.m. on February 3 the *Nimrod* was moored to the bay ice, ready to land the stores.

THE LANDING OF STORES AND EQUIPMENT

With this work commenced the most uncomfortable fortnight, and the hardest work, full of checks and worries, that I or any other member of the party had ever experienced. If it had not been for the whole-hearted devotion of our party, and their untiring energy, we would never have got through the long toil of discharging.

The first thing to be landed was the motor-car, and after that came the ponies, for it was probable that any day might see the break-up of the bay ice, and there being only two fathoms of water along the shore, as we had ascertained by sounding down the tide crack, the ship could not go very close in. It would have been practically impossible to have landed the ponies in boats, for they were only half-broken in, and all in highly strung, nervous condition.

Joyce ran the dogs ashore and tied them up to rocks, all except Possum, who was still engaged with her little puppies. We worked till 3 a.m., landing pony fodder and general stores, and then knocked off and had some cocoa and a rest, intending to turn to at 6 a.m.

We had hardly started work again when a strong breeze sprung up with drifting snow. The ship began to bump heavily aginst the ice-foot and twice dragged her anchors out, so, as there seemed no possibility of getting ahead with the landing of the stores under these conditions, we steamed out and tied up at the main iceface, about six miles to the south, close to where we had lain for the past few days. It blew fairly hard all day and right through the evening, but the wind went down on the afternoon of the 5th, and we returned to the bay that evening. The poor dogs had been tied up all this time, without any shelter or food, so directly we made fast, Joyce was off ashore with a steaming hot feed for them. Scamp came running down to meet him, and Queenie got loose and played havoc amongst the penguins. They had killed over a hundred, and the skuas were massed in great numbers, taking full advantage of this disaster. We never saw Queenie again. She must have fallen over a cliff into the sea.

We lost no time in getting the ponies ashore. This was by no means an easy task, for some of the animals were very restive, and it required care to avoid accident to themselves or to us. Some time before we had thought of walking them down over a gang-plank on to the ice, but afterwards decided to build a rough horse-box, get them into this, and then sling it over the side by means of the main gaff. One after another the ponies were led out of the stalls into the horse-box and were slung over on to the ice.

Presently it came to Grisi's turn, and we looked for a lively time with this pony, for he was the most spirited and in the best condition of all. As the box was being hoisted up, his violent kicking threatening to demolish the somewhat frail structure, and it was with a devout feeling of thankfulness that I saw him safe on the ice. They all seemed to feel themselves at home, for they immediately commenced pawing at the snow as they are wont to do in their own far-away Manchurian home, where, in the winter, they scrape away the snow to get out the rough tussocky grass that lies underneath.

All this time the hut-party were working day and night, and the building was rapidly assuming an appearance of solidity. The uprights were in, and the brace ties were fastened together, so that if it came on to blow there was no fear of the structure being destroyed.

By this time there were several ugly looking cracks in the bay ice, and these kept opening and closing having a play of seven or eight inches between the floes. Mackay started to try and get the pony Chinaman across the crack when it was only about six inches wide, but the animal suddenly took fright, reared up on his hind legs, and backing towards the edge of the floe, which had at that moment opened to a width of a few feet, fell bodily into the ice-cold water.

It looked as if it was all over with poor Chinaman, but Mackay hung on to the head rope, and Davis, Mawson, Michell and one of the sailors who were on the ice close by, rushed to his assistance. The pony managed to get his fore feet on the edge of the ice-floe. After great difficulty a rope sling was passed underneath him, and then by tremendous exertion he was lifted up far enough to enable him to scramble on the ice. There he stood, wet and trembling in every limb. A few seconds later the floe closed up against the other one. It was providential that it had not done so during the time that the pony was in the water, for in that case the animal would inevitably have been squeezed to death between the two huge masses of ice. A bottle of brandy was thrown on to the ice from the ship, and half its contents were poured down Chinaman's throat.

A BLIZZARD: THE DEPARTURE OF THE *NIMROD*

About five o'clock on the afternoon of February 18, snow began to fall, with a light wind from the north, and as at times the boat could hardly be seen from the ship, instructions were given to the boat's crew that whenever the *Nimrod* was not clearly visible they were to wait alongside the shore until the snow squall had passed and she appeared in sight again. Within half an hour it was blowing a furious blizzard, and every sign of land, both east and west, was obscured in the scudding drift.

All night the gale raged with great fury. The speed of the gusts at times must have approached a force of a hundred miles an hour. The tops of the seas were cut off by the wind, and flung over the decks, mast, and rigging of the ship, congealing at once into hard ice, and the sides of the vessels were thick with the frozen sea water. 'The masts were grey with the frozen spray, and the bows were a coat of mail.' Very soon the cases and sledges lying on deck were hard and fast in a sheet of solid ice, and the temperature had dropped below zero. Harbord, who was the officer on watch, on whistling to call the crew aft, found that the metal whistle stuck to his lips, a painful intimation of the low temperature.

At 2 a.m. the weather suddenly cleared, and though the wind still blew strongly and gustily, it was apparent that the force of the gale had been expended. We could now see our position clearly. The wind and current, in spite of our efforts to keep our position, had driven us over thirty miles to the north, and at this time we were abeam of Cape Bird. The sea was rapidly decreasing in height, enabling us to steam for Cape Royds.

We arrived there in the early morning, and I went ashore at Back Door Bay, after pushing the whale boat through pancake ice and slush, the result of the gale.

On going down to our main landing-place, the full effect of the blizzard became apparent. There was hardly a sign to be seen of the greater part of our stores. At first it appeared that the drifting snow had covered the cases and bales and the coal, but a closer inspection showed that the real disappearance of our stores from view was due to the sea. Such was the force of the wind blowing straight on to the shore from the south that the spray had been flung in sheets over everything and had been carried by the wind for nearly a quarter of a mile inland, and consequently in places, our precious stores lay buried to a depth of five or six feet in a mass of frozen sea water.

At 10 p.m. the *Nimrod's* bows were pointed to the north, and she was moving rapidly away from the winter quarters with a fair wind. Within a month I hoped she would be safe in New Zealand, and her crew enjoying a well-earned rest. We could hope for no word of news from civilisation until the *Nimrod* came south again in the following summer, and before that we had a good deal of difficult work to do, and some risks to face.

FIRST DAYS IN WINTER QUARTERS

The inside of the hut was not long in being fully furnished, and a great change it was from the bare shell of our first days of occupancy. The first thing done was to peg out a space for each individual, and we saw that the best plan would be to have the space allotted in sections, allowing two persons to share one cubicle. This space for two men amounted to six feet six inches in length and seven feet in depth from the wall of the hut towards the centre. There were seven of these cubicles, and a space for the leader of the expedition; thus providing for the fifteen who made up the shore-party.

My room contained the bulk of our library, the chronometers, the chronometer watches, barograph, and the electric-recording thermometer; there was ample room for a table, and the whole made a most comfortable cabin.

The wall of Adams' and Marshall's cubicle, which was next to my room, was fitted with shelves made out of Venesta cases, and there was so much neatness and order about this apartment that it was known by the address, 'No. 1 Park Lane.' In front of the shelves hung little gauze curtains, tied up with blue ribbon, and the literary tastes of the occupants could be seen at a glance from the bookshelves. In Adams' quarter the period of the French Revolution and the Napoleonic era filled most of his bookshelves, though a complete edition of Dickens came in a good second. Marshall's shelves were stocked with bottles of medicine, medical works, and some general literature. The dividing curtain of duck was adorned by Marston with life-sized coloured drawings of Napoleon and Joan of Arc.

The next cubicle on the same side was occupied by Marston and Day, and as the former was the artist and the latter the general handy man of the expedition, one naturally found an ambitious scheme of decoration. This cubicle was known as 'The Gables'.

Next came one of the first cubicles that had been built. Joyce and Wild occupied the 'Rogues' Retreat', a painting of two very tough characters drinking beer out of pint mugs, with the inscription *The Rogues' Retreat* painted underneath, adorning the entrance to the den. The first bed had been built in Wild's store-room for secrecy's sake; it was to burst upon the view of every one, and to create mingled feelings of admiration and envy, admiration for the splendid design, envy of the unparalleled luxury provided by it. However, in building it, the designer forgot the size of the doorway he had to take it through, and it had ignominiously to be sawn in half before it could be passed out of the store-room into the hut. The printing press and type case for the polar paper occupied one corner of this cubicle.

The next and last compartment was the dwelling-place of the Professor and Mawson. It would be difficult to do justice to the picturesque confusion of this compartment; one hardly likes to call it untidy, for the things that covered the bunks by daytime could be placed nowhere else conveniently. A miscellaneous assortment of cameras, spectroscopes, thermometers, microscopes, electrometers and the like lay in profusion on the blankets. The name given, though not by the owners, to this cubicle was 'The Pawn Shop'.

In order to give as much free space as possible in the centre of the hut we had the table so arranged that it could be hoisted up over our heads after meals were over. This gave ample room for the various carpentering and engineering efforts that were constantly going on. Murray built the table out of the lids of packing-cases, and though often scrubbed, the stencilling on the cases never came out. We had no table-cloth, but this was an advantage, for a well-scrubbed table had a cleaner appearance than would be obtained with such washing as could be done in an Antarctic laundry.

As the winter came on and the light grew faint outside, the hut became more and more like a workshop, and it seems strange to me now, looking back to those distant days, to remember the amount of trouble and care that was taken to furnish and beautify what was only to be a temporary home. During our first severe blizzard, the hut shook and trembled so that every moment we expected the whole thing to carry away, and there is not the slightest shadow of a doubt that if we had been located in the open, the hut and everything in it would have been torn up and blown away. Even with our sheltered position I had to lash the chronometers to the shelf in my room, for they were apt to be shaken off when the walls trembled in the gale. When the storm was over we put a stout wire cable over the hut, burying the ends in the ground and freezing them in, so as to afford additional security in case heavier weather was in store for us in the future.

SLEDGING EQUIPMENT: PONIES AND DOGS

In considering the various methods of haulage in the Antarctic the experience of the National Antarctic Expedition proved of very great value. Only twenty dogs were taken with the *Discovery*, and the trouble they gave and their eventual collapse and failure are matters of common knowledge amongst those interested in Antarctic exploration. The knowledge I gained of the Barrier surface on that occasion suggested to me the feasibility of using ponies for traction purposes, for I had heard that in Siberia and Northern Manchuria ponies of a peculiarly hardy and sturdy stock did excellent work in hauling sledges and carrying packs over snow and ice at very low temperatures and under very severe weather conditions.

It seems to be generally assumed that a Manchurian pony can drag a sledge over a broken trail at the rate of twenty or thirty miles a day, pulling not less than twelve hundred pounds. Some authorities even put the weight to be hauled at eighteen hundred pounds, but this is, I think, far too heavy a load. It was a risk to take ponies from the far north through the tropics and then across two thousand miles of stormy sea on a very small ship, but I felt that if it could be done it would be well worth the trouble, for, compared with the dog, the pony is a far more efficient animal, one pony doing the work of at least ten dogs on the food allowance for ten dogs, and travelling a longer distance in a day.

We established ourselves at the winter quarters with eight ponies, but unfortunately we lost four of them within a month of our arrival. The loss was due, in the case of three of the four, to the fact that they were picketed when they first landed on sandy ground, and it was not noticed that they were eating the sand. I had neglected to see that the animals had a supply of salt given to them, and as they found a saline flavour in the volcanic sand under their feet, due to the fact that the blizzards had sprayed all the land near the shore with sea water, they ate it at odd moments. All the ponies seem to have done this, but some were more addicted to the habit than the others. Several of them became ill, and we were quite at a loss to account for the trouble until Sandy died. Then a post-mortem examination revealed the fact that his stomach contained many pounds of sand, and the cause of the illness of the other ponies became apparent. We shifted them at once from the place where they were picketed, so that they could get no more sand, and gave them what remedial treatment lay in our power, but two more died in spite of all our efforts. The loss of the fourth pony was due to poisoning. The Manchurian ponies will eat anything at all that can be chewed, and this particular animal seems to have secured some shavings in which chemicals had been packed. The post-mortem examination showed that there were distinct signs of corrosive poisoning. The losses were a matter of deep concern to us.

We were left with four ponies, Quan, Socks, Grisi and Chinaman, and it is a rather curious fact that the survivors were the white or light-coloured animals, while disaster had befallen all the dark animals.

The four ponies were very precious in our eyes, and they were watched and guarded with keen attention. Every one of them seemed to possess more cunning and sense than the ordinary broken-in horse at home, and this cunning, when put into practice to gain any end of their own, was a constant source of petty annoyance to us. Quan was the worst offender, his particular delight being to bite through his head rope and attack the bales of fodder stacked behind him; then, when we put a chain on to prevent this, he deliberately rattled it against the side of the hut, which kept us awake. The wall of the hut was sheathed with galvanised iron, and shortly after the ponies entered the stable, as they started to gnaw the ropes, a line of wire had been stretched fore and aft along the tables to which to make fast the head rope. Quan used to take this line between his teeth and pull back as far as possible and then let it go with a bang. We tried keeping his nose-bag on, but within a few hours he would have worked a hole in this and started again on the rope. On going into the stables to try and stop his mischief, one's annoyance invariably passed away on seeing the intelligent look on the delinquent's face, as he rolled his eye round and leered at one as though to say:'Ha! Got the best of you again'.

Grisi was our best-looking pony, with a very pretty action and in colour a dapple grey; his conduct in the stables, however, was not friendly to the other ponies and we had to build him a separate stall in the far corner, as on the slightest provocation he would lash out with his hind feet. He became rather nervous and high-strung during the dark months, though we kept a lamp continually burning in the ponies' quarters. Socks was a pretty little pony, shaped something like a miniature Clydesdale, very willing to work and always very fiery. After leading him along when out walking, it seemed a great change to take great raw-boned good-natured old Quan, who, in spite of his ugly appearance, was a general favourite. The last of our remaining ponies, Chinaman, was a strong beast, sulky in appearance, but in reality one of the best of the horses; he also had a penchant for biting through his head rope, but a chain stopped this.

We had been able to obtain only nine dogs, five bitches and four dogs, but so prolific were they that before mid-winter we had a young family of nine pups, five of these being born on the *Nimrod*. There were many more births, but most of the puppies came to an untimely end, there being a marked difference between the mothers as regards maternal instincts. Gwendoline, known as the 'mad bitch', took no care at all of her pups, whilst Daisy not only mothered her own but also a surviving puppy belonging to Gwen, which was taken from her when the culpable carelessness she had exhibited in the rearing of her offspring had resulted in the death of the remainder.

The presence of the dogs around winter quarters and on our walks was very cheerful, and gave a homelike feeling to the place, and our interest in the pups was always fresh, for as they gradually grew up each one developed characteristics and peculiarities of its own. Names were given to them regardless of their sex. Roland, for example, did not belong to the sterner sex, and was in her earlier days a very general favourite. She had a habit of watching for the door to be opened, and then launching herself, a white furry ball, into the midst of the party in the hut. Ambrose, a great big sleepy dog, was so named by Adams, perhaps owing to his portly proportions, which might bear resemblance to the well-favoured condition of a monk. Somehow or another the name Ambrose seemed to suit him. He had a trick of putting his head between one's legs whenever we were standing about outside, so when in the dark we felt a dog about our knees, we knew it was Ambrose. Ambrose had a brother and sister, but they were name-less, shining only in the reflected glory of the great Ambrose, being known as 'Ambrose's brother' or 'Ambrose's sister.'

All the pups were white or would have been white if some of them had not elected to sleep in the dustbin where the warm ashes were thrown at night time; indeed, the resting-places these little creatures found were varied and remarkable. Most of them learnt by sad experience the truth of the ancient words:

Such are the perils that environ
The man who meddles with cold iron,

for sometimes an agonising wail would proceed from a puppy and the poor little beast would be found with its tongue frozen fast to a tin in which it had been searching for some succulent remains. I have mentioned the puppies' usefulness in keeping watch on the ponies. They did the same service as regards the older dogs, which were tied up, for if by chance one of these dogs got adrift, he was immediately pursued by a howling mob of puppies; when the larger puppies were eventually chained up, the smaller ones watched them, too, with jealous eye. After enjoying some months of freedom, it seemed to be a terrible thing to the young dogs when first a collar was put on and their freedom was taken from them, and even less did they enjoy the experience of being taken to the sledge and there taught to pull.

Our experience on the *Discovery* expedition, specially during the long southern journey when we had so much trouble with our mixed crowd of dogs, rather prejudiced me against these animals as a means of traction, and we only took them as a stand-by in the event of the ponies breaking down.

The Geographical South Pole was by no means the only prize to be attempted in the coming season. While Shackleton himself led the Southern Party, other members of the expedition would be trying for the Magnetic Pole, surveying the Western Mountains, looking for minerals in the Dry Valley and generally carrying out a whole range of scientific observations. One such challenge lay near to hand. Just a few miles to the east of Cape Royds, the towering mass of Mount Erebus, still an active volcano, rose to a height of some thirteen thousand feet above them. It had never before been climbed. As the days grew longer, an attempt on that smoking summit seemed more and more attractive. From Shackleton's point of view it would give him the opportunity to test the calibre of some of his team without stretching his limited resources. He resisted the temptation to go himself, and chose Professor David to lead the assault party with Mawson and Mackay. Adams, Marshall and Brocklehurst were to act as a support party, bringing up additional stores.

There was not a single experienced mountaineer among them. Nevertheless the attempt proved a triumphant success. In the event the two parties joined up. They made a thorough examination of both the extinct and active craters, measured the height of the mountain accurately for the first time (13,370 feet above sea level) and glissaded their way down again, arriving at winter quarters just nine days later. The only casualty was Brocklehurst, who suffered from frostbitten feet. Unluckily for him, he lost not only some of his toes but also his place on the team which would be trying for the South Pole itself.

Shackleton now turned all his attention to the great journeys which lay ahead.

SOUTHERN DEPOT JOURNEY

By the middle of September a good supply of provisions, oil, and gear had been stored at Hut Point in preparation for the sledge journeys. All the supplies required for the southern journey had been taken there, in order that the start might be made from the most southern base available. During this period, while the men were gaining experience and getting into training, the ponies were being exercised regularly along the sea ice from winter quarters across to Cape Barne, and I was more than satisfied with the way in which they did their work. I felt that the little animals were going to justify the confidence I had reposed in them when I had brought them all the way from Manchuria to the bleak Antarctic. I tried the ponies with loads of varying weights in order to ascertain as closely as possible how much they could haul with maximum efficiency, and after watching the results of the experiments very carefully came to the conclusion that a load of 650 lb. per pony should be the maximum. It was obvious that if the animals were overloaded their speed would be reduced, so that there would be no gain to us, and if we were to accomplish a good journey to the south it was important that they should not be tired out in the early stages of the march over the Barrier surface. The weight I have mentioned was to include that of the sledge itself, which I have already stated was about 60 lb. When I came to consider the question of weight, I realised the full seriousness of the loss the expedition had sustained when the other four ponies were lost during the winter, for I saw that we would not be able to take with us towards the Pole as much food as I should have liked.

During the month of May, Day had taken the engine out of the motor-car, a task of no little difficulty in a temperature below zero, and after cleaning every part thoroughly, had packed it away in a case for the winter. On September 14, when the light was beginning to get stronger, he got the engine back into the car, working in a temperature of minus 10° Fahr., and began preparations for the journeys over the ice. The car made its first journey of importance on September 19, and by that time experiments had proved that an extensive reduction in weight was necessary if the machine was to accomplish anything at all. Day therefore proceeded to strip it of every bit of wood or metal not absolutely essential to running efficiency.

In its final form the bare chassis carried the engine and one seat for the driver. We had wheels of several types, but soon found that ordinary wheels with rubber tyres and non-skid chains gave the best results. At a temperature of minus 30° Fahr. the tyres became quite hard, with no spring in them, but we had no tyre troubles at all, even when the ice was very rough.

On September 19 the motor-car took Day, Brocklehurst and Adams, with a sledge on which were packed 750 lb. of stores, to lay a depot at Glacier Tongue for the southern journey. There was a stiff breeze blowing, with a temperature of minus 23° Fahr., but the car ran well for eight miles as far as Inaccessible Island over the sea ice. Then it got into the heavy sastrugi caused by the wind blowing between Inaccessible Island and Tent Island, and was stopped by soft snow, into which it ploughed deeply. An easier route was found about a mile further north, at a point where the sastrugi were less marked. The car reached a point a quarter of a mile distant from the Tongue, and the sledge was hauled the rest of the way by the men, as the surface was very soft. The return journey presented fewer difficulties, for Day was able to drive in the outward tracks. The total distance covered by the car that day was at least thirty miles, and the speed had ranged from three to fifteen miles an hour. The three men left the winter quarters at 9.30 a.m., and arrived back at 6.45 p.m., having accomplished an amount of work that would have occupied six men for two or three days without the assistance of the car.

About September 14 we started to make active preparations for the depot journey. I decided to place a depot one hundred geographical miles south of the *Discovery* winter quarters, the depot to consist of pony maize. I picked a depot party consisting of Adams,

Marshall, Wild, Joyce and Marston, with myself as the sixth man.

The depot party left Cape Royds on September 22, with a load of about 170 lb. per man, and made the first part of the journey in the motor-car. Day was able to get the machine, with the sledges towed behind and all the members of the party either on the car or the sledges, as far as Inaccessible Island, moving at a speed of about six miles an hour. I heard afterwards that the car ran back to the hut, a distance of eight miles, in twenty minutes. We took the sledges on ourselves over a fairly good surface, and spent the first night at the *Discovery* hut. Three of the puppies had followed the car when we started away from the winter quarters, and they had firmly refused to go back with it, apparently because Joyce had been in the habit of feeding them, and they were not willing to leave him. They followed us right to Hut Point, the first long march of their short lives, and after devouring all the meat and biscuits we would give them, they settled down in a corner of the hut for the night. We could not take the poor little animals out on to the Barrier with us, though they would have followed us readily enough, and we decided that the only thing to do was to shut them up in the hut until we came back. There was plenty of snow there, so that they would not want for water, and we opened a box of biscuits and some tinned meat, and left the food where they could reach it. Their anxious barks and whines followed us as we moved off southwards. [In fact they were gone for three weeks! *Ed.*]

The journey was a severe one, for the temperature got down to fifty-nine degrees below zero Fahr., with blizzard winds, but as we travelled over ground that had become fairly familiar in the course of the previous expedition, I will not deal with our experiences in any great detail. The main depot was laid in latitude 79.36° South, longitude 168° East, a distance of about one hundred and twenty geographical miles from the winter quarters.

On our return we found our little friends, the puppies, safe and sound in the hut, and their delight at seeing us again was simply huge. Directly they heard us approaching they started to make every effort in their power to attract attention, and the moment the door was opened they rushed out and fairly threw themselves upon us. They twined their fat little bodies round our boots and yelped in an ecstasy of welcome. Poor little dogs, they had, no doubt, been lonely and frightened during the three weeks they had spent in the hut, though physically they seemed to have been comfortable enough. They had eaten all the meat left for them, but they still had biscuits, and they had put on flesh.

Their coats were quite black owing to their having lain amongst the fragments of coal on the floor.

The next day we started for Cape Royds, and had the good fortune to meet the motor-car, driven by Day, at a point about a mile and a half south of Cape Barne. The sledges were soon hitched on behind, and we drove back triumphantly to the winter quarters. It was October 13 and we had travelled 320 statute miles since we left the hut twenty-two days before.

PREPARATION FOR THE SOUTHERN JOURNEY

The southern sledging-party was to leave the winter quarters on October 29, and immediately on the return of the depot party we started to make the final preparations for the attempt to reach the South Pole. I decided that four men should go south, I myself to be one of them, and that we should take provisions for ninety-one days; this amount of food, with the other equipment, would bring the load per pony up to the weight fixed as a result of experiments as the maximum load.

The men selected to go with me on the southern journey were Adams, Marshall and Wild. A supporting-party was to accompany us for a certain distance in order that we might start fairly fresh from a point beyond the rough ice off Minna Bluff, and we would take the four ponies and four sledges. It was with some regret that I decided that the motor-car would have to stay behind. The trials that we had made in the neighbourhood of the winter quarters had proved that the car could not travel over a soft snow surface, and the depot journey had shown me that the surface of the Barrier was covered with soft snow, much softer and heavier than it had been in 1902, at the time of the *Discovery* expedition. In fact I was satisfied that, with the Barrier in its then condition, no wheeled vehicle could travel over it. The wheels would simply sink in until the body of the car rested on the snowy surface.

The provisioning of the Southern Party was a matter that received long and anxious consideration. Marshall went very carefully into the question of the relative food-values of the various supplies, and we were able to derive much useful information from the experience of previous expeditions.

The daily allowance of food for each man on the journey, as long as full rations were given, was to be as follows:

	Oz.
Pemmican	7·5
Emergency ration	1·5
Biscuit	16.0
Cheese or chocolate	2.0
Cocoa	·7
Plasmon	1.0
Sugar	4·3
Quaker Oats	1.0
	34.0

The clothing worn by each man when we started on the southern journey was very light. We had experimented on the spring sledging journey, and had proved that it was quite possible, even in very low temperatures, to abandon the heavy pilot cloth garments, which tire the wearer by their own weight, and to march in woollen undergarments and windproof overalls. The personal equipment of the members of the Southern Party was as follows:

Woollen pyjama trousers	Burberry overalls
Woollen singlet	Balaclava
Woollen shirt	Burberry head covering
Woollen guernsey	Woollen mits
Two pairs thick socks	Fur mits
One pair finnesko	

Each man had his spare clothing and his personal belongings in a bag, the total weight of which was about seventeen pounds. The contents of each of these bags, in addition to diaries, letters and similar personal possessions, was as follows:

Pyjama sleeping-jacket	Two pairs goggles, one smoked,
Pyjama trousers, spare	one coloured
Eight pairs woollen socks	Roll lamp-wick, for tying on
Three pairs finnesko	mits and finnesko
Supply sennegrass	Sledge flag
Three pairs mittens	Tobacco and matches
Spare woollen helmet	
One pair spiked ski-boots	
Woollen muffler	

It was necessary to prepare for the non-return of the Southern Party, although we were taking no gloomy view of our prospects, and I therefore left full instructions for the conduct of the expedition in the event of accident. My instructions to Murray on this point were as follows:

In the event of the non-arrival of the Southern Party by February 25 you are to land sufficient coal and provisions to support a party of seven men for one year at Cape Royds. You are then to pick three men to stay behind, and you will pick these men from volunteers. If there are no volunteers, which is highly improbable, you are to select three men and order them to stay. You will give these three men instructions to proceed at once to the south on the 168th meridian in search of the Southern Party, the leader using discretion as to the time they should take over the search. You are to leave all the dogs ashore to assist this party. You will instruct them to search for the remains of the Southern Party in the following summer. You are to use your discretion as to any other orders you may think it desirable to issue. The *Nimrod* is to land as much sugar, fruit and jam as possible. There are ample provisions otherwise, but anything in the way of dainties or special vegetables should be landed. There are sufficient ordinary vegetables. The *Nimrod* is also to land any clothing that you may think necessary for the party of three men remaining behind. . . . In the event of J. B. Adams returning and my non-return, he is in full command of the whole expedition, and has my instructions in the matter. The ship must on the 1st of March steam to the entrance of McMurdo Sound to see the ice conditions, and if there is no heavy pack likely to hold her up, she can return to Cape Royds again; but I think that the utmost limit for the date to which you should remain is the 10th of March, 1909, as if we have not returned by then something very serious must have happened.

FIRST DAYS OF THE SOUTHERN MARCH

The events of the southern journey were recorded day by day in the diary I wrote during the long march. I read this diary when we had got back to civilisation, and arrived at the conclusion that to rewrite it would be to take away the special flavour which it possesses. It was written under conditions of much difficulty, and often of great stress, and these conditions I believe it reflects. I am therefore publishing the diary with only such minor amendments to the phraseology as were necessary in order to make it easily understood. The reader will understand that when one is writing in a sleeping-bag, with the temperature very low and food rather short, a good proportion of the 'of's', 'and's' and 'the's' get left out.

The story will probably seem bald, but it is at any rate a faithful record of what occurred.

October 29, 1908. A glorious day for our start; brilliant sunshine and a cloudless sky, a fair wind from the north, in fact, everything that could conduce to an auspicious beginning. We had breakfast at 7 a.m., and at 8.30 the sledges that the motor was to haul to Glacier Tongue were taken down by the penguin rookery and over to the rough ice. As we left the hut where we had spent so many months in comfort, we had a feeling of real regret that never again would we all be together there. It was dark inside, the acetylene was feeble in comparison with the sun outside, and it was small compared to an ordinary dwelling, yet we were sad at leaving it. Last night as we were sitting at dinner the evening sun entered through the ventilator and a circle of light shone on the picture of the Queen. Slowly it moved across and lit up the photograph of his Majesty the King. This seemed an omen of good luck, for only on that day and at that particular time could this have happened, and today we started to strive to plant the Queen's flag on the last spot of the world.

Hardly had we been going for an hour when Socks went dead lame. This was a bad shock, for Quan had for a full week been the same. We had thought that our troubles in this direction were over. Socks must have hurt himself on some of the sharp ice. We had to go on, and I trust that in a few days he will be all right. I shall not start from our depot at Hut Point until he is better or until I know actually what is going to happen. The lameness of a pony in our present situation is a serious thing. If we had eight, or even six, we could adjust matters more easily, but when we are working to the bare ounce it is very serious.

At 1 p.m. we halted and fed the ponies. As we sat close to them on the sledge Gris suddenly lashed out, and striking the sledge with his hoof, struck Adams just below the knee. Three inches higher and the blow would have shattered his knee-cap and ended his chance of going on. As it was the bone was almost exposed, and he was in great pain, but said little about it.

October 30. At Hut Point. Another gloriously fine day. We started away for Hut Point at 10.30 a.m., leaving the supporting-party to finish grinding the maize. The ponies were in good fettle and went away well, Socks walking without a sledge, while Grisi had 500 lb., Quan 430 lb., and Chinaman 340 lb. Socks seems better today. It is a wonderful change to get up in the morning and put on ski boots without any difficulty, and to handle cooking vessels without 'burning' one's fingers on the frozen metal. I was glad to see all the ponies so well, for there had been both wind and drift during the night. Quan seems to take a delight in biting his tether when anyone is looking, for I put my head out of the tent occasionally during the night to see if they were all right, and directly I did so Quan started to bite his rope. At other times they were all quiet.

November 1. Had breakfast at 6 a.m., and Murray came on the car with me, Day driving. There was a fresh easterly wind. We left Cape Royds at 8 a.m., and arrived off Inaccessible Island at twenty minutes past eight, having covered a distance of eight miles. The car was running very well. Gris bolted with his sledge, but soon stopped. The ponies pulled very well, with a bad light and a bad surface. We arranged the packing of the sledges in the afternoon, but we are held up because of Socks. His foot is seriously out of order. It is almost a disaster, for we want every pound of hauling power. This evening it is snowing hard, with no wind. Adams' leg is much better. Wild noticed a seal giving birth to a pup.

November 2. Dull and snowy during the early hours of today. When we awoke we found that Quan had bitten through his tether and played havoc with the maize and other fodder. Directly he saw me coming down the ice-foot, he started off, dashing from one sledge to another, tearing the bags to pieces and trampling the food out. It was ten minutes before we caught him. Luckily, one sledge of fodder was untouched. He pranced round, kicked up his heels, and showed that it was a deliberate piece of destructiveness on his part, for he had eaten his fill. His distended appearance was obviously the result of many pounds of maize.

November 3. Started at 9.30 from Hut Point, Quan pulling 660 lb., Grisi 615 lb., Socks 600 lb., and Chinaman 600 lb. Five men hauled 660 lb., 153 lb. of this being pony feed for our party. It was a beautifully fine day, but we were not long under way when we found that the surface was terribly soft, the ponies at times sinking in up to their bellies and always over their hocks.

We picked up the other sledges at the Barrier junction, and Brocklehurst photographed us all, with our sledge-flags flying and the Queen's Union Jack. At 10.15 we left the sea ice, and instead of finding the Barrier surface better, discovered that the snow was even softer than earlier in the day. The ponies pulled magnificently, and the supporting-party toiled on painfully in their wake.

We camped at 6 p.m., and, after feeding the ponies, had our dinner, consisting of pemmican, emergency ration, plasmon biscuits and plasmon cocoa, followed by a smoke, the most ideal smoke a man could wish for after a day's sledging. As there is now plenty of biscuit to spare, we gave the gallant little ponies a good feed of them after dinner.

November 5. On turning out this morning, we found the weather overcast, with slight snow falling and only a few landmarks visible to the north, nothing to the south.

November 6. Lying in our sleeping-bags all day except when out feeding the ponies, for it has been blowing a blizzard, with thick drift, from south by west. It is very trying to be held up like this, for each day means the consumption of 40 lb. of pony feed alone. We only had a couple of biscuits each for lunch, for I can see that we must retrench at every setback if we are going to have enough food to carry us through. We started with ninety-one days' food, but with careful management we can make it spin out to 110 days. If we have not done the job in that time it is God's will. I read *Much Ado About Nothing* during the morning. The surface of the Barrier is better, for the wind has blown away a great deal of the soft snow, and we will, I trust, be able to see any crevasses before we are on to them. This is our fourth day out from Hut Point, and we are only twenty miles south.

November 7. Another disappointing day. The weather was thick and overcast, with no wind. Part of White Island could be seen, and Observation Hill, astern, but before us lay a dead white wall, with nothing, even in the shape of a cloud, to guide our steering. Almost immediately after we left we crossed a crevasse, and before we had gone half a mile we found ourselves in a maze of them, only detecting their presence by the ponies breaking through the crust and saving themselves, or the man leading a pony putting his foot through. The first one Marshall crossed with Grisi was 6 ft. wide, and when I looked down, there was nothing to be seen but a black yawning void. Just after this, I halted Quan on the side of one, as I thought in the uncertain light, but I found that we were standing on the crust in the centre, so I very gingerly unharnessed him from the sledge and got him across. Then the sledge, with our three months' provisions, was pulled out of danger. Following this, Adams crossed another crevasse, and Chinaman got his forefoot into the hole at the side. I, following with Quan, also got into difficulties, and so I decided that it was too risky to proceed, and we camped between two large crevasses.

We are now at last quite on our own resources, and as regards comfort in the tents are very well off, for with only two men in each tent, there is ample room. Adams is sharing one with me, whilst Marshall and Wild have the other. Wild is cook this week, so they keep the cooker and the primus lamp in their tent, and we go across to meals, after first feeding the ponies. Next week Adams will be cook, so the cooking will be done in the tent I am in. We will also shift about so that we will take turns with each other as tent-mates. On the days on which we are held up by weather we read, and I can only trust that these days may not be many. I am just finishing reading *The Taming of the Shrew*. I have Shakespeare's Comedies, Marshall has Borrow's *The Bible in Spain*, Adams has Arthur Young's *Travels in France*, and Wild has *Sketches by Boz*.

[The difficulties of travelling over snow and ice in a bad light are very great. When the light is diffused by clouds or mist, it casts no shadows on the dead white surface, which consequently appears to the eye to be uniformly level. Often as we marched the sledges would be brought up all standing by a sastrugus, or snow mound, caused by the wind, and we would be lucky if we were not tripped up ourselves. Small depressions would escape the eye altogether, and when we thought that we were marching along on a level surface, we would suddenly step down two or three feet. The strain on the eyes under these conditions is very great, and it is when the sun is covered and the weather is thickish that snow blindness is produced. Snow blindness, with which we all became acquainted during the southern journey, is a very painful complaint. The first sign of the approach of the trouble is running at the nose; then the sufferer begins to see double, and his vision gradually becomes blurred. The more painful symptoms appear very soon. The blood-vessels of the eyes swell, making one feel as though sand had got in under the lids, and then the eyes begin to water freely and gradually close up. The best method of relief is to drop some cocaine into the eye, and then apply a powerful astringent, such as sulphate of zinc, in order to reduce the distended blood-vessels. The only way to guard against an attack is to wear goggles the whole time, so that the eyes may not be exposed to the strain caused by the reflection of the light from all quarters. These goggles are made so that the violet rays are cut off, these rays being the most dangerous, but in warm weather, when one is perspiring on account of exertion with the sledges, the glasses fog, and it becomes necessary to take them off frequently in order to wipe them. The goggles we used combined red and green glasses, and so gave a yellow tint to everything and greatly subdued the light. When we removed them, the glare from the surrounding whiteness was intense, and the only relief was to get inside one of the tents, which were made of green material, very restful to the eyes. We noticed that during the spring journey, when the temperature was very low and the sun was glaring on us, we did not suffer from snow blindness. The glare of the light reflected from the snow on bright days places a very severe strain on the eyes, for the rays of the sun are flashed back from millions of crystals. The worst days, as far as snow blindness was concerned, were when the sun was obscured, so that the light came equally from every direction, and the temperature was comparatively high. *E.S.*]

November 9. A different story today. When we woke up at 4.30 a.m. it was fine, calm and clear, such a change from the last four days. We got breakfast at 5 a.m., and then dug the sledges out of the drift. At 8.30 a.m. we got under way, the ponies not pulling very well, for they had lost condition in the blizzard and were stiff. We got over the first few crevasses without difficulty, then all of a sudden Chinaman went down a crack which ran parallel to our course. Adams tried to pull him out and he struggled gamely, and when Wild and I, who were next, left our sledges and hauled along Chinaman's sledge, it gave him more scope, and he managed to get on to the firm ice, only just in time, for three feet more and it would have been all up with the southern journey. The three-foot crack opened out into a great fathomless chasm, and down that would have gone the horse, all our cooking gear and biscuits and half the oil, and probably Adams as well. But when things seem the worst they turn to the best, for that was the last crevasse we encountered, and with a gradually improving surface, though very soft at times, we made fair headway. At 6.20 p.m. we suddenly heard a deep rumble, lasting about five seconds, that made the air and the ice vibrate. It seemed to come from the eastward, and resembled the sound and had the effect of heavy guns firing. We conjecture that it was due to some large mass of the Barrier breaking away, and the distance must be at least fifty miles from where we are. It was startling, to say the least of it.

[On my return to the winter quarters I made inquiries as to whether the rumbling sound we had heard had been noticed at Cape Royds, but I found that no member of the party there had remarked anything out of the ordinary. Probably Mounts Erebus and Terror had intercepted the sound. There is no doubt that the Barrier ice breaks away in very large masses. We had an illustration of that fact in the complete disappearance of Barrier Inlet, the spot at which I had proposed to place the winter quarters. It is from the edge of the Barrier, not only in our quadrant locality, but also on the other side of the Antarctic area, that the huge tabular bergs found in the Antarctic waters are calved off. Fractures develop as the ice is influenced by the open water, and these fractures extend until the breaking-point is reached. Then a berg, or perhaps a series of bergs, is left free to float northwards. At the time when we heard and felt the concussion of a break, we were some fifty miles from the Barrier edge, so that the disturbance in the ice must have been extensive. *E.S.*]

STEADY PROGRESS: THE SIGHTING OF NEW LAND

November 10. Got up to breakfast at 6 a.m., and under way at 8.15 a.m. During the night we had to get out to the ponies. Quan had eaten away the straps on his rug, and Grisi and Socks were fighting over it. Quan had also chewed Chinaman's tether, and the latter was busy at one of the sledges, chewing rope. Happily he has not the same mischievous propensities as Quan, so the food-bags were not torn about. All these things mean work for us when the day's march is over, repairing the damage done. The ponies started away well, with a good hard surface to travel on, but a bad light, so we, being in finnesko, had frequent falls over the sastrugi. I at last took my goggles off, and am paying the penalty tonight, having a touch of snow-blindness. During the morning the land to the west became more distinct, and the going still better, so that when we camped for lunch, we had covered nine and a half statute miles. All the ponies, except Quan, showed the result of the Maujee ration, and are quite loose. Directly we started after lunch, we came across the track of an Adelie penguin. It was most surprising, and one wonders how the bird came out here. It had evidently only passed a short time before, as its tracks were quite fresh. It had been travelling on its stomach a good way, and its course was due east towards the sea, but where it had come from was a mystery, for the nearest water in the direction from which it came was over fifty miles away, and it had at least another fifty miles to do before it could reach food and water. The surface in the afternoon became appallingly soft, the ponies sinking in up to their hocks, but there was hard snow underneath. At 6 p.m. we camped, with a march for the day of 15 m. 1550 yd. statute.

November 13. No diary yesterday, for I had a bad attack of snow-blindness, and am only a bit better tonight. We did a good march yesterday of over fifteen miles over fair surface, and again today did fifteen miles, but the going was softer. The ponies have been a trouble again. I found Quan and Chinaman enjoying the former's rug. They have eaten all the lining. The weather has been beautifully fine, but the temperature down to 12° below zero. The others' eyes are all right. Wild, who has been suffering, has been better today. Snow-blindness is a particularly unpleasant thing. One begins by seeing double, then the eyes feel full of grit; this makes them water and eventually one cannot see at all. All yesterday aftrnoon, though I was wearing goggles, the water kept running out of my eyes, and, owing to the low temperature, it froze on my beard. However, the weather is beautiful, and we are as happy as can be, with good appetites, too good in fact for the amount of food we are allowing ourselves. We are on short rations, but we will have horse meat in addition when the ponies go under. We have saved enough food to last us from our first depot into the Bluff, where, on the way back, we will pick up another depot that is to be laid out by Joyce during January next. I trust we will pick up the depot tomorrow night and it will be a relief, for it is a tiny speck in this snowy plain, and is nearly sixty miles from the nearest land. It is much the same as picking up a buoy in the North Sea with only distant mountains for bearings.

November 14. Another beautiful day, but with a low temperature (minus 7° Fahr. at 6 p.m.). During the morning there was a wind from the west-south-west, bitterly cold on our faces and burst lips, but the sun was warm on our backs. We expected to see the depot tonight or tomorrow morning, but during the afternoon, when we halted for a spell, we found that our 'ready use' tin of kerosene had dropped off a sledge, so Adams ran back three miles and found it. This caused a delay, and we camped at 6 p.m. We were just putting the position on the chart after dinner when Wild, who was outside looking through the Goertz glasses, shouted out that he could see the depot, and we rushed out. There were the flag and sledge plainly to be seen through the glasses. It is an immense relief to us, for there is stored at the depot four days' pony feed and a gallon of oil. We will sleep happily tonight. The Barrier surface now is covered with huge sastrugi, rounded off and running west-south-west and east-north-west, with soft snow between. We have never seen the surface alike for two consecutive days. The Barrier is as wayward and as changeful as the sea.

November 15. Another beautiful day. We broke camp at 8 a.m., and reached our depot at 9.20 a.m. We found everything intact, the flag waving merrily in the breeze, the direction of which was about west-south-west. We camped there and at once proceeded to re-distribute weights and to parcel our provisions to be left there. We found that we had saved enough food to allow for three days' rations, which ought to take us into the Bluff on our return, so we made up a bag of provisions and added a little oil to the tin we had been using from, leaving half a gallon to take us the fifty odd miles to the Bluff on the way back. We then depoted our spare gear and finnesko, and our tin of sardines and pot of black currant jam. We had intended these provisions for Christmas Day, but the weight is too much; every ounce is of importance.

November 16. It has been a wonderful and successful week, so different to this time six years ago, when I was toiling along five miles a day over the same ground. Tonight one can see the huge mountain range to the south of Barne Inlet. In order to further economise food we are saving three lumps of sugar each every day, so in time we will have a fair stock. The great thing is to advance our food-supply as far south as possible before the ponies give out. Every one is in splendid health, eyes all right again, and only minor troubles, such as split lips, which do not allow us to laugh. Wild steered all day, and at every hourly halt I put the compass down to make the course we are going straight as a die to the south. Chinaman, or 'The Vampire', as Adams calls him, is not so fit; he is stiff in the knees and has to be hauled along. Quan, *alias* 'Blossom', is A1, but one cannot leave him for a moment, otherwise he would have his harness chewed up. Within the last week he has had the greater part of a horse-cloth, about a fathom of rope, several pieces of leather, and odds and ends such as a nose-bag buckle, but his digestion is marvellous, and he seems to thrive on his strange diet. He would rather eat a yard of creosoted rope than his maize and Maujee, indeed he often, in sheer wantonness, throws his food all over the snow.

November 18. It is possible that we have reached the windless area around the Pole, for the Barrier is a dead, smooth, white plain, weird beyond description, and having no land in sight, we feel such tiny specks in the immensity around us. Overhead this afternoon, when the weather cleared, were wonderful lines of clouds, radiating from the south-west, travelling very fast to the north-east. It seems as though we were in some other world, and yet the things that concern us most for the moment are trivial, such as split lips and big appetites. Already the daily meals seem all too short, and we wonder what it will be like later on, when we are really hungry. I have had that experience once, and my companions will soon have it again with me. All the time we are moving south to our wished-for goal, and each day we feel that another gain has been made. We did 15 miles 500 yards today.

November 20. The surface has been the worst we have encountered so far, terribly soft, but we did 15 miles 800 yards (statute) for the day. The latter part of the afternoon was better. It seems to savour of repetition to write each day of the heavy going and the soft surface, but these factors play a most important part in our daily work, and it causes us a great deal of speculation as to what we will eventually find as we get further south. The whole place and conditions seems so strange and so unlike anything else in the world in our experience, that one cannot describe them in fitting words. At one moment one thinks of Coleridge's *Ancient Mariner*: 'Alone, alone; all, all alone, alone on a wide, wide sea', and then when the mazy clouds spring silently from either hand and drift quickly across our zenith, not followed by any wind, it seems uncanny. There comes a puff of wind from the north, another from the south, and anon one from the east or west, seeming to obey no law, acting on erratic impulses. It is as though we were truly at the world's end, and were bursting in on the birthplace of the clouds and the nesting home of the four winds, and one has a feeling that we mortals are being watched with a jealous eye by the forces of nature. To add to these weird impressions that seem to grow on one in the apparently limitless waste, the sun tonight was surrounded by mock suns and in the zenith was a bow, turning away from the great vertical circle around the sun. These circles and bows were the colour of the rainbow. We are all fairly tired tonight, and Wild is not feeling very fit, but a night's rest will do him good. The ponies are all fit except poor old Chinaman, and he must go tomorrow. He cannot keep up with the others, and the bad surface has played him out.

November 21. Started at 7.30 a.m. as we had to come to camp early tonight, and we wanted to get a good latitude observation at noon. We came to camp at 12.30 p.m., just as the weather cleared a little, and we could see land on our right hand, but only the base of the mountains, so could not identify them. Chinaman came up at last, struggling painfully along, so when we made our depot this evening he was shot. We will use the meat to keep us out longer, and will save on our dried stores. This is now our second depot, and we intend to leave about 80 lb. of pony meat, one tin of biscuits (27 lb.), some sugar and one tin of oil to see us back to Depot A. It is late now, for all arrangements for the depot took time. There was a lot of work in the arranging of the sledges for the remaining three ponies: packing stores, skinning Chinaman and cutting him up, all in a low temperature.

[The killing of ponies was not pleasant work, but we had the satisfaction of knowing that the animals had been well fed and well treated up to the last, and that they suffered no pain. When we had to kill a pony, we threw up a snow mound to leeward of the camp, so that no smell of blood could come down wind, and took the animal behind this, out of sight of the others. As a matter of fact, the survivors never displayed any interest at all in the proceedings, even the report of the revolver used in the killing failing to attract their attention. The sound did not travel far on the wide open plain. The revolver was held about 3 in. from the forehead of the victim and one shot was sufficient to cause instant death. The throat of the animal was cut immediately and the blood allowed to run away. Then Marshall and Wild would skin the carcase, and we took the meat off the legs, shoulders and back. In the case of Chinaman the carcase was opened and the liver and undercut secured, but the job was such a lengthy one that we did not repeat it in the case of the other animals. Within a very short time after killing, the carcase would be frozen solid, and we always tried to cut the meat up into as small pieces as possible before this occurred, for the cutting became very much more difficult after the process of freezing was complete. *E.S.*]

November 22. A beautiful morning. We left our depot with its black flag flying on the bamboo lashed to a discarded sledge, stuck upright in the snow, at 8.20 a.m. We have now three ponies dragging 500 lb. each, and they did splendidly through the soft snow. The going, I am thankful to say, is getting better, and here and there patches of harder surface are to be met with. The outstanding feature of today's march is that we have seen new land to the south – land never seen by human eyes before. The land consists of great snow-clad heights beyond Mount Longstaff, and also far inland to the north of Mount Markham. We were rather longer at lunch camp, for we tried to pull out Adams' tooth, which has given him great pain, so much that he has not slept at night at all. But the tooth broke, and he has a bad time now.

November 23. Our record march today, the distance being 17 miles 1650 yards statute. It has been a splendid day for marching, with a cool breeze from the south and the sun slightly hidden. The horses did very well indeed, and the surface has improved, there being fairly hard sastrugi from the south. Marshall has just succeeded in pulling out Adams' tooth, so now the latter will be able to enjoy horse-meat. This evening we had it fried, and so saved all our other food except biscuits and cocoa. It is my week as cook now, and Wild is my tent companion.

BEYOND ALL FORMER FOOTSTEPS

November 26. A day to remember, for we have passed the 'farthest South' previously reached by man. Tonight we are in latitude 82° 18½' South, longitude 168° East, and this latitude we have been able to reach in much less time than on the last long march with Captain Scott, when we made latitude 82° 16½' our 'farthest South'. We celebrated the breaking of the 'farthest South' record with a four-ounce bottle of Curaçoa, sent us by a friend at home. After this had been shared out into two tablespoonfuls each, we had a smoke and a talk before turning in. One wonders what the next month will bring forth. We ought by that time to be near our goal, all being well.

[It falls to the lot of few men to view land not previously seen by human eyes, and it was with feelings of keen curiosity, not unmingled with awe, that we watched the new mountains rise from the great unknown that lay ahead of us. Mighty peaks they were, the eternal snows at their bases, and their rough-hewn forms rising high towards the sky. No man of us could tell us what we would discover in our march south, what wonders might not be revealed to us, and our imaginations would take wings until a stumble in the snow, the sharp pangs of hunger, or the dull ache of physical weariness brought back our attention to the needs of the immediate present. As the days wore on, and mountain after mountain came into view, grimly majestic, the consciousness of our insignificance seemed to grow upon us. We were but tiny black specks crawling slowly and painfully across the white plain, and bending our puny strength to the task of wresting from nature secrets preserved inviolate through all the ages. *E.S.*]

November 27. Started at 8 a.m., the ponies pulling well over a bad surface of very soft snow. The weather is fine and clear save for a strong mirage, which throws all the land up much higher than it really is. All day we have seen new mountains arise, and it is causing us some anxiety to note that they tend more and more to the eastward, for that means an alteration of our course from nearly due south. Still they are a long way off, and when we get up to them we may find some strait that will enable us to go right through them and on south. One speculates greatly as we march along, but patience is what is needed. I think that the ponies are feeling the day-in, day-out drudgery of pulling on this plain. Poor beasts, they cannot understand, of course, what it is all for, and the wonder of the great mountains is nought to them, though one notices them at times looking at the distant land.

November 28. When we camped tonight Grisi was shot. He had fallen off during the last few days, and the snow-blindness was bad for him, putting him off his feed. He was the one chosen to go at the depot we made this evening. This is Depot C, and we are leaving one week's provisions and oil, with horsemeat, to carry us back to Depot B. We will go on tomorrow with 1200 lb. weight (nine weeks' provisions), and we four will pull with the ponies, two on each sledge.

November 29. The worst feature of today's march was the terribly soft snow in the hollows of the great undulations we were passing. During the afternoon one place was so bad that the ponies sank in right up to their bellies, and we had to pull with might and main to get the sledges along at all. The ponies were played out by 5.45 p.m., especially old Quan, who nearly collapsed, not from the weight of the sledge, but from the effort of lifting his feet and limbs through the soft snow. The weather is calm and clear, but very hot, and it is trying to man and beast. A time is coming, I can see, when we will have to ascend the mountains, for the land runs round more and more in an easterly direction. Still after all we must not expect to find things cut and dried and all suited to us in such a place.

December 1. Poor old Quan was quite finished when we came to camp at 6 p.m., having done 12 miles 200 yards, so he was shot. We all felt losing him, I particularly, for he was my special horse ever since he was ill last March. I had looked after him, and in spite of all his annoying tricks he was a general favourite. He seemed so intelligent. Still it was best for him to go, and like the others he was well fed to the last. We have now only one pony left, and are in latitude 83° 16' South. Ahead of us we can see the land stretching away to the east, with a long white line in front of it that looks like a giant Barrier, and nearer a very crusted-up appearance, as though there were great pressure ridges in front of us. It seems as though there is now going to be a change in some gigantic way in keeping with the vastness of the whole place. At one moment our thoughts are on the grandeur of the scene, the next on what we would have to eat if only we were let loose in a good restaurant. We are very hungry these days, and we know that we are likely to be for another three months.

December 2. Started at 8 a.m., all four of us hauling one sledge, and Socks following behind with the other. He soon got into our regular pace, and did very well indeed. Socks, the only pony left now, is lonely. He whinnied all night for his lost companion.

There is a red hill about 3000 ft. in height, which we hope to ascend tomorrow, so as to gain a view of the surrounding country. Then we will make our way, if possible, with the pony up a glacier ahead of us on to the land ice, and on to the Pole if all goes well. It is an anxious thing for us, for time is precious and food more so; we will be greatly relieved if we find a good route through the mountains.

December 4. Unable to write yesterday owing to bad attack of snow-blindness, and not much better tonight, but I must record the events of the two most remarkable days that we have experienced since leaving the winter quarters. After breakfast at 5.30 a.m. yesterday, we started off from camp, leaving all camp gear standing and good feed by Socks to last him the whole day.

Crossing several ridges of ice-pressure and many more crevasses, we eventually at 12.30 p.m. reached an area of smooth blue ice in which were embedded several granite boulders, and here we obtained a drink of delicious water formed by the sun playing on the rock face and heating the ice at the base. After travelling for half a mile, we reached the base of the mountain which we hoped to climb in order to gain a view of the surrounding country. This hill is composed of granite, the red appearance being no doubt due to iron. At 1 p.m. we had a couple of biscuits and some water, and then started to make our way up the precipitous rock face. This was the most difficult part of the whole climb, for the granite was weathered and split in every direction, and some of the larger pieces seemed to be just nicely balanced on smaller pieces, so that one could almost push them over by a touch. With great difficulty we clambered up this rock face, and then ascended a gentle snow slope to another rocky bit, but not so difficult to climb. From the top of this ridge there burst upon our view an open road to the south, for there stretched before us a great glacier running almost south and north between two huge mountain ranges. As far as we could see, except towards the mouth, the glacier appeared to be smooth, yet this was not a certainty, for the distance was so great. Eagerly we clambered up the remaining ridges and over a snow-slope, and found ourselves at the top of the mountain, the height being 3350 ft. according to aneroid and hypsometer. From the summit we could see the glacier stretching away south inland till at last it seemed to merge in high inland ice. Where the glacier fell into the Barrier about north-east bearing, the pressure waves were enormous, and for miles the surface of the Barrier was broken up. This was what we had seen ahead of us the last few days, and we now understood the reason of the commotion on the Barrier surface.

It is all so interesting and everything is on such a vast scale that one cannot describe it well. We four are seeing these great designs and the play of nature in her grandest moods for the first time, and possibly they may never be seen by man again.

ON THE GREAT GLACIER

December 5. Broke camp sharp at 8 a.m. and proceeded south down an icy slope to the main glacier. The ice was too slippery for the pony, so Wild took him by a circuitous route to the bottom on snow. At the end of our ice slope, down which the sledge skidded rapidly, though we had put on rope brakes and hung on to it as well as we could, there was a patch of soft snow running parallel with the glacier, which here trended about south-west by south. Close ahead of us were the massed-up, fantastically shaped and split masses of pressure across which it would have been impossible for us to have gone, but, fortunately, it was not necessary even to try, for close into the land was a snow slope free from all crevasses, and along this gentle rise we made our way. After a time this snow slope gave place to blue ice, with numberless cracks and small crevasses across which it was quite impossible for the pony to drag the sledge without a serious risk of a broken leg in one of the many holes, the depth of which we could not ascertain. We therefore unharnessed Socks, and Wild took him over this bit of ground very carefully, whilst we others first hauled our sledge and then the pony sledge across to a patch of snow under some gigantic granite pillars over 2000 ft. in height, and here, close to some thaw water, we made our lunch camp. I was still badly snow-blind, so stayed in camp whilst Marshall and Adams went on to spy out a good route to follow after lunch was over. When they returned they informed me that there was more cracked-up blue ice ahead, and that the main pressure of the glacier came in very close to the pillar of granite that stood before us, but that beyond that there appeared to be a snow slope and good going. The most remarkable thing they reported was that as they were walking along, a bird, brown in colour with a white line under each wing, flew just over their heads and disappeared to the south. It is, indeed, strange to hear of such an incident in latitude 83° 40′ South. They were sure it was not a skua gull, which is the only bird I could think of that would venture down here, and the gull might have been attracted by the last dead pony, for when in latitude 80° 30′ South, on my last southern trip, a skua gull arrived shortly after we had killed a dog.

After lunch we started again, and by dint of great exertions managed, at 6 p.m., to camp after getting both sledges and then the pony over another couple of miles of crevassed blue ice. We then went on and had a look ahead, and saw that we are going to have a tough time tomorrow to get along at all. I can see that it will, at least, mean relaying three or four times across nearly half a mile of terribly crevassed ice, covered in places with treacherous snow, and razor-edged in other places, all of it sloping down towards the rock *débris* strewn shore on the cliff side. We are camped under a wonderful pillar of granite that has been rounded by the winds into a perfectly symmetrical shape, and is banded by lines of gneiss. There is just one little patch of snow for our tents, and even that bridges some crevasses. Providence will look over us tonight, for we can do nothing more. One feels that at any moment some great piece of rock may come hurtling down, for all round us are pieces of granite, ranging from the size of a hazel-nut to great boulders twenty to forty tons in weight, and on one snow slope is the fresh track of a fallen rock. Still we can do no better, for it is impossible to spread a tent on the blue ice, and we cannot get any further tonight. We are leaving a depot here. My eyes are my only trouble, for their condition makes it impossible for me to pick out the route or do much more than pull. The distance covered today was 9 miles with 4 miles relay.

December 7. Started at 8 a.m., Adams, Marshall and self pulling one sledge. Wild leading Socks behind. We travelled up and down slopes with very deep snow, into which Socks sank up to his belly, and we plunged in and out continuously, making it very trying work. Passed several crevasses on our right hand and could see more to the left. The light became bad at 1 p.m., when we camped for lunch, and it was hard to see the crevasses, as most were more or less snow covered. After lunch the light was better, and as we marched along we were congratulating ourselves upon it when suddenly we heard a shout of 'help' from Wild. We stopped at once and rushed to his assistance, and saw the pony sledge with the forward end down a crevasse and Wild reaching out from the side of the gulf grasping the sledge. No sign of the pony. We soon got up to Wild, and he scrambled out of the dangerous position, but poor Socks had gone. Wild had a miraculous escape. He was following up our tracks, and we had passed over a crevasse which was entirely covered with snow, but the weight of the pony broke through the snow crust and in a second all was over. Wild says he just felt a sort of rushing wind, the leading rope was snatched from his hand, and he put out his arms and just caught the further edge of the chasm. Fortunately for Wild and us, Socks' weight snapped the swingle-tree of the sledge, so it was saved, though the upper bearer is broken. We lay down on our stomachs and looked over into the gulf, but no sound or sign came to us; a black bottomless pit it seemed to be. We hitched the pony sledge to ourselves and started off again, now with a weight of 1000 lb. for the four of us. Camped at 6.20 p.m., very tired, having to retreat from a maze of crevasses and rotten ice on to a patch where we could pitch our tents. We are indeed thankful for Wild's escape. When I think over the events of the day I realise what the loss of the sledge would have meant to us. We would have had left only two sleeping-bags for the four of us, and I doubt whether we could have got back to winter-quarters with the short equipment. Our chance of reaching the Pole would have been gone. We take on the maize to eat ourselves. There is one ray of light in this bad day, and that is that anyhow we could not have taken Socks on much further. We would have had to shoot him tonight, so that although his loss is a serious matter to us, for we had counted on the meat, still we know that for traction purposes he would have been of little further use. When we tried to camp tonight we stuck our ice-axes into the snow to see whether there were any more hidden crevasses, and everywhere the axes went through. It would have been folly to have pitched our camp in that place, as we might easily have dropped through during the night. We had to retreat a quarter of a mile to pitch the tent. It was very unpleasant to turn back, even for this short distance, but on this job one must expect reverses.

December 9. Another splendid day as far as the weather is concerned, and much we needed it, for we have had one of our hardest day's work and certainly the most dangerous so far. We started at 7.45 a.m. over the blue ice, and in less than an hour were in a perfect maze of crevasses, some thinly bridged with snow and others with a thicker and therefore more deceptive covering. Marshall went through one and was only saved by his harness. He had quite disappeared down below the level of the ice, and it was one of those crevasses that open out from the top, with no bottom to be seen, and I daresay there was a drop of at least 1000 ft. Soon after, Adams went through, then I did. The situation became momentarily more dangerous and uncertain. The sledges, skidding about, came up against the sheer, knife-like edges of some of the crevasses, and thus the bow of the second sledge, which had been strained when Socks fell, gave way. We decided to relay our gear over this portion of the glacier until we got on to safer ground, and it was well past eleven o'clock before we had got both sledges on to better ice. We camped at 11.45 a.m. to get the sun's meridian altitude, and, to save time while watching the sun's rise and fall, decided to lunch at noon. The latitude was found to be 84° 2′ South, which is not so bad considering that we have been hauling our heavy load of 250 lb. per man uphill for the last two days. At noon we were nearly 2500 ft. above sea-level. In the afternoon we had another heavy pull, and now are camped between two huge crevasses, but on a patch of hard snow. The distance today was 11 miles 1450 yards plus two miles relay. The talk now is mainly about food and the things we would like to eat, and at meal-times our hoosh disappears with far too great speed. We are all looking forward to Christmas Day, for then, come what may, we are going to be full of food.

December 10. Falls, bruises, cut shins, crevasses, razor-edged ice, and a heavy upward pull have made up the sum of the day's trials, but there has been a measure of compensation in the wonderful scenery, the marvellous rocks and the covering of a distance of 11 miles 860 yards towards our goal. We started at 7.30 a.m. amongst crevasses, but soon got out of them and pulled up a long slope of snow. Our altitude at noon was 3250 ft. above sea-level. Then we slid down a blue ice slope, after crossing crevasses. Marshall and I each went down one. We lunched at 1 p.m. and started at 2 p.m. up a long ridge by the side moraine of the glacier. It was heavy work, as the ice was split and presented knife-like edges between the cracks, and there were also some crevasses. Adams got into one. The going was terribly heavy, as the sledges brought up against the ice-edges every now and then, and then there was a struggle to get them started again. We changed our foot-gear, substituting ski-boots for the finnesko, but nevertheless had many painful falls on the treacherous blue ice, cutting our hands and shins. We are all much bruised. We camped on a patch of snow by the land at 6 p.m. The rocks of the moraine are remarkable, being of every hue and description. I cannot describe them, but we will carry specimens back for the geologists to deal with. The main rocks of the 'Cloud-Maker', the mountain under which we are camped, appear to be slates, reef-quartz and a very hard, dark brown rock, the name of which I do not know.

December 12. Our distance – three miles for the day – expresses more readily than I can write it the nature of the day's work. We started at 7.40 a.m. on the worst surface possible, sharp-edged blue ice full of chasms and crevasses, rising to hills and descending into gullies; in fact, a surface that could not be equalled in any polar work for difficulty in travelling. Our sledges are suffering greatly, and it is a constant strain on us both to save the sledges from breaking or going down crevasses, and to save ourselves as well. We are a mass of bruises where we have fallen on the sharp ice, but, thank God, no one has even a sprain. It has been relay work today, for we could only take on one sledge at a time, two of us taking turns at pulling the sledge whilst the others steadied and held the sledge to keep it straight. Thus we would advance one mile, and then return over the crevasses and haul up the other sledge. By repeating this today for three miles we marched nine miles over a surface where many times a slip meant death.

December 14. This has been one of our hardest day's work so far. We have been steering all day about south-south-west up the glacier, mainly in the bed of an ancient moraine, which is full of holes through which the stones and boulders have melted down long years ago. It has been snowing all day with a high temperature, and this has made everything very wet. We have ascended over 1000 ft. today, our altitude at 6 p.m. being 5600 ft. above sea-level, so the mountains to the west must be from 10,000 to 15,000 ft. in height, judging from their comparative elevation. My knee is better today. We have had a heavy pull and many falls on the slippery ice. Just before camping, Adams went through some snow, but held up over an awful chasm. Our sledges are much the worse for wear, and the one with the broken bow constantly strikes against the hard, sharp ice, pulling us up with a jerk and often flinging us down. Tonight our hopes are high that we are nearly at the end of the rise and that soon we will reach our longed-for plateau. Then southward indeed! Food is the determining factor with us. We did 7½ miles today.

December 16. We have now traversed nearly one hundred miles of crevassed ice, and risen 6000 ft. on the largest glacier in the world. One more crevassed slope, and we will be on the plateau, please God. We are all fit and well. The temperature tonight is plus 15° Fahr., and the wind is blowing freshly from the south-west. There are splendid ranges of mountains to the west-south-west, and we have an extended view of glacier and mountains. Ahead of us lie three sharp peaks, connected up and forming an island in what is apparently inland ice or the head of the glacier. These mountains are not beautiful in the ordinary acceptance of the term, but they are magnificent in their stern and rugged grandeur. No foot has ever trod on their mighty sides, and until we reached this frozen land no human eyes had seen their forms.

December 17. We made a start at 7.20 a.m. and had an uphill pull all the morning over blue ice with patches of snow, which impeded our progress until we learned that the best way was to rush the sledges over them, for it was very difficult to keep one's footing on the smooth ice, and haul the sledges astern over the snow. We have burned our boats behind us now as regards warm clothing, for this afternoon we made a depot in by the rocks of the island we are passing, and there left everything except the barest necessaries. After dinner tonight Wild went up the hill-side in order to have a look at the plateau. He came down with the news that the plateau is in sight at last, and that tomorrow should see us at the end of our difficulties. He also brought down with him some very interesting geological specimens, some of which certainly look like coal. The quality may be poor, but I have little doubt that the stuff is coal. If that proves to be the case, the discovery will be most interesting to the scientific world.

ON THE PLATEAU TO THE FARTHEST SOUTH

December 18. Almost up! The altitude tonight is 7400 ft. above sea-level. That has been one of our hardest days, but worth it, for we are just on the plateau at last. We started at 7.30 a.m., relaying the sledges, and did 6 miles 600 yards, which means nearly 19 miles for the day of actual travelling. All the morning we worked up loose, slippery ice, hauling the sledges up one at a time by means of the alpine rope, then pulling in harness on the less stiff rises. All the afternoon we relayed up a long snow slope, and we were hungry and tired when we reached camp. We have been saving food to make it spin out, and that increases our hunger; each night we all dream of foods. We save two biscuits per man per day, also pemmican and sugar, eking out our food with pony maize, which we soak in water to make it less hard. All this means that we have now five weeks' food, while we are about 300 geographical miles from the Pole, with the same distance back to the last depot we left yesterday, so we must march on short food to reach our goal.

December 21. Midsummer Day, with 28° of frost! We have frostbitten fingers and ears, and a strong blizzard wind has been blowing from the south all day, all due to the fact that we have climbed to an altitude of over 8000 ft. above sea-level. From early morning we have been striving to the south, but six miles is the total distance gained, for from noon, or rather from lunch at 1 p.m., we have been hauling the sledges up, one after the other, by standing pulls across crevasses and over great pressure ridges. When we had advanced one sledge some distance, we put up a flag on a bamboo to mark its position, and then roped up and returned for the other. It is a wonderful sight to look down over the glacier from the great altitude we are at, and to see the mountains stretching away east and west, some of them over 15,000 ft. in height. We are very hungry now, and it seems as cold almost as the spring sledging. Our beards are masses of ice all day long. Thank God we are fit and well and have had no accident, which is a mercy, seeing that we have covered over 130 miles of crevassed ice.

December 22. One sledge today, when coming down with a run over a pressure ridge, turned a complete somersault, but nothing was damaged, in spite of the total weight being over 400 lb. We are now dragging 400 lb. at a time up the steep slopes and across the ridges, working with the alpine rope all day, and roping ourselves together when we go back for the second sledge, for the ground is so treacherous that many times during the day we are saved only by the rope from falling into fathomless pits. Wild describes the sensation of walking over the surface, half ice and half snow, as like walking over the glass roof of a station. The usual query when one of us falls into a crevasse is: 'Have you found it?' One gets somewhat callous as regards the immediate danger, though we are always glad to meet crevasses with their coats off, that is, not hidden by the snow covering. Tonight we are camped in a filled-in crevasse. Away to the north down the glacier a thick cumulus cloud is lying, but some of the largest mountains are standing out clearly. Immediately behind us lies a broken sea of pressure ice. Please God, ahead of us there is a clear road to the Pole.

December 23. Today's crevasses have been far more dangerous than any others we have crossed, as the soft snow hides all trace of them until we fall through. Constantly today one or another of the party has had to be hauled out from a chasm by means of his harness, which had alone saved him from death in the icy vault below. We started at 6.40 a.m. and worked on steadily until 6 p.m., with the usual lunch hour in the middle of the day. The pony maize does not swell in the water now, as the temperature is very low and the water freezes. The result is that it swells inside after we have eaten it.

December 24. Tonight we are 9095 ft. above sea-level, and the way before us is still rising. I trust that it will soon level out, for it is hard work pulling at this altitude. So far there is no sign of the very hard surface that Captain Scott speaks of in connection with his journey on the Northern Plateau. There seem to be just here regular layers of snow, not much wind-swept, but we will see better the surface conditions in a few days. Tomorrow will be Christmas Day, and our thoughts turn to home and all the attendant joys of the time. One longs to hear 'the hansoms slurring through the London mud'. Instead of that we are lying in a little tent, isolated high on the roof of the end of the world, far, indeed, from the ways trodden of men. Still, our thoughts can fly across the wastes of ice and snow and across the oceans to those whom we are striving for and who are thinking of us now. And, thank God, we are nearing our goal. The distance covered today was 11 miles 250 yards.

December 25. Christmas Day. There has been from 45° to 48° of frost, drifting snow and a strong biting south wind, and such has been the order of the day's march from 7 a.m. to 6 p.m. up one of the steepest rises we have yet done, crevassed in places. Now, as I write, we are 9500 ft. above sea-level, and our latitude at 6 p.m. was 85° 55′ South.

We had a splendid dinner. First came hoosh, consisting of pony ration boiled up with pemmican and some of our emergency Oxo and biscuit. Then in the cocoa water I boiled our little plum pudding, which a friend of Wild's had given him. This, with a drop of medical brandy, was a luxury which Lucullus himself might have envied; then came cocoa, and lastly cigars and a spoonful of *crème de menthe* sent us by a friend in Scotland. We are full tonight, and this is the last time we will be for many a long day. After dinner we discussed the situation, and we have decided to still further reduce our food. We have now nearly 500 miles, geographical, to do if we are to get to the Pole and back to the spot where we are at the present moment. We have one month's food, but only three weeks' biscuit, so we are going to make each week's food last ten days. We will have one biscuit in the morning, three at midday, and two at night. It is the only thing to do. Tomorrow we will throw away everything except the most absolute necessities. Already we are, as regard clothes, down to the limit, but we must trust to the old sledge-runners and dump the spare ones. One must risk this. We are very far away from all the world, and home thoughts have been much with us today, thoughts interrupted by pitching forward into a hidden crevasse more than once. Ah, well, we shall see all our own people when the work here is done. Marshall took our temperatures tonight. We are all 2° sub normal, but as fit as can be. It is a fine open-air life and we are getting south.

December 28. If the Barrier is a changing sea, the plateau is a changing sky. During the morning march we continued to go up hill steadily, but the surface was constantly changing. We are now 10,199 ft. above sea-level and the plateau is gradually flattening out, but it was heavy work pulling this afternoon. The high altitude, and a temperature of 48° of frost made breathing and work difficult. We are getting south – latitude 86° 31′ South tonight. The last sixty miles we hope to rush, leaving everything possible, taking one tent only and using the poles of the other as marks every ten miles, for we will leave all our food sixty miles off the Pole except enough to carry us there and back. I think the country is flattening out more and more, and hope tomorrow to make fifteen miles, at least.

December 29. Yesterday I wrote that we hoped to do fifteen miles today, but such is the variable character of this surface that one cannot prophesy with any certainty an hour ahead. A strong southerly wind, with from 44° to 49° of frost, combined with the effect of short rations, made our distance 12 miles 600 yards instead. We have reached an altitude of 10,310 ft., and an uphill gradient gave us one of the most severe pulls for ten hours that would be possible. It looks serious, for we must increase the food if we are to get on at all, and we must risk a depot at seventy miles off the Pole and dash for it then. Our sledge is badly strained, and on the abominably bad surface of soft snow is dreadfully hard to move. I have been suffering from a bad headache all day, and Adams also was worried by the cold. I think that these headaches are a form of mountain sickness, due to our high altitude. The others have bled from the nose, and that must relieve them. Physical effort is always trying at a high altitude, and we are straining at the harness all day, sometimes slipping in the soft snow that overlies the hard sastrugi. My head is very bad. The sensation is as though the nerves were being twisted up with a corkscrew and then pulled out. Marshall took our temperatures tonight, and we are all at about 94°, but in spite of this we are getting south. We are only 198 miles off our goal now. If the rise would stop the cold would not matter, but it is hard to know what is a man's limit. We have only 150 lb. per man to pull, but it is more severe work than the 250 lb. per man up the glacier was. The Pole is hard to get.

December 30. We only did 4 miles 100 yards today. We started at 7 a.m., but had to camp at 11 a.m., a blizzard springing up from the south. It is more than annoying. I cannot express my feelings. We were pulling at last on a level surface, but very soft snow, when at about 10 a.m. the south wind and drift commenced to increase, and at 11 a.m. it was so bad that we had to camp. And here all day we have been lying in our sleeping-bags trying to keep warm and listening to the threshing drift on the tent-side. I am in the cooking-tent, and the wind comes through, it is so thin. Our precious food is going and the time also, and it is so important to us to get on. We lie here and think of how to make things better, but we cannot reduce food now, and the only thing will be to rush all possible at the end. We will do, and are doing all humanly possible. It is with Providence to help us.

December 31. The last day of the old year, and the hardest day we have had almost, pushing through soft snow uphill with a strong head wind and drift all day. My head has been very bad all day, and we are all feeling the short food, but still we are getting south. We are in latitude 86° 54′ South tonight, but we have only three weeks' food and two weeks' biscuit to do nearly 500 geographical miles. We can only do our best. Too tired to write more tonight. We all get iced-up about our faces, and are on the verge of frostbite all the time. Please God the weather will be fine during the next fourteen days. Then all will be well. The distance today was eleven miles.

[If we had only known that we were going to get such cold weather as we were at this time experiencing, we would have kept a pair of scissors to trim our beards. The moisture from the condensation of one's breath accumulated on the beard and trickled down on the Burberry blouse. Then it froze into a sheet of ice inside, and it became very painful to pull the Burberry off in camp. Little troubles of this sort would have seemed less serious to us if we had been able to get a decent feed at the end of the day's work, but we were very hungry. *E.S.*]

January 2. Terribly hard work today. We started at 6.45 a.m. with a fairly good surface, which soon became very soft. We were sinking in over our ankles, and our broken sledge, by running sideways, added to the drag. We have been going uphill all day, and tonight are 11,034 ft. above sea-level. It has taken us all day to do 10 miles 450 yards, though the weights are fairly light. My head is giving me trouble all the time. Wild seems the most fit of us. God knows we are doing all we can, but the outlook is serious if this surface continues and the plateau gets higher, for we are not travelling fast enough to make our food spin out and get back to our depot in time. I cannot think of failure yet. I must look at the matter sensibly and consider the lives of those who are with me. I feel that if we go on too far it will be impossible to get back over this surface, and then all the results will be lost to the world. We can now definitely locate the South Pole on the highest plateau in the world, and our geological work and meteorology will be of the greatest use to science, but all this is not the Pole. Man can only do his best, and we have arrayed against us the strongest forces of nature.

January 4. The end is in sight. We can only go for three more days at the most, for we are weakening rapidly. Short food and a blizzard wind from the south, with driving drift, at a temperature of 47° of frost have plainly told us today that we are reaching our limit, for we were so done up at noon with cold that the clinical thermometer failed to register the temperature of three of us at 94°. We started at 7.40 a.m., leaving a depot on this great wide plateau, a risk that only this case justified, and one that my comrades agreed to, as they have to every one so far, with the same cheerfulness and regardlessness of self that have been the means of our getting as far as we have done so far. Pathetically small looked the bamboo, one of the tent poles, with a bit of bag sown on as a flag, to mark our stock of provisions, which has to take us back to our depot, one hundred and fifty miles north. We lost sight of it in half an hour, and are now trusting to our footprints in the snow to guide us back to each bamboo until we pick up the depot again. The main thing against us is the altitude of 11,200 ft. and the biting wind. Our faces are cut, and our feet and hands are always on the verge of frostbite. Our fingers, indeed, often go, but we get them round more or less. I have great trouble with two fingers on my left hand. They have been badly jammed when we were getting the motor up over the ice face at winter quarters, and the circulation is not good. Our boots now are pretty well worn out, and we have to halt at times to pick the snow out of the soles. There is half a gale blowing dead in our teeth all the time. We hope to reach within 100 geographical miles of the Pole; under the circumstances we can expect to do very little more. I am confident that the Pole lies on the great plateau we have discovered, miles and miles from any outstanding land. The temperature tonight is minus 24° Fahr.

January 5. Today head wind and drift again, with 50° of frost, and a terrible surface. I realise that the food we have been having has not been sufficient to keep up our strength, let alone supply the wastage caused by exertion, and now we must try to keep warmth in us, though our strength is being used up. My head still gives me great trouble. I began by wishing that my worst enemy had it instead of myself, but now I don't wish even my worst enemy to have such a headache; still, it is no use talking about it. Self is a subject that most of us are fluent on. We find the utmost difficulty in carrying through the day, and we can only go for two or three more days. Never once has the temperature been above zero since we got on to the plateau, though this is the height of summer. We have done our best, and we thank God for having allowed us to get so far.

January 6. This must be our last outward march with the sledge and camp equipment. Tomorrow we must leave camp with some food, and push as far south as possible, and then plant the flag. Today's story is 57° of frost, with a strong blizzard and high drift; yet we marched 13¼ geographical miles through soft snow, being helped by extra food. This does not mean full rations, but a bigger ration than we have been having lately. The pony maize is all finished. The most trying day we have yet spent, our fingers and faces being frost-bitten continually. Tomorrow we will rush south with the flag. We are at 88° 7′ South tonight. It is our last outward march. Blowing hard tonight. I would fail to explain my feelings if I tried to write them down, now that the end has come. There is only one thing that lightens the disappointment, and that is the feeling that we have done all we could. It is the forces of nature that have prevented us from going right through. I cannot write more.

January 7. A blinding, shrieking blizzard all day, with the temperature ranging from 60° to 70° of frost. It has been impossible to leave the tent, which is now snowed up on the lee side. We have been lying in the bags all day, only warm at food time, with fine snow making through the walls of the worn tent and covering our bags. We are greatly cramped. Adams is suffering from cramp every now and then. We are eating our valuable food without marching. The wind has been blowing eighty to ninety miles an hour. We can hardly sleep. Tomorrow I trust this will be over. Directly the wind drops we march as far south as possible, then plant the flag, and turn homeward. Our chief anxiety is lest our tracks may drift up, for to them we must trust mainly to find our depot; we have no land bearings in this great plain of snow. It is a serious risk that we have taken, but we had to play the game to the utmost, and Providence will look after us.

January 8. Again all day in our bags, suffering considerably physically from cold hands and feet, and from hunger, but more mentally, for we cannot get on south, and we simply lie here shivering. Every now and then one of our party's feet go, and the unfortunate beggar has to take his leg out of the sleeping-bag and have his frozen foot nursed into life again by placing it inside the shirt, against the skin of his almost equally unfortunate neighbour. We must do something more to the south, even though the food is going, and we weaken lying in the cold, for with 72° of frost, the winds cut through our thin tent, and even the drift is finding its way in and on to our bags, which are wet enough as it is. Cramp is not uncommon every now and then, and the drift all round the tent has made it so small that there is hardly room for us at all. The wind has been blowing hard all day; some of the gusts must be over seventy or eighty miles an hour. This evening it seems as though it were going to ease down, and directly it does we shall be up and away south for a rush. I feel that this march must be our limit. We are so short of food, and at this high altitude, 11,600 ft., it is hard to keep any warmth in our bodies between the scanty meals. We have nothing to read now, having depoted our little books to save weight, and it is dreary work lying in the tent with nothing to read, and too cold to write much in the diary.

January 9. Our last day outwards. We have shot our bolt, and the tale is latitude 88° 23′ South, longitude 162° East. The wind eased down at 1 a.m., and at 2 a.m. were up and had breakfast. At 4 a.m. started south, with the Queen's Union Jack, a brass cylinder containing stamps and documents to place at the furthest south point, camera, glasses and compass. At 9 a.m. we were in 88° 23′ South, half running and half walking over a surface much hardened by the recent blizzard. It was strange for us to go along without the nightmare of a sledge dragging behind us. We hoisted her Majesty's flag and the other Union Jack afterwards, and took possession of the plateau in the name of his Majesty. While the Union Jack blew out stiffly in the icy gale that cut us to the bone, we looked south with our powerful glasses, but could see nothing but the dead white snow plain. There was no break in the plateau as it extended towards the Pole, and we feel sure that the goal we have failed to reach lies on this plain. We stayed only a few minutes, and then, taking the Queen's flag and eating our scanty meal as we went, we hurried back and reached our camp about 3 p.m. We were so dead tired that we only did two hours' march in the afternoon and camped at 5.30 p.m. The temperature was minus 19° Fahr. Fortunately for us, our tracks were not obliterated by the blizzard; indeed, they stood up, making a trail easily followed. Homeward bound at last. Whatever regrets may be, we have done our best.

As Dr Eric Marshall wrote in his diary, the four men were now further from civilisation, geographically speaking, than any human beings had ever been before. What effect did it have on them? Shackleton's published diary describes graphically enough the physical hardships they were undergoing. But it tells us little, if anything, about their personal relationships. For an insight into that, we must turn to the diaries of the other members of the party. The two that have survived are those of Marshall and Wild.

Of all the members of the expedition, no one recorded his experiences in language quite so outspoken or vitriolic as Dr Eric Marshall. Even before the *Nimrod* reached the ice, he began to take a dislike to his leader, which may well have reciprocated. In fact, had it not been for his qualifications as senior surgeon, photographer and cartographer, it may be that Shackleton would never have chosen him for the Southern Journey at all.

As early as 26 February, when the party had only just arrived at Cape Royds, Marshall wrote in his diary:

> Sh. awakes surly in the morning . . . improved slightly as the day went on. He seldom puts his hand to any work, save when a cinematograph is working. His spasm then lasts five minutes.

And on the very next day, Marshall wrote:

> What a different show this is to what I anticipated when I first joined the expedition. I thought I should be under a *man*.
>
> Soon disillusioned, but always hoping he would be all right on ice. . . . Vacillating, erratic and a liar, easily scared, moody and surly; a boaster. Some chance of success if he does not start on Southern Journey as he hints, on which all my ambitions are centred. There were times when more than one of us thought of returning with *Nimrod*.

A month later, Marshall was still recording his thoughts in much the same vein:

> Must have a talk with Sh. some time. By God he has not played the game and is not capable of doing so; and he's a consummate liar and a practised hypocrite. When he took me on he thought he had got a fool. No doubt he was right. He had got a man who was fool enough, 1: to take him at his word, 2: to disregard and refute certain reports we had heard of him, 3: to spend £90 in preparation and waiting

for the Expedition, 4: to have the best interests of the Expedition at heart, 5: to have sacrificed an appointment and prospects in order to join hands with a coward and a cad, who was incapable of keeping his word. By God I have been a damned fool to trust him. He is incapable of a decent action or thought.

As a judge of his fellow men, Marshall could certainly be a trifle capricious. Of Douglas Mawson, who went on to become one of the greatest Antarctic explorers of all time, Marshall wrote, shortly after meeting him:

Mawson is useless and objectionable, lacking in guts and manners. Could leave him behind without a regret.

And of Lieutenant Adams, with whom he shared a cubicle in the hut, and a tent for much of the Southern Journey, he had this to say in his diary:

. . . Argumentative, childish, hopeless; idiot at critical times.

Even under normal circumstances, Dr Marshall might not have been everybody's choice as an ideal travelling companion.

It was part of Shackleton's policy to alternate tent-mates on the Southern Journey, and so lessen the chance of factions developing within the group. He was not entirely successful. More and more as the days went by, Frank Wild became Shackleton's man, and remained so for the rest of his life. For their part, Adams and Marshall also became something of a 'pair'.

On long expeditions, the pettiest things, like the size of another man's cocoa mug, can develop into obsessions. Reading Wild's diary today, it is clear that he convinced himself that Adams and Marshall were not pulling their weight; and in the pages of his diary he worked himself up into a personal fury on the subject, using a cipher to prevent the others from reading his thoughts.

Extracts from Wild's and Marshall's diaries, placed in chronological sequence, make fascinating reading; and provide an insight wholly missing from Shackleton's narrative.

5 November 1908 [Marshall]
Shackleton moaning over snow blindness, which he has only himself to thank for.

10 November 1908 [Wild]
Poor Chinaman is getting worse, but he has only one more day to do. He is like his boss (Adams), too damned slack in harness.

9 December 1908 [Wild]
Sh. and I are pulling at least two thirds of the load. The big hog (Marshall) does not even pull his own food. A. does little better.

10 December 1908 [Marshall]
Hope there won't be more than a day or two of this killing heavy work.

[Wild]
Marshall is just as bad again. I could shoot him.

12 December 1908 [Marshall]
Heart-breaking work, with more in view for tomorrow.

13 December 1908 [Wild]
If Joyce and Marston were here instead of A. and M. I reckon we should be at least forty miles further ahead.

14 December 1908 [Marshall]
Without exaggeration, this must have been the hardest week's work ever done in the Antarctic. . . . Following Shackleton to the Pole is like following an old woman . . . always pausing.

17 December 1908 [Marshall]
A most tiring day . . . An hour before lunch I had to fall back to the rear sledge, as it was quite impossible to stand up without nails.

19 December 1908 [Wild]
Yesterday while the rest of us were tearing our hearts out up the steep slopes, M. was walking along with a slack trace. Once it was so slack that Shackleton fell over it.

21 December 1908 [Marshall]
Sh. as cook is hopeless. He is feeling our high altitude.

23 December 1908 [Marshall]
Pretty good going with both sledges until later part of the afternoon, when we ran into pressure.

[Wild]
(A page has been torn out, perhaps because it was

libellous; then the diary continues, obviously about Marshall.)

I have quite made up my mind to show him up before all hands when we return. I sincerely wish he would fall down a crevasse about a thousand feet deep; he certainly does not pull the weight of the extra tent and his kit, and that leaves the weight of his food for us to pull.

10 January 1909 [Marshall]
Pretty fast travelling with wind just abaft-beam. Sail, improvised out of floor cloth and tent poles, proved a great help.

[Wild]
I had thought that with a full belly ahead of us as an incentive M. would have done a bit of pulling on the homeward track, but he does not even keep the slack in now. Nearly all the afternoon his trace was dragging.

24 January 1909 [Marshall]
Course straight. Going strong. Perfect weather. Depot appears to be twelve miles away.

[Wild]
M. is certainly bucking up. He has been pulling almost his share today, so I think he must be getting scared about the food.

31 January 1909 [Marshall]
Only three hauling, as Wild is quite unfit for work.

[Wild]
Shackleton privately forced upon me his one breakfast biscuit, and would have given me another tonight, had I allowed him. I do not suppose that anyone else in the world can thoroughly realise how much generosity and sympathy was shown by this. I do, and by God I shall never forget it. Thousands of pounds would not have bought that one biscuit.

Here now is Shackleton's own account of the journey back. As hunger and exhaustion began to have their effect, his diary entries became much shorter.

THE RETURN MARCH

January 10. We started at 7.30 a.m. with a fair wind, and marched all day, with a stop of one hour for lunch, doing over 18½ geographical miles to the north. It has, indeed, been fortunate for us that we have been able to follow our outward tracks, for the force of the gale had torn the flags from the staffs. We will be all right when we pick up our depot. It has been a big risk leaving our food on the great white plain, with only our sledge tracks to guide us back. Tonight we are all tired out, but we have put a good march behind us. The temperature is minus 9° Fahr.

January 11. A good day. We have done nearly 17 geographical miles. We have picked up our depot and now are following the sledge tracks to the north. The temperature has been minus 15° Fahr. There has been tremendous wind here, and the sastrugi are enormous.

January 13. It was heavy pulling all day, but we did a good distance in spite of it, getting 15 miles 1650 yards to the north. We have the sail up continually, but I cannot say that it has been very much help today. The temperature, minus 18° Fahr. nearly all the time, makes things very cold, and we ourselves slept badly last night. I did not sleep at all, for both my heels are frost-bitten and have cracked open, and I also have cracks under some of my toes; but we can march all right, and are moving over the ground very fast. We must continue to do so, for we have only about 20 lb. of biscuit to last us over 140 miles, and I expect there will be little in the locker by the time we strike our glacier head depot. The surface has been very severe today.

January 14. A strong following blizzard all day gave us our best day's run of the whole trip, 20 miles 1600 yards in ten hours. We decided to cut down the rations by another biscuit, as we have only six days' biscuit left on short ration, and 120 miles to go before we reach the depot, so we feel very hungry, and with the temperature minus 18° Fahr. to minus 21° Fahr. all day in the wind, one easily gets frost-bitten.

January 15. Started in a strong blizzard at 7.30 a.m. with a temperature of minus 23° Fahr., and marched steadily till noon, doing 9½ miles; then marched from 1.30 p.m. till 6 p.m., making a total distance for the day of 20 miles, statute. It has been thick, with a pale sun only shining through, but we are still able to follow our old sledge tracks, though at times they are very faint. Unfortunately, when we halted at 3.30 p.m. for a spell, we found that the sledge meter had disappeared, and discovered that it had broken off short at the brass fitting. This is a serious loss to us, for all our Barrier distances between depots are calculated on it, and although we have another depoted at the foot of the glacier we do not know the slip. We now must judge distance till we get a sight of land.

January 17. At 10 a.m. we came up to our Christmas camp, and there took on a bamboo we had left, and which now comes in useful for our sail. This sail is now a great help. We dropped over 500 ft. today, and in three days ought to reach our depot at this rate.

January 18. Our best day, 26½ miles down-hill, with a strong following wind. We have nearly got to the end of the main icefall. With luck we may reach the depot tomorrow night. With food now in hand, we had a decent feed tonight. I have been very unlucky today, falling into many crevasses and hurting my shoulder badly. I have also had many falls, besides the trouble with the bad heels on the hard stuff.

January 19. Another record day, for we have done about twenty-nine miles to the north, rushing under sail down icefalls and through crevasses, till, at 6 p.m., we picked up our sledge tracks of December 18 outwards. We camped, dead beat, at 6.30 p.m., and had a good hoosh. We have descended to 7500 ft., and the temperature tonight is minus 14° Fahr. We are now only 8½ miles from our depot, which we will reach tomorrow morning, all being well. This strong blizzard wind has been an immense help this way, though not outwards for us.

January 20. Although we have not covered so much ground today, we have had an infinitely harder time. A gale was blowing, and often fierce gusts came along, sweeping the sledge sideways, and knocking us off our feet. We all had many falls, and I had two specially heavy ones which shook me up severely. When we reached the steep slopes where we had roped the sledges up on our outward journey, we lowered the sledge down by means of the alpine rope, using an ice-axe as a bollard to lower by. On several occasions one or more of us lost our footing, and were swept by the wind down the ice-slope, with great difficulty getting back to our sledge and companions. We arrived at our depot at 12.30 p.m. with sore and aching bodies.

January 24. One of our hardest day's work, and certainly the longest, for we started at 6.45 a.m., went on till 12.50 p.m., had lunch, started at 2 p.m., went on till 6 p.m., had a cup of tea, and went on till 9 p.m. Then we had our single pot of hoosh and one biscuit, for we have only two days' food left and one day's biscuit on much reduced ration, and we have to cover forty miles of crevasses to reach our depot before we can get any more food. I am now all right again, though rather weak. We had a terribly hard time in the crevassed ice this morning, and now our sledge has not much more than half a runner on one side, and is in a very shaky state. However, I believe we are safe now. The distance today was sixteen miles, statute.

January 26 and 27. Two days written up as one, and they have been the hardest and most trying we have ever spent in our lives, and will ever stand in our memories. Tonight (the 27th) we have had our first solid food since the morning of the 26th. We came to the end of all our provisions except a little cocoa and tea, and from 7 a.m. on the 26th till 2 p.m. on the 27th we did sixteen miles over the worst surfaces and most dangerous crevasses we have ever encountered, only stopping for tea or cocoa till they were finished, and marching twenty hours at a stretch, through snow 10 to 18 in. thick as a rule, with sometimes 2½ ft. of it. We fell into hidden crevasses time after time, and were saved by each other and by our harness. In fact, only an all-merciful Providence has guided our steps to tonight's safety at our depot. Adams fell exhausted in his harness, but recovered and went on again. Wild did the same the night before.

January 28. We are now safe, with six days' food and only fifty miles to the depot, but Wild has developed dysentery. We are at a loss to know what is the cause of it. It may possibly be due to the horse-meat. Just before we left the glacier I broke through the soft snow plunging into a hidden crevasse. My harness jerked up under my heart, and gave me rather a shake up. It seemed as though the glacier were saying: 'There is the last touch for you; don't you come up here again.' It was with a feeling of intense relief that we left this great glacier, for the strain has been hard, and now we know that except for blizzards and thick weather, which two factors can alone prevent us from finding our depots in good time, we will be all right.

January 29. We are having a most unfriendly greeting from the Barrier. We got up as usual and had breakfast at 5.30 a.m., the weather thick and overcast, but the land showing enough for us to steer by. We got away at 7.20 a.m., and soon after it began to snow, which in a temperature of plus 30° Fahr. melted on the sledge and all our gear, making everything into a miserably wet state. We had to put the compass down every now and then, for it became too thick to see any landmarks, and at 9.30 the wind suddenly sprang up from the east, cold and strong, freezing solid all our wet clothes, and the various things on the sledge. It was blowing a blizzard with snow and heavy drift in less than five minutes from the time the wind started, and with difficulty we managed to get up one tent and crawl into it, where we waited in the hope that the weather would clear.

January 30. Wild is seedy today, but we hope that as soon as he reaches Grisi Depot he will be better. We have no variety of food, and only have four miserably thin biscuits a day to eke out the horse-meat. The plasmon is all finished and so are we ourselves by the end of the day's march. The sledge also is in a terribly bad state, but as soon as we reach the depot all will be well.

January 31. Started at 7 a.m., Wild bad with dysentery. Picked up mound 4 p.m., and camped at 6 p.m. Very bad surface. Did 13½ miles.

February 1. Started 7 a.m.; awful surface at times. Wild very bad. Picked up mound. Camped 6 p.m., having done nearly fourteen miles.

February 2. Started at 6.40 a.m. Camped 7 p.m. at depot. Wild and self dysentery; dead tired, bad surface, with undulations. Did 13½ miles.

February 4. Cannot write more. All down with acute dysentery; terrible day. No march possible; outlook serious. . . . Fine weather.

February 5. Eight miles today; dead tired. Dysentery better, but Adams not too right. Camped at 5.30 p.m. We are picking up the mounds well. Too weak on half ration to write much. Still hanging on to geological specimens. Please God we will get through all right. Great anxiety.

February 7. Blowing hard blizzard. Kept going till 6 p.m. Adams and Marshall renewed dysentery. Dead tired. Short food; very weak.

February 8. Did twelve miles. We had fine weather after 10 a.m. Started from camp in blizzard. Adams and Marshall still dysentery; Wild and I all right. Feel starving for food. Talk of it all day. Anyhow, getting north, thank god. Sixty-nine miles to Chinaman depot.

February 9. Strong following blizzard, and did 14½ miles to north. Adams not fit yet. All thinking and talking of food.

February 10. Strong following wind. Did 20 miles 300 yards. Temperature plus 22° Fahr. All thinking and talking of food.

February 11. All our thoughts are of food. We ought to reach the depot in two days. Now we are down to half a pannikin of meat and five biscuits a day. Adams not all right yet, and Wild shaky tonight.

February 13. Breakfast at 4.40 a.m. We packed up, with a cold wind blowing, and reached the depot, with all our food finished, at 11.30 a.m. There we got Chinaman's liver, which we have had tonight. It tasted splendid. We looked round for any spare bits of meat, and while I was digging in the snow I came across some hard red stuff, Chinaman's blood frozen into a solid core. We dug it up, and found it a welcome addition to our food. It was like beef-tea when boiled up. The distance today was twelve miles, with a light wind.

February 15. My birthday today. I was given a present of a cigarette made out of pipe tobacco and some coarse paper we had with us. It was delicious. A hard pull today, and my head is very bad again. The distance was 12¼ miles, with a fairly good surface and fine weather. We are picking up our mounds with great regularity. The land can be seen faintly through the haze in the distance.

February 16. A fair surface today, but no wind. The sastrugi are disappearing. We are appallingly hungry. We are down to about half a pannikin of half-cooked horse-meat a meal and four biscuits a day. When we break camp in the morning we pull the tent off the poles and take it down before we move the things inside, for the effort of lifting the sleeping-bags, &c., through the doorway is too great.

February 17. We all have tragic dreams of getting food to eat, but rarely have the satisfaction of dreaming that we are actually eating. Last night I did taste bread and butter. We look at each other as we eat our scanty meals and feel a distinct grievance if one man manages to make his hoosh last longer than the rest of us.

February 19. We sighted Mount Erebus in the morning. The old landmarks are so pleasant. Camped at 6 p.m., temperature minus 10° Fahr. We ought to reach Depot A tomorrow.

February 20. It was dull and overcast today, and we could see only a little way. Still we made progress, and at 4 p.m. we reached Depot A. We had run out of food when we reached the depot today, and we have had a good hoosh tonight. The unaccustomed pemmican fat made me feel quite queer, but I enjoyed the pudding we made out of biscuits and the tin of jam which we originally intended to have for Christmas Day, but which we left behind when on the way south in order to save weight. Our depoted tobacco and cigarettes were here, and it is difficult to describe the enjoyment and luxury of a good smoke. I am sure that the tobacco will make up for the shortage of food. I do not doubt but that the Bluff Depot will have been laid all right by Joyce.

February 22. A splendid day. We did 20½ miles, and on the strength of the distance had a good feed. About 11 a.m. we suddenly came across the tracks of a party of four men, with dogs. Evidently the weather has been fine and they have been moving at a good pace towards the south. We could tell that the weather has been fine, for they were wearing ski boots instead of finnesko, and occasionally we saw the stump of a cigarette. The length of the steps showed that they were going fast. We are now camped on the tracks, which are fairly recent, and we will try to follow them to the Bluff, for they must have come from the depot. We found three small bits of chocolate and a little bit of biscuit at the camp after carefully searching the ground for such unconsidered trifles, and we 'turned backs' for them. I was unlucky enough to get the bit of biscuit, and a curious unreasoning anger took possession of me for a moment at my bad luck. It shows how primitive we have become, and how much the question of even a morsel of food affects our judgment.

THE FINAL STAGE

February 23. Started at 6.45 a.m. in splendid weather, and at 11 a.m., while halting for a spell, Wild saw the Bluff Depot miraged up. It seemed to be quite close, and the flags were waving and dancing as though to say, 'Come, here I am, come and feed'. It was the most cheerful sight our eyes had ever seen, for we had only a few biscuits left. These we at once devoured. A flashing light appeared to be on the depot, and when we reached it at 4 p.m., this turned out to be a biscuit tin, which had been placed in the snow so as to catch the light of the sun. It was a great cheerful eye twinkling at us. The depot had appeared much closer than it really was, because we were accustomed to judging from the height of an ordinary depot, whereas this one was built on a snow mound over 10 ft. high, with two bamboos lashed together on top, and three flags. It was a splendid mark. Joyce and his party have done their work well. Now we are safe as regards food, and it only remains for us to reach the ship. I climbed up on the top of the depot, and shouted out to those below of the glorious feeds that awaited us. First I rolled down three tins of biscuits, then cases containing luxuries of every description, many of them sent by friends. There were Carlsbad plums, eggs, cakes, plum puddings, gingerbread and crystallised fruit, even fresh boiled mutton from the ship. After months of want and hunger, we suddenly found ourselves able to have meals fit for the gods, and with appetites that the gods might have envied. Apart from the luxuries there was ample supply of ordinary sledging rations. Tonight we improvised a second cooking-stand out of a biscuit tin, and used our second primus to cook some of the courses. Our dream food has come true, and yet after we had eaten biscuits and had two pannikins of pemmican, followed by cocoa, our contracted bodies would not stand the strain of more food, and reluctantly we had to stop. I cannot tell what a relief it has been to us. There is nothing much in the way of news from the ship, only just a letter saying that she had arrived on January 5, and that all was well.

February 24. Though we have plenty of weight to haul now we do not feel it so much as we did the smaller weights when we were hungry. We have good food inside us, and every now and then on the march we eat a bit of chocolate or biscuit. Warned by the experience of Scott and Wilson on the previous southern journey, I have taken care not to overeat. Adams has a wonderful digestion, and can go on without any difficulty. Wild's dysentery is a bit better today.

February 25. We turned out at 4 a.m. for an early start, as we are in danger of being left if we do not push ahead rapidly and reach the ship. On going into the tent for breakfast I found Marshall suffering from paralysis of the stomach and renewed dysentery, and while we were eating a blizzard came up. If Marshall is not better tonight, I must leave him with Adams and push on, for time is going on, and the ship may leave on March 1, according to orders, if the Sound is not clear of ice. He is in a bad way still, but thinks that he could travel tomorrow.

February 27 (1 a.m.). The blizzard was over at midnight, and we got up at 1 a.m., had breakfast at 2, and made a start at 4.

March 5. Marshall was unable to haul, his dysentery increasing, and he got worse in the afternoon, after lunch. At 4 p.m. I decided to pitch camp, leave Marshall under Adams' charge, and push ahead with Wild, taking one day's provisions and leaving the balance for the two men at the camp. I hoped to pick up a relief party at the ship. We dumped everything off the sledge except a prismatic compass, our sleeping-bags and food for one day, and at 4.30 p.m. Wild and I started, and marched till 9 p.m. Then we had a hoosh, and marched until 2 a.m. of the 28th, over a very hard surface. We stopped for one hour and a half off the north-east end of White Island, getting no sleep, and marched till 11 a.m., by which time our food was finished. We kept flashing the heliograph in the hope of attracting attention from Observation Hill, where I thought that a party would be on the look-out, but there was no return flash. We thought once that we saw a party coming over to meet us, and our sledge seemed to grow lighter for a few minutes, but the 'party' turned out to be a group of penguins at the ice-edge. The weather was so thick that we could not see any distance ahead, and we arrived at the ice edge suddenly. The ice was swaying up and down and there was grave risk of our being carried out. I decided to abandon the sledge, as I felt sure that we would get assistance at once when we reached the hut, and time was becoming important. It was necessary that we should get food and shelter speedily. Wild's feet were giving him a great deal of trouble. We reached the top of Ski Slope at 7.45 p.m., and from there we could see the hut and the bay. There was no sign of the ship, and no smoke or other evidence of life at the hut. We hurried on to the hut, our minds busy with gloomy possibilities, and found not a man there. There was a letter stating that the Northern Party had reached the Magnetic Pole, and that all the parties had been picked up except ours. The letter added that the ship would be sheltering under Glacier Tongue until February 26. It was now February 28, and it was with very keen anxiety in our minds that we proceeded to search for food. If the ship was gone, our plight, and that of the two men left out on the Barrier, was a very serious one.

We improvised a cooking vessel, found oil and a Primus lamp, and had a good feed of biscuit, onions and plum pudding, which were amongst the stores left at the hut. We were utterly weary, but we had no sleeping-gear, our bags having been left with the sledge, and the temperature was very low. We found a piece of roofing felt, which we wrapped round us, and then we sat up all night, the darkness being relieved only when we occasionally lighted the lamp in order to secure a little warmth. We tried to burn the magnetic hut in the hope of attracting attention from the ship, but we were not able to get it alight. We tried, too, to tie the Union Jack to Vince's cross, on the hill, but we were so played out that our cold fingers could not manage the knots. It was a bad night for us, and we were glad indeed when the light came again. Then we managed to get a little warmer, and at 9 a.m. we got the magnetic hut alight, and put up the flag. All our fears vanished when in the distance we saw the ship, miraged up. We signalled with the heliograph, and at 11 a.m. on March 1 we were on board the *Nimrod* and once more safe amongst friends. I will not attempt to describe our feelings. Every one was glad to see us, and keen to know what we had done. They had given us up for lost, and a search-party had been going to start that day in the hope of finding some trace of us. I found that every member of the expedition was well, that the plans had worked out satisfactorily, and that the work laid down had been carried out. The ship had brought nothing but good news from the outside world. It seemed as though a great load had been lifted from my shoulders.

The first thing was to bring in Adams and Marshall, and I ordered out a relief party at once. I had a good feed of bacon and fried bread, and started at 2.30 p.m. from the Barrier edge with Mackay, Mawson and McGillan, leaving Wild on the *Nimrod*. We marched until 10 p.m., had dinner and turned in for a short sleep. We were up again at 2 a.m. the next morning (March 2), and travelled until 1 p.m., when we reached the camp where I had left the two men. Marshall was better, the rest having done him a lot of good, and he was able to march and pull. We reached the winter quarters at 9.50, and Marshall was put to bed. Mackay and I lighted a carbide flare on the hill by Vince's cross, and after dinner all hands turned in except Mackay and myself. A short time after Mackay saw the ship appear. It was now blowing a hard blizzard, but Mackintosh had seen our flare from a distance of nine miles. Adams and I went on board the *Nimrod*, and Adams, after surviving all the dangers of the interior of the Antarctic continent, was nearly lost within sight of safety. He slipped at the ice-edge, owing to the fact that he was wearing new finnesko, and he only just saved himself from going over. He managed to hang on until he was rescued by a party from the ship.

A boat went back for Marshall and the others, and we were all safe on board at 1 a.m. on March 4.

[Subsequent calculations have shown that the distances given in my diary of the southern journey were not always quite accurate. The calculations were made under circumstances of special difficulty, and were not checked until after my return to civilisation. The reader will notice that some of the distances are given in statute miles and others in geographical miles. After the last meridian altitude was taken at the plateau depot and until the return to the same depot the distances were noted in geographical miles. I have thought it best to let the diary figures stand. *E.S.*]

Those who are interested in following up the experiences of other members of the *Nimrod* expedition will find them recounted in the second volume of *Heart of the Antarctic*, together with a summary of the scientific data collected. I have not included them here because they were not part of Shackleton's personal experience.

However, in the first chapter of the second volume, before handing over to Professor David, Shackleton set aside his personal diary, and attempted a summary of conclusions on his own journey to the south. Here are some of them.

SOME NOTES ON THE SOUTHERN JOURNEY

Food

We brought back with us from the journey towards the Pole vivid memories of how if feels to be intensely, fiercely hungry. During the period from November 15, 1908, to February 23, 1909, we had but one full meal, and that was on Christmas Day. Even then we did not keep the sense of repletion for very long for within an hour or two it seemed to us that we were as hungry as ever. Our daily allowance of food would have been a small one for a city worker in a temperate climate, and in our case hunger was increased by the fact that we were performing vigorous physical labour in a very low temperature. We looked forward to each meal with keen anticipation, but when the food was in our hands it seemed to disappear without making us any the less ravenous. We would gnaw carefully round the sides of our biscuits, making them last as long as possible. Marshall used sometimes to stand his pannikin of hoosh in the snow a little while, because it got thicker as it cooled, but it was a debatable point whether this paid. One seemed to be getting more solid food, but there was a loss of warmth, and in the minus temperatures on the plateau we found it advisable to take our hoosh very hot. We would make the biscuits last as long as possible, and sometimes we tried to save a bit to eat in the sleeping-bag later on, but it was hard to do this. If one of us dropped a crumb, the others would point it out, and the owner would wet his finger in his mouth and pick up the morsel. Not the smallest fragment was allowed to escape.

We used to 'turn backs' in order to ensure equitable division of the food. The cook would pour the hoosh into the pannikins and arrange the biscuits in four heaps. Perhaps someone would suggest that one pannikin had rather less in it than another, and if this view was endorsed by the others there would be a readjustment. Then when we were all satisfied that the food had been divided as fairly as possible, one man would turn his back, and another, pointing at one pannikin or group of biscuits, would say, 'Whose?' The man who had his back turned, and therefore could not see the food, would give a name, and so the distribution would proceed, each of us always feeling sure that the smallest share had fallen to our lot. At lunch-time there would be chocolate or cheese to distribute on alternate days, and we much preferred the chocolate days to the cheese days. The chocolate seemed more satisfying, and it was more easily divided. The cheese broke up into very small fragments on the march, and the allowance, which amounted to two spoonfuls per man, had to be divided up as nearly as possible into four equal heaps. The chocolate could be easily separated into sticks of equal size. It can be imagined that the cook for the week had no easy task. His work became more difficult still when we were using pony-meat, for the meat and blood, when boiled up, made a delightful broth, while the fragments of meat sunk to the bottom of the pot. The liquor was much the better part of the dish, and no one had much relish for the little dice of tough and stringy meat, so the cook had to be very careful indeed. Poor old Chinaman was a particularly tough and stringy horse.

We used the meat immediately we had started to kill the ponies in order to save the other food, for we knew that the meat contained a very large percentage of water, so that we would be carrying useless weight with it. The reader will understand that the loss of Socks, which represented so many pounds of meat, was a very severe blow to us, for we had after that to use sledging stores at the depots to make up for the lost meat. If we had been able to use Socks for food, I have no doubt that we would have been able to get further south, perhaps even to the Pole itself, though in that case we could hardly have got back in time to catch the ship before she was forced to leave by the approach of winter.

When we were living on meat our desire for cereals and farinaceous foods became stronger; indeed any particular sort of food of which we were deprived seemed to us to be the food for which nature craved. When we were short of sugar we would dream of sweet-stuffs, and when biscuits were in short supply our thoughts were concerned with crisp loaves and all the other good things displayed in the windows of the bakers' shops. During the last weeks of the journey outwards, and the long march back, when our allowance of food had been reduced to twenty ounces per man a day, we really thought of little but food. The glory of the great mountains that towered high on either side, the majesty of the enormous glacier up which we travelled so painfully, did not appeal to our emotions to any great extent. Man becomes very primitive when he is hungry and short of food, and we learned to know what it is to be desperately hungry. I used to wonder sometimes whether the people who suffer from hunger in the big cities of civilisation felt as we were feeling, and I arrived at the conclusion that they did not, for no barrier of law and order would have been allowed to stand between us and any food that had been available.

No French chef ever devoted more thought to the invention of new dishes than we did. Sometimes there would be an argument as to whether a suggested dish was really an original invention, or whether it did not too nearly resemble something that we had already tasted in happier days. The 'Wild roll' was admitted to be a high-water mark of gastronomic luxury. Wild proposed that the cook should take a supply of well-seasoned minced meat, wrap it in rashers of fat bacon, and place around the whole an outer covering of rich pastry, so that it would take the form of a big sausage-roll. Then this roll would be fried with plenty of fat. My best dish, which I must admit I put forward with a good deal of pride as we marched over the snow, was a sardine pasty, made by placing well-fried sardines inside pastry. At least ten tins of sardines were to be emptied on to a bed of pastry, and the whole then rolled up and cooked, preparatory to its division into four equal portions. I remember one day Marshall came forward with a proposal for a thick roll of suet pudding with plenty of jam all over it, and there arose quite a heated argument as to whether he could fairly claim this dish to be an invention, or whether it was not the jam roll already known to the housewives of civilisation. There was one point on which we were all agreed, and that was that we did not want any jellies or things of that sort at our future meals. The idea of eating such elusive stuff as jelly had no appeal to us at all.

I daresay that all this sounds very greedy and uncivilised to the reader who has never been on the verge of starvation, but as I have said before, hunger makes a man primitive. We did not smile at ourselves or at each other as we planned wonderful feats of over-eating. We were perfectly serious about the matter, and we noted down in the back pages of our diaries details of the meals that we had decided to have as soon as we got back to the places where food was plentiful.

The dysentery from which we suffered during the latter part of the journey back to the coast was certainly due to the meat from the pony Grisi. This animal was shot one night when in a greatly exhausted condition, and I believe that his flesh was made poisonous by the presence of the toxin of exhaustion, as is the case with animals that have been hunted. The manner in which we managed

1 Ernest Shackleton in his early thirties and in determined mood.

2 Shackleton's ship Nimrod *leaving Lyttelton Harbour on New Zealand's South Island, New Year's Day 1908. She was given a tumultuous send-off by the local people.*

3 Frank Wild with a pair of huskies. The British never achieved the same success as the Norwegians with dog teams. They were said to be too sentimental about them.

4 *Ross Island, Antarctica; winter quarters for successive attempts to reach the South Pole. On the western side is the 13,200 ft volcano, Mt Erebus. The first ascent was made by members of Shackleton's expedition in 1908.*

5 *An ice pressure ridge, stretching from the Barne Glacier towards Cape Royds on Ross Island, photographed by Herbert Ponting in 1911.*

6 *An aerial view of Ross Island, looking due East towards Mt Erebus. Scott's*
Discovery *Expedition hut was built near the tip of the peninsula in the*
foreground, on the northern side. In the lower right-hand side of the picture the
division between the seasonal sea-ice and the permanent Ross Ice Shelf can be
seen. This is the Barrier. To the north of it, the ice might be 15 ft thick; to the
south, up to 200 ft thick.

7 *The Beardmore Glacier seen from the air. Over a hundred miles in length, it is among the largest in the world.*

8 *Shackleton's party reach their 'Furthest South' on 6 January 1909: Latitude 88°23′S 162°E, less than 100 miles from the South Pole. (l to r) Adams, Wild, Shackleton. The photograph was taken by Marshall.*

9 *One of Herbert Ponting's famous photographs taken in 1911, during the Terra Nova Expedition. He called it 'Ramparts of the South Pole'. In fact it is the foot of the Barne Glacier, where it meets the Ross Sea.*

10 *The departure of* Endurance *from Millwall Docks, London, on 1 August 1914, bound for the Weddell Sea. General mobilisation for war against Germany had been ordered a few days earlier.*

11 *Shackleton with his wife Emily on board* Endurance *before setting sail.*

12 The way South. Endurance *picks her way through the pack-ice guarding the entrance to the Weddell Sea, 10 December 1914.*

13 Endurance *in trouble, February 1915. With every implement they can lay their hands on, the crew try to cut a way forward through the encroaching pack-ice.*

14 Endurance *beset in the ice as the long winter night descends. The huskies are taken off the ship's deck and installed in 'dogloos' alongside. April 1915.*

15 Once Endurance *was firmly beset in the ice, the forehold was cleared of stores and converted into a general mess-room for officers and scientists. It was nicknamed 'The Ritz'.*

16 Hurley's photograph of Endurance *by moonlight, stuck fast in the ice.*

17 Waiting in vain for Endurance *to break free. A game of football relieves the monotony, October 1915.*

18 An ominous sign: 'rafting' ice near Endurance, *forced up by immense pressure acting on the surface of the pack, November 1915.*

19 Endurance *doomed but defiant, November 1915.*

20 Endurance *keeling over.*

21 and 22 *The last days of* Endurance. *She was abandoned on 27 October 1915 and finally sank on 21 November.*

23 *Elephant Island seen from an ice grotto, April 1916.*

24 *The 'hut' on Elephant Island, constructed out of the two upturned boats lashed together and covered by a sail.*

25 The James Caird *sets out on her 800-mile journey to South Georgia, 24 April 1916. The extra deck cover built by the carpenter McNeish, just before the voyage, can be clearly seen.*

26 Shackleton, with a faithful companion, on his last voyage in the Quest, *September 1921.*
27 The memorial cross to Shackleton on South Georgia.

to keep on marching when suffering, and the speed with which we recovered when we got proper food, were rather remarkable, and the reason, no doubt, was that the dysentery was simply the result of the poison, and was not produced by organic trouble of any sort. We had a strong wind behind us day after day during this period, and this contributed in a very large measure to our safety, for in the weakened condition we had then reached we could not have made long marches against a head-wind, and without long marches we would have starved between the depots.

The Sun

When we were travelling along during the early part of the journey over the level Barrier surface, we felt the heat of the sun severely, though as a matter of fact the temperature was generally very low, sometimes as low as zero Fahr. though the season was the height of summer. It was quite usual to feel one side of the face getting frozen while the other side was being sun-burned. The ponies would have frozen perspiration on their coats on the sheltered side, while the sun would keep the other side hot and dry, and as the day wore on and the sun moved round the sky the frosted area on the animals would change its position in sympathy.

Equipment

In reviewing the experience gained on the southern journey, I do not think that I could suggest any improvement in equipment for any future expedition. The Barrier surface evidently varies in a remarkable fashion, and its condition cannot be anticipated with any degree of certainty. The traveller must be prepared for either a hard surface or a very soft one, and he may get both surfaces in the course of one day's march. The eleven-foot sledge is thoroughly suitable for the work, and our method of packing the stores and hauling the sledges did not develop any weak points. We would have been glad to have had crampons for use on the glacier; what would be better still would be heavy alpine boots with nails all round, for very often the surface would give little grip to crampons, which would only touch the rough ice at one or two points. The temperature is too cold to permit of the explorer wearing ordinary leather boots, and some boot would have to be designed capable of keeping the feet warm and carrying the nails all round. A mast consisting of a bamboo lashed to the forward oil-box proved as efficient as could be required for use in connection with a sail on the sledges. It was easily rigged and had no elaborate stays. I would suggest no change in the clothing, for the light woollen under-clothing, with thin windproof material out-side, proved most satisfactory in every way. We could certainly not have travelled so fast had we been wearing the regulation pilot cloth garment generally used in polar exploration. Our experience made it obvious that a party which hopes to reach the Pole must take more food per man than we did, but how the additional weight is to be provided for is a matter for individual considera-tion. I would not take cheese again, for although it is a good food, we did not find it as palatable as chocolate, which is practically as sustaining. Our other foods were all entirely satisfactory.

Duties

Each member of the Southern Party had his own particular duties to perform. Adams had charge of the meteorology, and his work involved the taking of temperatures at regular intervals, and the boiling of the hypsometer, sometimes several times in a day. He took notes during the day, and wrote up the observations at night in the sleeping-bag. Marshall was the cosmographer and took the angles and bearings of all the new land; he also took the meridian altitudes and the compass variation as we went south. When a meridian altitude was taken, I generally had it checked by each member of the party, so that the mean could be taken.

Marshall's work was about the most uncomfortable possible, for at the end of a day's march, and often at lunch-time, he would have to stand in the biting wind handling the screws of the theodolite. The map of the journey was prepared by Marshall, who also took most of the photographs. Wild attended to the repair of the sledges and equipment, and also assisted me in the geological observations and the collection of specimens. It was he who found the coal close to the Upper Glacier Depot. I kept the courses and distances, worked out observations and laid down our directions. We all kept diaries.

BETWEEN *NIMROD* AND *ENDURANCE*

by Christopher Ralling

Shackleton's homecoming after the *Nimrod* Expedition was a triumph of almost Roman proportions. Emily met him at Dover and the two of them travelled by train to London, where a delegation from the Royal Geographical Society and other notables were waiting on the platform at Charing Cross. The reception party included Sir Clements Markham and Captain Scott. In the station yard a huge crowd was waiting to greet the returning hero. Legend had it that the horses were taken out of the carriage shafts and eager young men replaced them, setting off at a brisk trot in the direction of Trafalgar Square, while the crowd surged around them. True or not, it was the sort of legend that now began to attach itself to this new-found national celebrity. His unaffected warmth and straight-forwardness and his undoubted patriotism fitted the mood of the country; and he responded to it.

The news of the Expedition's success had been broken by the *Daily Mail* in an exclusive story, which Shackleton had cabled from New Zealand, but by the time he reached London, every newspaper was full of eulogies. A quotation which none of his chroniclers has been able to resist, appeared in the *Sphere*:

> So long as Englishmen are prepared to do this kind of thing
> . . . we need not lie awake all night, every night, dreading the
> hostile advance of 'the boys of the dachsund breed'.

Although the war was still some five years away, perhaps it caught the mood of the time. They were heady days. For the moment, those elusive ninety-seven miles which had robbed him and his companions of the ultimate prize were forgotten. As far as the general public was concerned, the Expedition had been an unqualified success.

But for Shackleton, life was never destined to be quite so straightforward. Nor would he ever fully understand the mind and workings of the geographical Establishment. Whether it was over-exuberance or an impish desire to 'cock a snook' at those who had offered him so little assistance when he was setting out, he had sent a message to the Society's Secretary, Scott-Keltie, advising him to 'book the Albert Hall and get the King'. It had been frostily received.

Bad manners was one thing; deliberate falsification of results quite another. And within the Royal Geographical Society there was undoubtedly a faction which came to believe that Shackleton had done just that. It wounded him deeply. The prime mover appears to have been the Grand Old Man of the Society, Sir Clements Markham himself. In September 1909 he wrote to the current President, Major Leonard Darwin:

> As I am responsible for having started all this Antarctic business, I think it right that I should send you a note of what I think of recent developments. Shackleton's failure to reach the South Pole when it could have been done by another, and is really a matter of calculation, rather aggravates me. It will rouse ignorant admiration if the trumpets are blown loud enough, which they are sure to be. But I cannot accept the latitudes. For 88.20 they must have gone, dragging a sledge and on half rations, at the rate of fourteen miles a day in a straight line, up a steep incline 9,000 feet above the sea, for twenty days. I do not believe it.

The 'another' in this letter was, of course, Markham's own protégé, Scott, who to his credit seems to have remained aloof from the whispering campaign which now grew up around Shackleton's claims. The basis of the allegation was that he had deliberately added a few miles to each day's total. The only possible motive would have been to get within the magic 'last hundred miles' of the Pole. Ninety-seven, so the argument ran, sounds a great deal better than one hundred and fifty.

For this modest deception, Shackleton would have had to obtain the fraudulent collusion of his three companions, who as we have seen, were in no mood to collaborate on anything, except their own survival. Nevertheless, the seeds of suspicion, once sown, began to spread. Today they probably have more to tell us about the extraordinary influence Sir Clements Markham wielded in the Society (even after, in his own words, he had become 'an extinct volcano') than anything else. In Sir Clements' eyes, Shackleton had thoroughly 'muddied the waters'. He had broken his word in going back to McMurdo; and now, honestly or otherwise, he had completely stolen the limelight, while failing to finish the job. At the height of his resentment, he even put it about that Shackleton had never sat the examination for his Master's Certificate in the Merchant Marine. It was totally untrue.

Shackleton's public reply to those who were questioning his claims appeared in the *Geographical Journal*. It was brisk and formal, almost to the point of curtness.

> The latitude observations made on the Southern Journey were taken with the thedolite, as were all the bearings, angles and azimuths. Variation was ascertained by means of a compass attached to the theodolite, and the steering compasses were checked accordingly. At noon each day the prismatic compasses were placed in the true meridian, and checked against the theodolite compass and the steering compasses. The last latitude observation taken on the outward journey was taken at 87° 22′ S. and the remainder of the distance towards the south was calculated by sledge meter and dead reckoning. The accuracy of the sledge meter had been proved by the fact that the daily record of distance travelled agreed roughly with the observations for position. We took only one observation on the return journey, on 31 January, and then found that our position had been accurately recorded by the sledge meter.

Doubts may have remained, but the matter was never raised again. For the rest of his life Shackleton's relationship with the Royal Geographical Society remained one of guarded mistrust.

Meanwhile, Captain Scott refused to be caught up in the swirling currents of congratulation and recrimination that eddied around Shackleton's feet. His mind was clear. It was better by far to complete the missing miles to the Pole rather than argue about them. Within a few days of their return, a dinner was given at the Savage Club for members of the expedition. In his welcoming speech, Scott seized his opportunity. 'What matters now,' he said, 'is that the Pole should be attained by an Englishman. I personally am prepared, and have been for the last two years, to go forth in search of that object.'

Then, on 1 July 1909, just two weeks after Shackleton's return, Scott staked out his claim in the form of a letter.

Dear Shackleton,

If, as I understand, it does not cut across any future plans of yours, I propose to organise the Expedition to the Ross Sea which, as you know, I have had so long in preparation, so as to start next year.

My plan is to establish a base in King Edward VII Land and to push South and East. I cannot but think that late in the season with a heavier ship than the 'Nimrod' it will be possible to establish the base.

The prospect offers good geographical work as well as a chance of reaching a high latitude, and I am sure you will wish me success; but of course I should be glad to have your assurance that I am not disconcerting any plan of your own.

Shackleton gave himself four days to think about this before replying, equally formally:

Dear Captain Scott,

. . . I understand that you have already your expedition in preparation, and it will not interfere with any plans of mine. If I do any further exploration it will not be until I have heard news of your expedition, presuming that you start next year. I may later on attempt the circumnavigation of the Antarctic Continent but my ideas as regards this are indefinite.

I wish you every success in your endeavour to penetrate the ice and to land on King Edward VII Land and to attain a high latitude from that base. I quite agree with you that good geographical work can be done from that quarter, and it will have a newer interest than McMurdo Sound.

The past hangs heavily over these letters. Both men had learned something from the painful experience of their last ill-fated agreement. But the rivalry remained. The idea that Britain's two most celebrated explorers should take part in a joint endeavour, perhaps starting from different bases, was clearly out of the question.

Their personal relationship had not been improved by a small, but to Scott extremely irritating, incident which had happened some months before. He had received a letter through the post addressed in Shackleton's handwriting, and with one of the specially printed King Edward VII Land stamps on the envelope. Inside was a blank piece of paper.

The most probable explanation is that this was one of many such envelopes sent home to selected people who would put a special value on the stamp. Shackleton may have intended to include some sort of explanatory note, but forgotten to do so.

But coming from the man who had just usurped his base, Scott considered it at best a practical joke in very poor taste, and at worst a deliberate insult.

So far as we know, the matter was never mentioned between them, so Shackleton had no opportunity to explain or apologise.

Each man now had one more momentous journey before him. Each would be confronted by failure, but a failure of epic proportions.

As the world knows, Scott was beaten by Amundsen in his race for the Pole, and on the journey back, perished with his four companions. Shackleton, in his bid to make the first trans-Antarctic crossing, sighted land just once, never landed a single man on the Continent itself, and was forced to watch his brand-new ship crushed to death in the merciless pack ice of the Weddell Sea. These are the facts; as bald as the facts of Dunkirk. But out of these apparent failures have come the two great stories of Antarctic endeavour, which are never likely to be surpassed.

But two more years were to pass before the beginning of this next climactic phase in British exploration. For Shackleton, much of the time had to be spent lecturing in Britain, Europe and America in an attempt to recover the costs of the *Nimrod* expedition. Good lecturer though he was, the task became increasingly irksome.

There were a few gratifying moments. His bluff sailor's manner seems to have found favour with the King, who first of all made him a Commander of the Royal Victorian Order, and subsequently a Knight of the Realm. The Prime Minister too, responded to popular clamour, and came forward with a Government grant of £20,000 to help cover the Expedition's expenses. But in spite of all the popular acclaim, the old restlessness which seemed to afflict him whenever he came home for any length of time, began to creep back.

As always, he was full of schemes for making a fortune as quickly as possible. Cigarette promotion, a taxi-cab company, even a mining concession in Hungary were all vigorously pursued at intervals between his lecturing commitments. The result, much to the unspoken sadness of Emily, was that he spent less and less time with his family.

It was a time of strain for both of them, which Shackleton did his best to alleviate sometimes, by elaborate practical jokes. On one memorable occasion, he went to a theatrical costumiers and had himself made up and fitted out to resemble an elderly relative returning from abroad. In this guise he arrived at his own house, where he was announced as 'Sir Ernest's uncle, back from South America'. The children, and for a brief moment Emily as well, were completely taken in. But such pranks, endearing as they were, concealed frustrations of a deeper kind. The endless round of lecturing was paying fewer and fewer dividends. Once it was over, he would not know where to turn. In November 1910, he wrote to Emily from Germany:

> Last night was bad, the arrangements were awful and a very poor attendance and they made a worse job of the moving pictures than they did at Buda Pest: it was most unsatisfactory and I was particularly anxious to have things right now, as I can see a strong anti-English feeling in Germany now, quite different to when I was here in January. When the picture of the Queen's flag is shown there is a stony silence, and altogether it seems different; there are no social arrangements and this may be due to the lack of my gracious lady's presence. If things do not get better soon I will think very seriously of chucking the whole thing and not wear myself out on it, and on these unsatisfactory meetings . . .

It seems likely that Emily at this time knew better than Shackleton himself that the only cure for a man of his restless and striving nature would be to return to the one place in the world where he felt completely fulfilled, the Antarctic. Painful though it must have been for her, she even suggested that he should consider going on the expedition that Mawson was to lead in the following year. (Mawson was one of the two Australians who had been with him on the *Nimrod*.) His reply is most revealing:

> No darling, I don't want to go with Mawson: that time has gone. I want to consolidate our world and make our future lives comfortable and there is much to do. I feel that another Expedition, unless it crosses the Continent, is not much.

Emily must have read this passage with a wry smile. This was the man she knew all too well; resolutely insisting that his domestic responsibilies must come first, yet unable to conceal the idea which was already germinating in his head.

For the moment, however, the baton had been passed to Scott, and Shackleton's life passed into a relatively fallow and unrewarding period. It seems an appropriate moment, therefore, to break off from giving an account of his daily life, and take a look at the inner man, as revealed in his poetry.

He had no pretensions in this direction beyond the simple wish, on occasion, to express his feelings in verse; and he would certainly have been embarrassed to see his efforts collected together for general publication. But no representative selection of his writing would be complete without including some of the poems he wrote for the two expedition journals that were produced in Antarctica, *Aurora Australis* and *The South Polar Times*; and others that he wrote purely for himself.

The credit for collecting them together belongs entirely to Margery Fisher, who has kindly given permission for them to be reprinted here, together with her own introductory notes.

1 *A Tale of the Sea*
(A copy of this poem in Shackleton's handwriting survives among the Shackleton family papers, with the date February 1895. It is superscribed Emily A. Dorman 15th March 1899. In 1895 Shackleton was scarcely twenty-one years of age and serving as Third Officer on the *Monmouthshire* in the Far East. We here reproduce the poem from Shackleton's copy, with his own characteristic punctuation.)

> I slept and dreamt of the ocean:
> Of tarry sailors joys:
> Of the tales which they loved to fashion
> Of days when they were boys:
> And I laughed aloud in my sleep:
> 'In those days they said they were men:
> Is there one who has a record
> Of worth: for a poets pen'?
>
> The dream soon faded and left me:
> But it returned again
> And I smelt the Galleys odour

Heard curses of sailor men.
Heard moaning of bitter salt winds:
Shrieking of gathering gales:
Wings of wild sea birds rising,
Beat the waves like threshers flails.

Then I saw a great long line
Of ghostly ships from the North;
Come churning the seas to foam
Splashing their bows with froth.
Dipping now into the hollows:
Now on the top they rise;
Pointing their booms to the ocean's bed
And anon to the wind swept skies.

They in the foremost ships,
With tattered sails, and torn,
Thus spoke from the high poop aft:
Where the deck with their tread was worn:
Where nailed to the rotting flagstaffs:
The old white Ensigns flew
Badge of our English freedom
Over all waters blue.

'We fell for our countrys glory
And not for the yellow gold:
No: not as reward for greed:
Has the Arctic o'er us rolled:
We fell for the light of science,
To make clear the hidden paths
When the iceberg crunches our timbers,
As though they were only laths.'

Then they told me a wondrous tale
And I strove to write it down
But my pen refused its duty:
And I lost my chance for renown
But since that vision left me:
I have looked on those sailor men
As worthy the brightest idyll.
That poet could ever pen.

Oh! the deepest blue of the sky:
Oh! the greenest sward on the lea:
To me seems dull and paltry,
Since I dreamt of that tossing sea,
For now I know it is peopled
With wandering souls of the past:
Blown to & fro on its surface
At the mercy of every blast.

2 *Fanning Isle*

(This was a favourite poem of Lady Shackleton's. The verses were given to a friend from South Australia shortly after Shackleton's arrival in London in 1903, and may therefore be presumed to have been written during his voyage across the Pacific on the *Oratava* on his way to San Francisco, in February 1903. The subtitle of the poem is 'A Link in the All-British Cable'.)

Surf-bound, lonely islet,
Set in a summer sea,
Work of a tiny insect,
A lesson I learn from thee.
For to your foam-white shores
The deep sea cables come.
Through slippery ooze, by feathery palms,
Flies by the busy hum
Of the nations linked together,
The young, with the older lands,
A moment's space, and the Northern tale
Is placed in Southern hands.
So, green isle small and lonely,
I find as I think it o'er
That your place in the scheme of nations
Shows to me more and more
That every deed of Nature
Helps to the finished plan,
That starts with the lowly worm
And will end in the perfect man:
That the smallest leads to the greatest,
And your worth may now be seen
As the pulsing heart of the ocean
Goes by your island green.

3 *Two Ways*

(We have found this poem only in the *Sunday Express* of 5 February 1922, with no note of how it came to the paper or why it is not to be found among the other poems preserved by his wife. The poem was printed as a facsimile from a manuscript, inscribed at the end 'E. H. Shackleton, *S. S. India*, 12.11.07'.)

You may love the calm and peaceful days,
And the glorious tropic nights
When the roof of the Earth with broad stars blaze
And the Moon's long path of light
Steals in a shining silver streak,
From the far horizon line
And on the brink of the ocean's rim
Still greater planets shine.
But all the delight of summer seas,
And the sun's westing gold
Are nought to me for I know a sea
With a glamour and glory untold.

The gloom and cold of the long stern night
The work with its strain and stress
Hold sterling worth and sheer delight,
And these soft bright times hold less.
For all is new on our ice bound shore
Where white peaks dare the stars
There strong endeavour and steady hand
Alone can unloose the bars.
Then by faith unswerving we may attain
To the oft wished for distant goal,
And at last to our country's gain
Hold with our flag the Southern Pole.

4 *To the Great Barrier*

(This long romantic poem, with its echoes of Swinburne and Tennyson, was written for the *South Polar Times*, the magazine of Scott's expeditions, and was included in the August number of 1902, over the signature NEMO.)

Mother of mighty icebergs, these Kings of the Southern Seas,
Mystery, yet unfathomed, though we've paid in full our fees,
Eyes strained by ceaseless watching, when the low grey fog doth
    screen

Your walls from our aching vision, and the great grim giants you
    wean
Away from your broad white bosom, where for aeons untold is
    laid
Each yearly tribute of fallen snows, that this wonderful plain has
    made.
We have felt, more than seen, the danger, close ahead of our
    long jib boom,
But a turn of the icy wheel has made for us more sea room.
We have sailed from your farthest West, that is bounded by fire
    and snow,
We have pierced to your farthest East, till stopped by the hard,
    set floe.
We have steamed by your wave worn caverns; dim, blue,
    mysterious halls,
We have risen above your surface, we have sounded along your
    walls.
And above that rolling surface we have strained our eyes to see
But league upon league of whiteness was all there seemed to be.
Ah, what is the secret you're keeping, to the Southward beyond
    our ken?
This year shall your icy fastness resound with the voices of
    men?
Shall we learn that you come from the mountains? Shall we call
    you a frozen sea?
Shall we sail to the Northward and leave you, still a Secret for
    ever to be?

5 *L'Envoi*
(This poem represents Shackleton's most ambitious attempt to
sum up the feelings which the Antarctic had called forth in him. It
was also written for the *South Polar Times* over the signature
NEMO, and was included after the end-piece of the last number
produced on Scott's first expedition (August 1903), after Shackleton had been invalided home to England.)

Slowly, though touched with glamour, the winter night went by,
    And we longed to see the sunlight sweep up in the Northern
    sky.
Still we wait in this icy fastness till the good sun sets us free.
    When no longer the tumbling billow is chained to a frozen
    sea.
Then shall our hardened bows dip gladly once more to the foam

Of the Southward driving roller as the good ship strives for
    home.
Brothers, we then shall be parted in a world that is greater far
    Than this weird and wondrous region shut in with an icy
        bar.
We shall read then in other pages words fashioned with easier
        pen,
    Each day with its list of changes in a world of busy men.
But our hearts will still be faithful to this Southern land of ours,
    Though we wander in English meadows 'mid the scent of
        English flowers,
When the soft southerly breeze shakes the blossom away from
    the thorn,
    And flings from the wild rose cup, the shining gift of the
        morn;
And when the scarlet poppies peep through the golden wheat,
    As the stronger winds of Autumn march in with heavier
        feet;
And when the fields are snow clad, trees hard in a frosty rime,
    Our thoughts will wander Southward, we shall think of the
        grey old time;
Again in dreams go back to our fight with the icy foe;
    The crash of the steel clad bows; the sob of the tilted floe;
The tearing, rending asunder; the crack in the frozen field;
    The grating beneath the keel of the piece that sunk sooner
        than yield,
Our run through the ice free ocean till the snowy peaks
        appeared,
    Crowned by the gold of the morning, shod with the glaciers
        weird.
Then our joy at the furthest East where never yet man had
        been;
    When through the curtain of falling snow the bare, black
        rocks were seen;
We shall dream of the ever increasing gales, the birds in their
        Northward flight;
    The magic of twilight colours, the gloom of the long, long
        night.
We shall dream of those months of sledging through soft and
        yielding snow;
    The chafe of the strap on the shoulder; the whine of the
        dogs as they go.
Our rest in the tent after marching; our sleep in the biting cold;

The Heavens now grey with the snow cloud, anon to be
  burnished gold;
The threshing drift on the tent side exposed to the blizzard's
  might;
  The wind-blown furrows and snow drifts; the crystal's play
  in the light;
And when, in the fading firelight, we turn these pages o'er,
  We shall think of the times we wrote therein by that far off
  Southern shore.
With regret we shall close the story, yet ever in thought go back,
  And success for each comrade will pay for on Life's still
  unbeaten track;
And the love of men for each other that was born in that naked
  land,
  Constant through life's great changes will be held by our
  little band.
Though the grip of the frost may be cruel, and relentless its icy
  hold,
  Yet it knit our hearts together in that darkness stern and
  cold.

6 *Midwinter Night*
(This is the only example that survives of Shackleton's light verse.
The poem was contributed to *Aurora Australis*, the magazine of
Shackleton's British Antarctic Expedition of 1907–09. It is signed
'Veritas' but appears in the contents list under 'Nemo', the
pseudonym Shackleton had used in the *South Polar Times*. On 17
June 1908 Marshall wrote in his diary, 'Sh. composing poetry.
Rather good on night watchman.' The poem was illustrated by a
drawing by Marston.)

> The acetylene splutters and flickers,
> The night comes into its own.
> Outside Ambrose and Terror
> And snarling over a bone.
>
> And this is the tale the watchman,
> Awake in the dead of night,
> Tells of the fourteen sleepers
> Whose snoring gives him the blight.
>
> The revels of Eros and Bacchus
> Are mingled in some of their dreams,
> For the songs they gustily gurgle
> Are allied to bibulous themes.

And subjects re barmaids and bottles,
Whisky and barrels of beer,
Are mixed with amorous pleadings
That sound decidedly queer.

Darling you really love me?
Stutters one dreaming swain;
The watchman whispers 'Never',
And the dreamer writhes in pain.

From the corner cabin a mutter,
The listener knows not what;
It sounds like 'yon pale moon',
Or some other poetic rot.

Murder is done in another's dream
And falls from shuddering heights;
Erebus rises to dance on the sea
And the dreamer flees south in tights.

Another sails north on the broken ice
Just dressed in Nature's clothes,
Whilst seals and penguins grin in delight
And the frost plays hell with his toes.

And some see tailors they knew of yore,
Stalk in with their mile-long bills;
And everyone when morning broke
Made a rush for calomel pills.

7 *Erebus*
(This, probably Shackleton's best and most satisfying poem, was
also contributed to *Aurora Australis* over the signature 'Nemo'.)

Keeper of the Southern Gateway, grim, rugged, gloomy, and
 grand;
Warden of these wastes uncharted, as the years sweep on, you
 stand.
At your head the swinging smoke-cloud; at your feet the
 grinding floes;
Racked and seared by the inner fires, gripped close by the outer
 snows.
Proud, unconquered, and unyielding, whilst the untold aeons
 passed,
Inviolate through the ages, your ramparts spurning the blast,

Till men impelled by a strong desire, broke through your icy bars;
Fierce was the fight to gain that height where your stern peak
    dares the stars.
You called your vassals to aid you, and the leaping blizzard rose,
Driving in furious eddies, blinding, stifling, cruel snows.
The grasp of the numbing frost clutched hard at their hands
    and faces,
And the weird gloom made darker still dim seen perilous places.
They, weary, wayworn, and sleepless, through the long
    withering night,
Grimly clung to your iron sides till with laggard Dawn came the
    light;
Both heart and brain upheld them, till the long-drawn strain
    was o'er,
Victors then on your crown they stood, and gazed at the
    Western shore,
The distant glory of that land in broad spendour lay unrolled,
With icefield, cape and mountain height, flame rose in a sea of
    gold.
Oh! Herald of returning suns to the waiting lands below;
Beacon to their home-seeking feet, far across the Southern
    snow;
In the Northland, in the years to be, pale Winters first white
    sign
Will turn again their thoughts to thee, and the glamour that is
    thine.

The years of rivalry between Scott and Shackleton ended in the
Spring of 1913, when the news of Scott's death and that of his
companions reached London, almost a year after they had
perished on the Barrier. A full year before, the news of
Amundsen's triumph in reaching the South Pole became
known to the world. When the victorious Norwegian, by now
unquestionably the greatest Polar explorer of his age, stopped
off in London on his way home in November 1912, the reception he received was far from warm.

In some circles, Amundsen's sudden announcement that he
was going south instead of north, had been considered a 'dirty
trick'. The President of the Royal Geographical Society
decided not to receive him; and his action was widely
applauded.

It was left to Shackleton to introduce Amundsen's lecture at
the Queen's Hall, and afterwards to move the vote of thanks.

He was not to know that just three days before, a search party had found the bodies of Wilson, Bowers and Scott, still in their tent, and just eleven miles from the depot which would have saved them.

So the long rivalry between the two men ended in tragedy; and the prize of the Pole, for which they had both striven for twelve long years, was snatched by another. In scientific circles it had long been considered a somewhat artificial goal which appealed to the popular imagination, but diverted resources from more important scientific aims.

The same criticism was to be made of Shackleton's next great venture, to which he now turned all his energies. This was to be nothing less than a crossing of the Antarctic Continent.

The plan had originally been put forward as early as 1908, by a scientist named W. S. Bruce, but had foundered for lack of funds. Shackleton's popular reputation now gave it a much better chance of success. As soon as his fund-raising activities reached a reasonable level of buoyancy, he announced his plans in a letter to *The Times*.

> *29 December 1913*
> Sir,—It has been an open secret for some time past that I have been desirous of leading another expedition to the South Polar regions.
>
> I am glad now to be able to state that, through the generosity of a friend, I can announce that an expedition will start next year with the object of crossing the South Polar continent from sea to sea.
>
> I have taken the liberty of calling the expedition 'The Imperial Trans-Antarctic Expedition', because I feel that not only the people of these islands, but our kinsmen in all lands under the Union Jack will be willing to assist us towards the carrying out of the full programme of exploration to which my comrades and myself are pledged.

This was typical of Shackleton. Even though his position was infinitely stronger than it had been in 1907, he had decided once again to by-pass the machinations of The Royal Geographical Society, and appeal directly to the public's sense of patriotism.

But, 'hidebound and narrow' as he considered the Society to be, he could not avoid their involvement altogether. An Austrian party under Dr König also had plans to follow up some of their earlier exploration in the Weddell Sea. When

Shackleton's plans became known, it was to The Royal Geographical Society, not to Shackleton personally, that König protested.

The President of the Society, Lord Curzon, now found himself having to adopt the role of reluctant arbitrator between the Austrians and their territorial claims on the one hand, and Shackleton the indignant patriot, over whom he had no actual control, on the other. To the Society's surprise and relief, Shackleton was persuaded, not only to submit his plans for their scrutiny, but to present himself in person. This gave some of the senior members what they really wanted; the opportunity to examine his proposals in detail. The questions ranged much wider than Shackleton's right to establish a base in the Weddell Sea. The fact was that even some of his greatest admirers, like Hugh Robert Mill, considered that this time he was attempting far too much, and had not fully assessed the risks.

The plan was certainly ambitious. It required two ships for the establishment of separate bases on opposite sides of the Antarctic Continent. Shackleton's own party would set out to cross the Continent via the Pole, using dogs and mechanised transport. Meanwhile a second party would take the old route to the South from Ross Island, laying depots of food and fuel on top of the Beardmore Glacier. The question was whether the achievement of such a plan could ever justify the risks. Shackleton had no such doubts. At the first of two meetings that he attended, he spelt out his position in the plainest of terms:

> Some people condemn this object as spectacular and of no particular use, and consider that no expedition should set forth without the one object of being purely scientific. Until the South Pole had been reached, deep in the mind of every explorer who penetrated into the Antarctic was the desire to reach that goal ... My desire is to cross the Antarctic Continent, and in undertaking this expedition, the members of it are the agents of the British nation. If I said differently I would be untrue to my conviction. I have put the crossing of the continent as the great object of this expedition, and there is not one person in this room tonight, and there is not one individual who is under the Union Jack in any part of the Empire, who does not wish the British Flag to be the first national flag ever carried across the frozen waste.

At a second, private meeting a month later, Lord Curzon pressed Shackleton further on the question of the scientific worth of his plans:

PRESIDENT: I suppose you realise that if you found (a mountain range) and explored it, that would really be much more interesting than a mere journey straight across?

SHACKLETON: The journey across is the thing that I want to do.

PRESIDENT: I should not say too much about that. No doubt the public likes it and admires the British spirit, but the scepticism that exists among scientific bodies will be most satisfactorily met by the scientific work you may be able to do, or the geographical discoveries you make.

SHACKLETON: The answer I am going to make to you is . . . that I must have the public interested – I must have the man in the street interested. The man who gave me £10,000 wanted to see it done so that a British expedition should be first across. The scientific world is very hard to get money out of at all. If I were to go for a purely scientific purpose I should expect them to give me the money.

Then in a stinging rebuke, he advised the Society to stop trying to be the 'keeper of the conscience of the geographical world'.

As for the members who attended the meeting, they found his answers less than satisfactory. Scott-Keltie, the Secretary, noted 'the impossibility of getting any clear answers out of Shackleton. He always answered two or three questions together, or one question in two or three different places.'

But at least the Society had had its say, even though in the end it all proved to be of academic interest. The coming war removed the threat of a confrontation with the Austrians. As for Shackleton, once again he went his own way.

It was not going to be easy. In a few months, he had to find two ships, 120 dogs, and enough stores and equipment to last for two years, if necessary. He also had to select the right men for both sides of the Continent.

Even though he had been through it all before, he always found this the most wearing part of any expedition. As soon as they were on their way, he would, he knew, be filled with a sense of relief. But until then, the strain would be felt by everyone, particularly his own family.

One of the ships was already to hand. Douglas Mawson had returned to Australia after his own momentous adventures in Antarctica, and was quite ready for Shackleton to take over his ship *The Aurora* for the journey to the Ross Sea. To carry his own party, Shackleton managed to purchase a new Norwegian vessel of wooden construction, called *Polaris*. He renamed her *Endurance* after his own family motto: 'By endurance we conquer.' On her decks she would be carrying a small whaler and two cutters. To these he gave the names of his three chief financial backers: James Caird, Dudley Docker and Janet Stancombe-Wills. Their names were destined to pass into Antarctic legend.

As a picker of men, Shackleton was eccentric, to say the least. But this time he made very few mistakes. Naturally he turned first to tried and trusted comrades of old. Frank Wild was invited to be second-in-command. Ernest Joyce was spotted on top of a London bus and chased down the street. Marston and Mackintosh were also invited to take their chance under his leadership for a second time.

Some of the newcomers who applied were astonished at the questions they were asked.

Years later the physicist R. W. James recalled his own experience:

> So far as I remember, he asked me if my teeth were good, if I suffered from varicose veins, if I had a good temper and if I could sing. At this question I probably looked a bit taken aback, for I remember he said 'Oh, I don't mean any Caruso stuff; but I suppose you can shout a bit with the boys?' He then asked me if my circulation was good. I said it was except for one finger, which frequently went dead in cold weather. He asked me if I would seriously mind losing it. I said I would risk that. . . . After that he put out his hand and said 'Very well, I'll take you.'

The meteorologist Dr Hussey had a similar experience:

> He called for me, looked me up and down, walked up and down when he was talking to me, didn't seem to take any notice. Finally he said 'Yes, I like you. I'll take you.' He told me afterwards he took me because he thought I looked funny!

When Dr Macklin applied for the job of one of the expedition's surgeons, he received no reply to his letter and called at the office:

> He looked me up and down, asked me one or two ques-
> tions, and just abruptly, like that, said 'All right, I'll take
> you', without any other reference or requirement of any
> kind at all . . . One question was 'Is your eye-sight alright?'
> I was wearing specs. I said it was. He asked 'Why are you
> wearing spectacles?' For want of anything better, I said
> 'Many a wise face would look foolish without spectacles,'
> and he laughed.

One would dearly love to know what criteria he had for turning people down. Out of five thousand hopeful applicants he needed less than fifty.

Among the unlucky ones were three who wrote in January 1914:

> Dear Sir Ernest,
> We 'three sporty girls' have decided to write and beg of
> you, to take us with you on your expedition to the South
> Pole.
> We are three strong healthy girls, and also gay and
> bright, and willing to undergo any hardships, that you
> yourselves undergo.
> If our feminine garb is inconvenient, we should just love
> to don masculine attire.
> We have been reading all books and articles that have
> been written on dangerous expeditions by brave men to the
> Polar regions, and we do not see why men should have all
> the glory, and women none, especially when there are
> women just as brave and capable as there are men.

One might have hoped that this would have won them at least an interview, instead of the rather curt reply that there were 'no vacancies for the opposite sex on the Expedition'.

Frank Worsley's account of how he came to join was perhaps the strangest of all. It was also to prove one of the most significant:

> One night, I dreamed that Burlington Street was full of ice
> blocks, and that I was navigating a ship along it – an absurd
> dream. Sailors are superstitious, and when I woke up next
> morning I hurried like mad into my togs, and down

Burlington Street I went. I dare say that it was only a coincidence, but as I walked along reflecting that my dream had certainly been meaningless, and uncomfortable and that it had cost me time that I could have used to better purpose, a sign on a doorpost caught the eye. It bore the words 'Imperial Trans-Antarctic Expedition', and no sooner did I see it than I turned into the building with the conviction that it had some special significance for me.

Shackleton was there. He and I spent only a few minutes together, but the moment I set eyes on him I knew that he was a man with whom I should be proud to work. He quickly divined what I wanted, and presently said to me 'You're engaged. Join your ship until I wire for you.' . . . He wrung my hand in his hard grasp, and that was that. I was committed to my fate.

In due course Worsley was put in command of *Endurance* and was later to play a vital role in navigating the *James Caird* across those terrible seas to South Georgia.

Endurance was due to sail for South America early in August 1914. The timing could have hardly been worse. On the third of the month, the Government ordered general mobilisation. The Great Powers were poised for the titanic struggle that was to grip Europe for the next four years. For Shackleton and his men it was a moment of agonising decision. They were fit, highly trained men with a strong sense of duty to their country; and here they were on the very eve of sailing away to the other side of the world. The popular press, too, were not slow in offering moral advice. But on the other hand, a great deal of money had already been spent preparing for the Expedition, and the outcome of a war was not going to be decided by twenty-eight men.

Shackleton decided that he really had no choice. He called his men together and told them that he had decided to put *Endurance* at the disposal of the Admiralty. It was a decision with which they all concurred.

Within hours, the matter was resolved. Winston Churchill, the First Sea Lord, saw very clearly that British morale and prestige would be far better served if the Expedition went ahead. Nor did he want to give the Kaiser the satisfaction of seeing it cancelled. He responded with a characteristic telegram: 'Proceed.' At last the Imperial Trans-Antarctic Expedition was under way.

In the final months before sailing, Shackleton had had little time for normal family life. Even when he did find a day or two to spend with Emily, he was often tired and irritable. The domestic side of his life was under strain. He was well aware of it but such were the pressures on him, he could do little to put it right.

Now it was too late. Another two years of separation loomed ahead; years of fulfilment for him, but likely to be lonely ones for Emily, burdened now with their three children. However, it was not too late to write. From Vigo, and later from Buenos Aires, he sent her two letters into which he poured all his feelings.

> My darling I have been having a sort of reaction since I left after the strain of all those last months and could do nothing but sleep and sit down I am better now but am not inclined to write or even read and this is why I am not writing a longer letter: I have your last letter still and have read it many times and I will answer it fully from B.A. I realize all you say and I dont want you to say or think that you have been to blame in the rows that arose: I think I am solely to be blamed: I expect I have a peculiar nature that the years have hardened and yet when . . . you were (upset) just as I was going I found myself just as miserable: I dont want to go away into the South with any misunderstanding between us: I know that if you were married to a more domesticated man you would have been much happier and I also suppose I am just obsessed with my work and all I have to do. . . . one thing stands out quite clearly that I am to blame for all those uncomfortable months: just now my nerves are all on edge and it seemed to me that I could hardly have pulled through those last two months without a breakdown: Now I am better: and will see things in a clearer and calmer light. . . .

The second letter, which he posted before setting out on the last leg of the voyage to South Georgia, was probably the most serious attempt that he ever made to analyse his own motives and feelings. As a self-portrait it may seem a trifle maudlin. But the likeness is there.

> I am just glad to have the worry over and get out to my work and my own life; it seems a hard thing to say but this I know is my Ishmaelite life and the one thing that I am suited for and in which I yield to no one; I know well that I am wanting in many ways domestically: that for some time past

we have not seen eye to eye and that the fault lies with me that is the trouble and tragedy of life that one never stands still but always moves on one way or the other. I wonder if you know me really: I am not worth much consideration if I were really known and I have shown you that or rather tried to show it to you only you think differently dont you? I hardly know how to write only I dont want you to be all the time I am away worrying about me I am not worth your doing that: I have on the way out done a lot of thinking and all to no purpose I have tried to look at things for (*sic*) your point of view as well as mine and all to no purpose: and I go round and round in a circle You have sometimes asked me to pretend and simulate feelings but I would be worse than I am if I did so; that deep down in your heart you know; and yet I am not without feelings as you know on the day I left London for this voyage I am a curious mixture with something feminine in me as well as being a man, and I had an uncomfortable weak feeling at leaving which according to the plan on which I am supposed by myself to be working out my life: should not exist; anyhow you cannot say that I am not honest and I know that you are fond of me but that at times I upset you: I have a curious nature and I have tried to analyse without much success; I have committed all sorts of crimes in thought if not always in action and dont worry much about it, yet I hate to see a child suffer, or I to be false in any way: I am just good as an explorer and nothing else, I am hard also and damnably persistent when I want anything: altogether a generally unpleasing character: I love the fight and when things easy I hate it though when things are wrong I get worried. I am not going to write more in this strain I am a bit tired tonight and just wandering along . . . now that I am on my own work I will be better and more at peace and I dont think I will ever go on a long expedition again; I will be too old. . . .'

Shackleton chose to begin his own narrative of the Expedition as the *Endurance* slipped anchor in Grytviken Harbour and headed south for the icy wilderness of the Weddell Sea.

Had he chosen to begin his extraordinary story a little earlier, there was one moment of high comedy that he would have found hard to resist. Before they left Buenos Aires, a young ship's steward from the White Star line, hearing that Shackleton was in port, had come aboard in search of adventure. His name was Percy Blackborrow. There was certainly a vacancy for a likely lad, since one or two troublemakers had been paid off. But Commander Worsley regarded him as far too young and inexperienced. He was still only nineteen.

But Blackborrow was not to be put off so easily. With *Endurance* three days out into the southern ocean, a sailor reported to Worsley that he thought he'd seen a pair of legs in the locker room. Worsley went to investigate, and the boy was duly winkled out of his hiding place, together with his pet cat.

There was no question of turning back, so the last and youngest member of the expedition was signed on. 'If anyone has to be eaten,' Shackleton told him, 'you will be the first.' Percy Blackborrow's longing for adventure was about to be satisfied.

Selections from
SOUTH
by E. H. Shackleton

INTO THE WEDDELL SEA

I had decided to leave South Georgia about December 5th, 1914, and in the intervals of final preparation I scanned again the plans for the voyage to winter quarters. What welcome was the Weddell Sea preparing for us?

Following the advice of the whaling captains at South Georgia, who generously placed their knowledge at my disposal, I had decided to steer to the South Sandwich Group, round Ultima Thule, and work as far to the eastward as the fifteenth meridian west longitude before pushing south. The whalers warned me of the difficulty of getting through the ice in the neighbourhood of the South Sandwich Group, and they thought that the Expedition would have to push through heavy pack in order to reach the Weddell Sea. Probably the best time to get into the Weddell Sea would be about the end of February. Owing to the warnings of the whalers I decided to take the deckload of coal, for if we had to fight our way through to Coats' Land we should need all the fuel we could carry.

At length the day of departure arrived. I gave the order to heave anchor at 8.45 a.m. on December 5th, and the clanking of the windlass broke for us the last link with civilisation. The morning was dull and overcast, but hearts aboard the *Endurance* were light. The long days of preparation were over and the adventure lay ahead.

The wind freshened during the day and all square sail was set, with the foresail reefed in order to give the lookout a clear view ahead, for we did not wish to risk contact with a 'growler', one of those treacherous fragments of ice that float with surface awash. During December 6th we made good progress on a south-easterly course, but December 7th brought the first check. At six o'clock on that morning the sea, which had been green in colour on the previous day, changed suddenly to a deep indigo.

Sanders Island and Candlemas were sighted early in the afternoon, and large numbers of bergs, mostly tabular in form, lay to the west of the island. The presence of so many bergs was ominous, and immediately after passing between the islands we encountered stream-ice. All sail was taken in and we proceeded slowly under steam. At 8 p.m. the *Endurance* was confronted by a belt of heavy pack-ice, half a mile broad and extending north and south. There was clear water beyond, but the pack in our neighbourhood was impenetrable. This was disconcerting. The noon latitude had been 57° 26′ S., and I had not expected to find pack-ice nearly so far north.

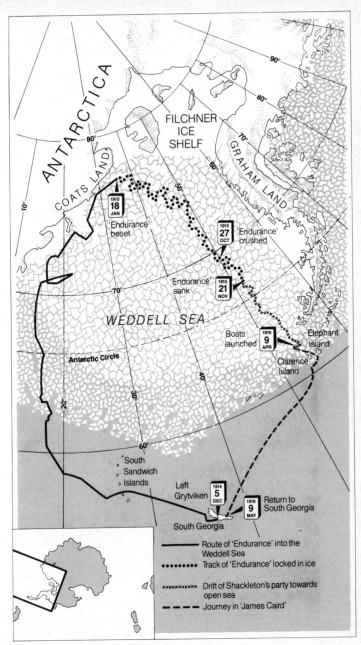

ANTARCTICA

COATS LAND

FILCHNER
ICE
SHELF

GRAHAM LAND

1915
18
JAN
'Endurance'
beset

1915
27
OCT
'Endurance'
crushed

'Endurance'
sank

1915
21
NOV

WEDDELL SEA

Boats
launched

1916
9
APR

Elephant
Island

Clarence
Island

Antarctic Circle

South
Sandwich
Islands

Left
Grytviken

1914
5
DEC

1916
9
MAY

Return to
South Georgia

South Georgia

⎯⎯⎯ Route of 'Endurance' into the
Weddell Sea

•••••••• Track of 'Endurance' locked in ice

×××××××× Drift of Shackleton's party towards
open sea

– – – Journey in 'James Caird'

During that night the situation became dangerous. We pushed into the pack in the hope of reaching open water beyond, and found ourselves in a pool which was growing smaller and smaller. Worsley and I were on deck all night, dodging the pack, but some anxious hours passed before we rounded it and were able to set sail once more.

This initial tussle with the pack had been exciting. Pieces of ice and bergs of all sizes were heaving and jostling against each other in the heavy south-westerly swell. In spite of all our care the *Endurance* struck large lumps stern on, but the engines were stopped in time and no harm was done.

Worsley, Wild and I, with three officers, kept three watches while we were working through the pack, so that we had two officers on deck all the time. The carpenter had rigged a six-foot wooden semaphore on the bridge to enable the navigating officer to give the seaman or scientists at the wheel the direction and the exact amount of helm required. This device saved time as well as the effort of shouting.

The morning of December 18th found the *Endurance* proceeding amongst large floes with thin ice between them, and shortly before noon further progress was barred by heavy pack, and we put an ice-anchor on the floe and banked the fires.

I had been prepared for evil conditions in the Weddell Sea, but had hoped that in December and January the pack would be loose, even if no open water was to be found. What we were encountering was fairly dense pack of a very obstinate character.

Pack-ice may be described as a gigantic and interminable jigsaw-puzzle devised by nature. The parts of the puzzle in loose pack have floated slightly apart and become disarranged; at numerous places they have pressed together again; as the pack gets closer the congested areas grow larger and the parts are jammed harder until it becomes 'close pack'; then the whole jigsaw-puzzle becomes so jammed that with care it can be crossed in every direction on foot. Where the parts do not fit closely there is, of course, open water, which freezes over in a few hours after giving off volumes of 'frost-smoke'. In obedience to renewed pressure this young ice 'rafts', thus forming double thicknesses of toffee-like consistency.

All through the winter the drifting pack changes – grows by freezing, thickens by rafting, and corrugates by pressure. If, finally, in its drift it impinges on a coast, such as the western shore of the Weddell Sea, terrific pressure is set up and an inferno of ice-blocks, ridges and hedgerows results, extending possibly for 150 or 200 miles off shore.

I have given this explanation so that the nature of the ice through which we had to push our way for hundreds of miles may be understood.

The conditions did not improve during December 19th, and after proceeding for two hours the *Endurance* was stopped again by heavy floes, and, owing to a heavy gale, we remained moored to a floe during the following day. The members of the staff and crew took advantage of the pause to enjoy a vigorous game of football on the level surface of the floe alongside the ship.

Monday, December 21st, was beautifully fine, and we made an early start through the pack. Petrels of several species, penguins and seals were plentiful, and we saw four small blue whales. At noon we entered a long lead to the southward and passed nine splendid bergs. One huge specimen was shaped like the Rock of Gibraltar but with steeper cliffs, and another had a natural dock which would have contained the *Aquitania*. Hurley brought out his kinematograph-camera to make a record of these bergs. We found long leads during the afternoon, but at midnight the ship was stopped by small, heavy ice-floes, tightly packed against an unbroken plain of ice. The outlook from the mast-head was not encouraging; the big floe was at least fifteen miles long and ten miles wide. I had never seen such an area of unbroken ice in the Ross Sea.

We waited with banked fires for an opportunity to proceed, and during the evening of December 22nd some lanes opened, and we were able again to move towards the south. So we struggled on until Christmas Day, when we were held up by more bad weather. However, we had a really splendid dinner, and in the evening everybody joined in a 'sing-song'.

NEW LAND

The condition of the pack improved in the evening of New Year's Day, and we progressed rapidly until a moderate gale came up from the east, with continuous snow. Early in the morning of January 2nd we got into thick old pack-ice. The position then was lat. 69° 49′ S., long. 15° 42′ W., and the run for the last twenty-four hours had been 124 miles S. 3° W., which was cheering.

This good run had made me hopeful of sighting the land on the following day, but we were delayed by heavy pack and also by the gale. I was becoming anxious to reach land on account of the dogs, with which I had been greatly pleased when we had started, but, owing to lack of exercise, they were now becoming run down.

Difficulties continued to beset us, and on the 4th we had been steaming and dodging about over an area of twenty square miles for fifty hours, trying to find an opening to the south, south-east, or south-west, but all the leads ran north, north-east, or north-west. It was as if the spirits of the Antarctic were pointing us to the backward track – the track we were determined not to follow.

Our desire was to make easting as well as southing, so that, if possible, we might reach the land east of Ross's farthest South, and well east of Coats' Land.

Solid pack, however, barred the way to the south, but on the 6th, with the ship moored to a floe, I took the opportunity to exercise the dogs. Their excitement when they got on to the floe was intense; several of them managed to get into the water, and their muzzles did not prevent them from having some hot fights. On the following day, when we were able to make some progress, killer-whales began to be active around us, and I had to exercise caution in allowing any one to leave the ship. These beasts have a habit of locating a resting seal by looking over the edge of a floe, and then striking through the ice from below in search of a meal; they would not distinguish between seal and man.

On the 8th and 9th fortune was with us, and the run southward in blue water, with a path clear ahead and the miles falling away behind us, was a joyful experience after the long struggle through the ice-lanes; but, like other good things, our spell of free movement had to end, and the *Endurance* encountered the ice again at 1 a.m. on the 10th.

At noon our position was lat. 72° 02′ S., long. 16° 07′ W., and we were now near the land discovered by Dr W. S. Bruce, leader of the *Scotia* Expedition, in 1904, and named by him Coats' Land. Dr Bruce encountered an ice-barrier in lat. 72° 18′ S., long. 10° W., and from his description of rising slopes of snow and ice, with shoaling water off the barrier-wall, the presence of land was clearly indicated. It was up those slopes, at a point as far south as possible, that I planned to begin the march across the Antarctic continent. All hands now were watching for the coast described by Dr Bruce, and at 5 p.m. the lookout reported an appearance of land to the south-south-east. It seemed to be an island or a peninsula with a sound on its south side. At the time we were passing through heavy loose pack, and shortly before midnight we broke into a lead of open sea along a barrier edge. The barrier was 70 feet high with cliffs of about 40 feet, and the *Scotia* must have passed this point when pushing to Bruce's farthest south on March 6th, 1904.

Thick and overcast weather impeded our progress on the following days, but on the 12th we were beyond the point reached by the *Scotia*, and the land underlying the ice-sheet, which we were skirting, was new. At 4 p.m. on the 13th, when we were still following the barrier to the south-west, we reached a corner and found it receding abruptly to the south-east. Our way was blocked by very heavy pack, and as we were unable to find an opening we moored the ship to a floe and banked fires.

Several young emperor penguins had been captured and brought aboard on the previous day, and two of them were still alive when the *Endurance* was brought alongside the floe. They promptly hopped on to the ice, turned round, bowed gracefully three times, and retired to the far side of the floe. There is something curiously human about the manners and movements of these birds. I was again concerned about the dogs. Some of them appeared to be ailing, and one dog had to be shot on the 12th.

We did not move the ship on the 14th, but on the following day conditions had improved, and in the evening the *Endurance* was moving southward with sails set and we continued to skirt the barrier in clear weather. I was watching for possible landing-places, though, as a matter of fact, unless compelled by necessity, I had no intention of landing north of Vahsel Bay, in Luitpold Land. Every mile gained towards the south meant a mile less sledging when the time came for the overland journey.

Shortly before midnight on the 15th we came abreast of the northern edge of a great glacier, projecting beyond the barrier into the sea. It was about 400 ft high, and at its edge was a large mass of thick bay-ice. The bay formed by the northern edge of this glacier would have made an excellent landing-place, for it was protected from the south-easterly wind and was open only to a northerly wind. I named the place Glacier Bay, and had reason later to remember it with regret.

The *Endurance* steamed along the front of this glacier for about seventeen miles, and at 4 a.m. on the 16th we reached the edge of another huge glacial overflow from the ice-sheet. We steamed along the front of this tremendous glacier for forty miles and then were held up by solid pack-ice, which appeared to be held by stranded bergs. No further advance was possible for that day, but the noon observation showed that we had gained 124 miles to the south-west during the preceding twenty-four hours. We pushed the ship against a small berg, and a blizzard from the east-north-east prevented us from leaving the shelter of the berg on the following day (Sunday, January 17th).

The land, when the air was clear, seemed to rise to 3,000 feet above the head of the glacier. Caird Coast, as I named it, connects Coats' Land, discovered by Bruce in 1904, with Luitpold Land, discovered by Filchner in 1912. We were now close to the junction with Luitpold Land.

The ship lay under the lee of the stranded berg until 7 a.m. on January 18th, by which time the gale had moderated so much that we could sail to the south-west through a lane which had opened along the glacier front, and on the morning of the 19th our position was lat. 76° 34' S., long. 31° 30' W. The weather was good, but as the ice had closed around the ship during the night, no advance could be made. A survey of the position on the 20th showed that the *Endurance* was firmly beset. As far as the eye could reach from the masthead the ice was packed heavily and firmly all round the ship in every direction.

Many uneventful days followed. Moderate breezes from the east and south-west had no apparent effect upon the ice, and the ship remained firmly held. On the 27th, the tenth day of inactivity, I decided to let the fires out. We had been burning half a ton of coal a day to keep steam in the boilers, and as the bunkers now contained only sixty-seven tons, representing thirty-three days' steaming, we could not afford this expenditure of coal.

During these days of waiting we gradually collected a stock of seal meat, which the dogs needed, and which also made a very welcome change from our rations.

Not until February 9th did I order steam to be raised in the hope of being able to proceed, but our effort failed. We could break the young ice, but the pack defied us and the ship became jammed against soft floe. As there seemed small chance of making a move, I had the motor crawler and warper put on the floe for a trial run. The motor worked most successfully, running at about six miles an hour over slabs and ridges of ice hidden by a foot or two of soft snow. The surface was worse than we should have expected to face on land or barrier-ice.

No important change in our situation took place during the second part of February. Early in the morning of the 14th I ordered a good head of steam on the engines and sent all hands on to the floe with ice-chisels, prickers, saws and picks. All that day and most of the next we worked strenuously to get the ship into the lead ahead of us. After terrific labour we got the ship a third of the way to the lead, but about 400 yards of heavy ice still separated the *Endurance* from the water, and reluctantly I was compelled to admit that further effort was useless. Every opening we made froze up again quickly owing to the unseasonably low temperature.

The abandonment of the attack was a great disappointment to all hands. The men had worked so splendidly that they had deserved success, but the task was beyond our powers. I had not yet abandoned hope of getting clear, but by this time I was beginning to count on the possibility of having to spend a winter in the inhospitable arms of the pack.

On the 22nd the *Endurance* reached the farthest south point of her drift, touching the 77th parallel of latitude in long. 35° W. The summer had gone; indeed, it had scarcely been with us at all. The temperatures were very low both day and night, and as the pack was freezing solidly around the ship, I could no longer doubt that the *Endurance* was confined for the winter.

'We must,' I wrote, 'wait for the spring, which may bring us better fortune. If I had guessed a month ago that the ice would grip us here, I would have established our base at one of the landing-places at the great glacier. But there seemed no reason to anticipate then that the fates would prove unkind. . . . My chief anxiety is the drift. Where will the vagrant winds and currents carry the ship during the long winter months that are ahead of us? We will go west, no doubt, but how far? And will it be possible to break out of the pack early in the spring and reach Vahsel Bay or some other suitable landing-place? These are momentous questions for us.'

On February 24th we ceased to observe ship routine, and the *Endurance* became a winter station. Orders were given for the after-hold to be cleared and the stores checked so that we might know exactly how we stood for a siege by an Antarctic winter. The dogs went off the ship on the following day, their kennels being placed on the floe along the length of a wire rope to which the leashes were fastened. They were obviously delighted to get off the ship, and we had already begun the training of teams. Hockey and football on the floe were our chief recreations, and all hands joined in many a strenuous game. We kept our wireless apparatus rigged, but without result. Evidently the distances were too great for our small plant.

WINTER MONTHS

March opened with a severe north-easterly gale which lasted until the 3rd. All hands were employed in clearing out the 'tween-decks, which was to be converted into a living-room and dining-room for officers and scientists. Here the carpenter erected the stove that had been intended for the shore hut, and the quarters were made very snug. The dogs seemed indifferent to the blizzard, and were content to lie most of the time curled into tight balls under the snow.

When the gale cleared we found that the pack had been driven in from the north-east and was more firmly consolidated than before. A new berg, probably fifteen miles in length, appeared on the northern horizon, and the sighting of it was of more than passing interest, since in that comparatively shallow sea it was possible for a big berg to become stranded. Then the island of ice would be a centre of tremendous pressure and disturbance amid the drifting pack. We had seen something already of the smashing effect of a contest between berg and floe, and did not wish to see the helpless *Endurance* involved in such a battle of giants.

The quarters in the 'tween-decks were completed by the 10th, and the men took possession of the cubicles which had been built. The largest cubicle contained Macklin, McIlroy, Hurley and Hussey; Clark and Wordie lived opposite in a room called 'Auld Reekie'. Next came the abode of the 'The Nuts', or engineers, followed by 'The Sailors' Rest', which was inhabited by Cheetham and McNeish.

The new quarters became known as 'The Ritz', and meals were served there instead of in the wardroom. Wild, Marston, Crean and Worsley established themselves in cubicles in the wardroom, and by the middle of the month all hands had settled down to the winter routine. I lived alone aft.

The training of the dogs in sledge teams continued. The orders used by the drivers were 'Mush' (go on), 'Gee' (right), 'Haw' (left), and 'Whoa' (stop). These are the words which Canadian drivers adopted long ago, borrowing them originally from England. The teams rapidly became efficient, but we were losing dogs owing to sickness.

During the night of the 3rd we heard the ice grinding to the eastward, and in the morning we saw that young ice was rafted 8 to 10 feet high in places. This was the first murmur of the danger which was so greatly to threaten us in later months. The ice was heard grinding and creaking during the 4th and the ship vibrated slightly. I gave orders that accumulations of snow, ice and rubbish alongside the *Endurance* should be shovelled away, so that in case of pressure there would be no weight against the topsides to check the ship rising above the ice.

The dogs had been divided into six teams of nine dogs each. Wild, Crean, Macklin, McIlroy, Marston and Hurley each had charge of a team, and were fully responsible for their own dogs. We were still losing dogs, and it was unfortunate that we had not the proper remedies for the disease from which they were suffering. By the end of April our mature dogs had decreased to fifty.

On the 14th a new berg, which was destined to give us cause for anxiety, appeared. It was a big berg, and during the day it increased its apparent altitude and slightly changed its bearing. Evidently it was aground and was holding its position against the drifting pack. During the next twenty-four hours the *Endurance* moved steadily towards the berg. We could see from the mast-head that the pack was piling and rafting against the mass of ice, and it was easy to imagine the fate of the ship if she entered the area of disturbance. She would be crushed like an egg-shell amid the shattering masses.

The drift of the pack was not constant, and during the succeeding days the berg, which was about three-quarters of a mile long on the side presented to us and probably considerably more than 200 feet high, alternately advanced and receded as the *Endurance* moved with the floe. On Sunday, April 18th, it was only seven miles distant from the ship, but a strong drift to the westward during the night of the 18th relieved our anxiety by carrying the *Endurance* to the lee of the berg, and before the end of the month it was no longer in sight.

We said good-bye to the sun on May 1st and entered the period of twilight, which would be followed by the darkness of midwinter. I wrote: 'One feels our helplessness as the long winter night closes upon us. By this time, if fortune had smiled upon the Expedition, we would have been comfortably and securely established in a shore base, with depots laid to the south, and plans made for the long march in the spring and summer. Where will we make a landing now? . . . Time alone will tell. I do not think any member of the Expedition is disheartened by our disappointment. All hands are cheery and busy, and will do their best when the time for acting comes. In the meantime we must wait.'

In those days the care of dog-teams was our heaviest responsibility, and a faint twilight round about noon of each day assisted us in the important work of exercising them. Whatever fate might be in store for us the conditioning and training of the dogs seemed essential, and whenever the weather permitted the teams were taken out by their drivers. Rivalries naturally arose, and on the 15th a great race, the 'Antarctic Derby', was run. Considerable betting took place, but the most thrilling wagers were those which concerned stores of chocolate and cigarettes.

A course of about 700 yards had been laid out, and five teams went to the starting point in the dim noon twilight, with a zero temperature and an aurora flickering faintly to the southward. Wild's time for the course was 2 minutes 16 seconds, and in a subsequent race against Hurley's team Wild's dogs completed the course in 2 minutes 9 seconds, although their load was 910 lb., or 130 lb. per dog.

On the evening of the 13th the most severe blizzard we had experienced in the Weddell Sea swept down upon us, and early in the following morning the kennels to the southern side of the ship were buried under 5 feet of drift. The ship was invisible at a distance of 50 yards, and I gave orders that nobody should go beyond the kennels, for it was impossible to preserve a sense of direction in the raging wind and suffocating drift. The temperature during the blizzard ranged from −21° to −33.5° Fahr., and by evening the gale had attained a force of sixty or seventy miles an hour, and the ship was trembling under the attack. We, however, were snug enough in our quarters aboard until the morning of the 14th, when all hands turned out to shovel the snow from deck and kennels. The temperature was then about −30° Fahr., and it was necessary to be on guard against frost-bite.

The weather did not clear until the 16th, and then we saw that the appearance of the surrounding pack had been altered completely by the blizzard. The 'island' floe containing the *Endurance* still stood fast, but cracks and masses of ice thrown up by pressure could be seen in all directions.

The ice-pressure, which was indicated by distant rumblings and by the appearance of formidable ridges, was now causing us more anxiety. The areas of disturbance were gradually approaching the ship. Early on the afternoon of the 22nd a 2-foot crack, running south-west and north-east for a distance of about two miles, approached to within 35 yards of the port quarter. I had all the sledges brought aboard and set a special watch in case it became necessary hurriedly to get the dogs off the floe.

In the morning we saw that our island had been reduced considerably during the night. Our long months of rest and safety seemed to have ended, and a period of stress to have begun. During the following day I had a store of sledging provisions, oil, matches, and other essentials, placed on the upper deck handy to the starboard quarter boat, so that we should be ready for a sudden emergency.

At this time I wrote: 'The ice for miles around is much looser. There are numerous cracks and short leads to the north-east and south-east. Ridges are being forced up in all directions. . . . It would be a relief to be able to make some effort on our own behalf; but we can do nothing until the ice releases our ship. If the floes continue to loosen, we may break out within the next few weeks and resume the fight. In the meantime the pressure continues, and it is hard to foresee the outcome. . . . All hands are cheered by the indication that the end of the winter darkness is near'.

The break-up of our floe came suddenly on Sunday, August 1st, just one year after the *Endurance* left the South-West India Docks on the voyage to the Far South. The position was lat. $72°$ $26'$ S., long. $48°$ $10'$ W. The morning brought a moderate south-westerly gale with heavy snow, and presently, after some warning movements of the ice, the floe began to break up all round us under pressure, and the ship listed over 10 degrees to starboard.

I had the dogs and sledges brought aboard at once and the gangway hoisted. The dogs seemed to realise their danger and behaved most peacefully. The pressure was rapidly cracking the floe, rafting it close to the ship and forcing masses of ice beneath the keel. The *Endurance* listed heavily to port against the gale, and, at the same time, was forced ahead, astern and sideways several times by the grinding floes. She received one or two hard nips, but resisted them without as much as a creak.

At one stage it looked as if the ship was to be made the plaything of successive floes, and I was relieved when she came to a standstill with a large piece of our old 'dock' under the starboard bilge. I had the boats cleared away ready for lowering, got up some additional stores, and set a double watch. Around us lay the ruins of 'Dog Town'; it was a sad sight, but my chief concern just then was about the safety of the rudder, which was being attacked viciously by the ice. I could see that some damage had been done, but it was at the time impossible to make a close examination.

After the ship had come to a standstill in her new position very heavy pressure was set up, but the *Endurance* had been built to withstand the attacks of the ice, and she lifted bravely as the floes drove beneath her. The effects of the pressure around us were awe-inspiring. Mighty blocks of ice, gripped between meeting floes, rose slowly until they jumped like cherry-stones squeezed between thumb and finger. The pressure of millions of tons of moving ice was crushing and smashing inexorably. If the ship was once gripped firmly her fate would be sealed.

By the afternoon of the 2nd the gale had moderated and the pressure had almost ceased. The gale had given us some northing, but it had also severely damaged the rudder of the *Endurance*.

Heavy masses of ice were still jammed against the stern, and it was consequently impossible to ascertain the extent of the damage.

I calculated that we were 250 miles from the nearest known land to the westward, and more than 500 miles from the nearest outpost of civilisation, Wilhelmina Bay. I hoped fervently that we should not have to undertake a march across the moving ice-fields. We knew the *Endurance* to be stout and true, but these were anxious days because no ship ever built by man could live, if taken fairly in the grip of the floes and prevented from rising to the surface of the grinding ice.

LOSS OF THE *ENDURANCE*

By the middle of September we were running short of fresh meat for the dogs. Nearly five months had passed since we had killed a seal, and penguins had seldom been seen. But on the 23rd we got an emperor penguin, and on the following day we secured a crab-eater seal. The return to seal-life was most opportune, as we wished to feed the dogs on meat, and seals also meant a supply of blubber to supplement our small remaining stock of coal.

During the last days of September the roar of the pressure grew louder, and I could see that the area of disturbance was rapidly approaching the ship. Stupendous forces were at work, and the fields of firm ice around the *Endurance* were steadily diminishing.

September 30th was a bad day, for at 3 p.m. cracks, which had opened during the night alongside the ship, began to work in a lateral direction. The ship sustained terrific pressure. The decks shuddered and jumped, beams arched, and stanchions buckled and shook. I ordered all hands to stand by in readiness for any emergency. But the ship resisted valiantly, and just when it seemed that the limit of her strength was being reached, one huge floe which was pressing down upon us cracked across and so gave relief.

'The behaviour of our ship in the ice,' Worsley wrote, 'has been magnificent. Since we have been beset her staunchness and endurance have been almost past belief again and again. . . . It will be sad if such a brave little craft should be finally crushed in the remorseless, slowly strangling grip of the Weddell pack, after ten months of the bravest and most gallant fight ever put up by a ship.'

The vital question for us was whether the ice would open sufficiently to release us before the drift carried us into the dangerous area which we were approaching? With anxious hearts we faced the month of October.

Two or three days later we had no doubt that the movement of the ice was increasing. Frost-smoke from opening cracks was showing in all directions during October 6. In one place it looked like a great prairie fire, at another it resembled a train running before the wind, the smoke rising from the engine straight upward; elsewhere the smoke columns gave the effect of warships steaming in line ahead.

The next attack of the ice came during the afternoon of October 19th. The two floes began to move laterally and exerted great pressure on the ship. Suddenly the floe on the port side cracked and huge pieces of ice shot up from under the port bilge. Within a few seconds the ship heeled over until she had a list of 30 degrees to port, being held under the starboard bilge by the opposing floe. Everything movable on deck and below fell to the lee side, and for a few minutes it looked as if the ship would be thrown upon her beam ends. The midship dog-kennels broke away and crashed down on the lee kennels, and the howls and barks of the frightened dogs helped to create a perfect pandemonium. Order, however, was soon restored.

If the ship had heeled any farther it would have been necessary to release the lee boats and pull them clear, and Worsley was watching to give the alarm. Dinner in the wardroom that evening was a curious affair, for most of the diners had to sit on the deck, their feet against battens and their plates on their knees. At 8 p.m. the floes opened, and within a few minutes the *Endurance* was again nearly upright. On Sunday, October 24th, the beginning of the end of the *Endurance* came. The position was lat. 69° 11′ S., long. 51° 5′ W.

We now had twenty-two and a half hours of daylight, and throughout the day we watched the threatening advance of the floes. At 6.45 p.m. the ship sustained heavy pressure in a dangerous position. The onslaught was almost irresistible. The ship groaned and quivered as her starboard quarter was forced against the floe, twisting the stern-post and starting the heads and ends of planking. The ice had lateral as well as forward movement, and the ship was twisted and actually bent by the stresses. She began to leak dangerously at once.

I had the pumps rigged, got up steam, and started the bilge pumps by 8 p.m. By that time the pressure had relaxed. The ship was making water rapidly aft, and all hands worked, watch and watch, during the night, pumping ship and helping the carpenter. By morning the leak was being kept in check.

On Monday, October 25th, the leak was kept under fairly easily, but the outlook was bad. Heavy pressure-ridges were forming in all directions, and I realised that our respite from pressure could not be prolonged. The pressure-ridges, massive and menacing, testified to the overwhelming nature of the forces at work. Huge blocks of ice, weighing many tons, were lifted into the air and tossed aside as other masses rose beneath them.

I scarcely dared to hope any longer that the *Endurance* would live, and during that anxious day I reviewed all my plans for the sledging journey which we should have to make if we had to take to the ice. As far as forethought could make us we were ready for any contingency. Stores, dogs, sledges and equipment were ready to be moved from the ship at a moment's notice.

The following day was bright and clear, and the sunshine was inspiring. But the roar of pressure continued, new ridges were rising, and as the day wore on I could see the lines of major disturbance were drawing nearer to the ship. The day passed slowly. At 7 p.m. very heavy pressure developed, with twisting strains which racked the ship fore and aft. The butts of planking were opened 4 or 5 inches on the starboard side, and at the same time we could see the ship bending like a bow under titanic pressure. Almost like a living creature she resisted the forces which would crush her; but it was a one-sided battle. Millions of tons of ice pressed inexorably upon the gallant little ship which had dared the challenge of the Antarctic. She was now leaking badly, and at 9 p.m. I gave the order to lower boats, gear, provisions and sledges to the floe, and move them to the flat ice a little way from the ship.

Then came a fateful day – Wednesday, October 27th.

'After long months of ceaseless anxiety and strain,' I wrote, 'after times when hope beat high and times when the outlook was black indeed, the end of the *Endurance* has come. But though we have been compelled to abandon the ship, which is crushed beyond all hope of ever being righted, we are alive and well, and we have stores and equipment for the task that lies before us. The task is to reach land with all the members of the Expedition. It is hard to write what I feel. To a sailor his ship is more than a floating home, and in the *Endurance* I had centred ambitions, hopes and desires. And now she is slowly giving up her sentient life at the very outset of her career. . . . The distance from the point where she became beset to the place where she now rests mortally hurt in the grip of the floes is 573 miles, but the total drift through all observed positions had been 1,186 miles, and we probably covered more than 1,500 miles.

'We are now 346 miles from Paulet Island, the nearest point

where there is any possibility of finding food and shelter. A small hut built there by the Swedish Expedition in 1902 is filled with stores left by the Argentine relief ship. . . . The distance to the nearest barrier west of us is about 180 miles, but a party going there would still be about 360 miles from Paulet Island, and there would be no means of sustaining life on the barrier. We could not take food enough from here for the whole journey; the weight would be too great. . . .

'The attack of the ice reached its climax at 4 p.m. The ship was hove stern up by the pressure, and the driving floe, moving laterally across the stern, split the rudder and tore out the rudder-post and stern-post. Then, while we watched, the ice loosened and the *Endurance* sank a little. The decks were breaking upwards and the water was pouring in below. Again the pressure began, and at 5 p.m. I ordered all hands on to the ice.

'At last the twisting, grinding floes were working their will on the ship. It was a sickening sensation to feel the decks breaking up under one's feet, the great beams bending and then snapping with a noise like heavy gun-fire. The water was overmastering the pumps, and to avoid an explosion when it reached the boilers I ordered the fires to be drawn and the steam let down. The plans for abandoning the ship in case of emergency had been well made, and men and dogs made their way to an unbroken portion of the floe without a hitch.

'Just before leaving I looked down the engine-room skylight as I stood on the quivering deck, and saw the engines dropping sideways as the stays and bed-plates gave way. I cannot describe the impression of relentless destruction which was forced upon me as I looked down and around. The floes, with the force of millions of tons of moving ice behind them, were simply annihilating the ship.'

Essential supplies had been placed on the floe about 100 yards from the ship, but after we had begun to pitch our camp there the ice started to split and smash beneath our feet. Then I had the camp moved to a bigger floe, and boats, stores and camp equipment had to be conveyed across a working pressure-ridge.

After the tents had been pitched I mustered all hands and explained the position as briefly and clearly as I could. I told them the distance to the Barrier and the distance to Paulet Island, and stated that I proposed to try to march with equipment across the ice in the direction of Paulet Island. I thanked the men for the steadiness they had shown under trying circumstances, and told them I did not doubt that we should all eventually reach safety provided that they continued to work their utmost and to trust me. Then we had supper, and all hands except the watch turned in.

But, for myself, I could not sleep, and the thoughts which came to me as I walked up and down in the darkness were not particularly cheerful. At midnight I was pacing the ice, listening to the grinding floe and the groans and crashes that told of the death-agony of the *Endurance*, when I noticed suddenly a crack running across our floe right through the camp. The alarm-whistle brought all hands tumbling out, and we moved everything from what was now the small portion of the floe to the larger portion. Nothing more could be done then, and the men turned in again; but there was little sleep.

Morning came in chill and cheerless, and all hands were stiff and weary after their first disturbed night on the floe. Just at daybreak I went over to the *Endurance* with Wild and Hurley to retrieve some tins of petrol, which could be used to boil up milk for the rest of the men.

Only six of the cabins had not been pierced by floes and blocks of ice. All the starboard cabins had been crushed, and the whole of the aft part of the ship had been crushed concertina fashion. The forecastle and 'The Ritz' were submerged, and the wardroom was three-quarters full of ice. The motor-engine forward had been driven through the galley. In short, scenes of devastation met me on every side. The ship was being crushed remorselessly.

Meanwhile Hurley had rigged his kinematograph camera, and was getting pictures of the *Endurance* in her death-throes. While he was thus engaged, the foretop and top-gallant mast came down with a run and hung in wreckage on the fore-mast, with the foreyard vertical. The mainmast followed immediately, snapping off about 10 feet above the main deck. The crow's-nest fell within 10 feet of where Hurley was turning the handle of his camera, but he did not stop the machine and so secured a unique, though sad, picture.

A quiet night followed, for, although the pressure was grinding around us, our floe was heavy enough to withstand the blows it received. 'We are,' I wrote on October 29th, 'twenty-eight men with forty-nine dogs. We have ten working sledges to relay with five teams. Wild's and Hurley's teams will haul the cutter with the assistance of four men. The whaler and the other boats will follow, and the men who are hauling them will be able to help with the cutter at the rough places. We cannot hope to make rapid progress, but each mile counts. Crean this afternoon has a bad attack of snow-blindness.'

At 3 p.m. on October 30th were got under way, leaving Dump Camp a mass of *débris*. The order was that personal gear must not exceed 2 lbs. per man, and this meant that nothing but bare necessaries could be taken on the march. I rather grudged the 2 lbs. allowance, being very anxious to keep weights at a minimum, but some personal belongings could fairly be regarded as indispensable.

Under such conditions a man needs something to occupy his thoughts, some tangible memento of his home and people beyond the seas. So sovereigns were thrown away and photographs kept.

I tore the fly-leaf out of the Bible which Queen Alexandra had given to the ship, with her own writing on it, and also the wonderful page of Job containing the verse:

Out of whose womb came the ice?
And the hoary frost of Heaven, who hath gendered it?
The waters are hid as with a stone,
And the face of the deep is frozen.

The other Bible, which Queen Alexandra had given for the use of the shore party, perished when the ship received her death-blow.

The pioneer sledge party, consisting of Wordie, Hussey, Hudson and myself, carrying picks and shovels, started to break a road through the pressure-ridges for the sledges carrying the boats. The boats, with their gear and the sledges beneath them, each weighed more than a ton. The sledges were the point of weakness. It seemed impossible to prevent them from smashing under their heavy loads when travelling over rough pressure-ice which stretched ahead of us probably for 300 miles.

OCEAN CAMP

In spite of the wet, deep snow, and the halts caused by having to cut a road through the pressure-ridges, we managed to march nearly a mile, but with relays and deviations the actual distance travelled was nearer six miles. As I could see that the men were exhausted I gave orders to pitch the tents under the lee of the two boats, which afforded some protection from the wet snow.

Next day broke cold and still, with the same wet snow, and I decided to find a more solid floe and camp there until conditions were more favourable for a second attempt to escape from our icy prison. To this end we moved our tents and all our gear to a thick, heavy floe about a mile and a half from the wreck, and camped there. This we named 'Ocean Camp'.

This floating lump of ice, about a mile square at first, but later splitting into smaller and smaller fragments, was to be our home for nearly two months. With a view to preserving our valuable sledging rations for the inevitable boat journey, I decided that we should live almost entirely on seals and penguins. During these two months we made frequent visits to the vicinity of the ship and retrieved much valuable clothing and food.

An attempt was next made to protect the cook against the inclemencies of the weather, and a party under Wild returned from a visit to the ship with the wheel-house practically complete. This, with the addition of some sails and tarpaulins stretched on spars, made a very comfortable storehouse and galley. Food, of course, was so important that I made a strict inventory of all that we possessed.

Although I had to keep in my mind the necessity for strict economy with our small store of food, I knew how important it was to keep the men cheerful, and that the depression occasioned by our surroundings and precarious position could be somewhat alleviated by increasing the rations, at least until we grew accustomed to our new mode of life. I know from the men's diaries that my efforts in this respect were successful. 'It is just,' one man wrote, 'like school days over again, and very jolly it is too, for the time being!'

In addition to our daily hunt for food, our time was passed in reading the few books we had managed to save from the ship. Our greatest treasure was a portion of the *Encyclopaedia Britannica*, which was continually used to settle our many arguments. The sailors on one occasion were heatedly discussing the subject of 'Money and Exchange', and when they discovered that the *Encyclopaedia* did not agree with their views they came to the conclusion that it must be wrong!

The two subjects of most interest to us were our rate of drift and the weather. Worsley's observations showed conclusively that the drift of our floe was almost entirely dependent upon the winds and was not much affected by the currents. Our hope, of course, was to drift northwards to the edge of the pack, and then, when the ice was loose enough, to take to the boats and row to the nearest land. We started off in fine style, drifting north about twenty-two miles in two or three days, but our average rate of progress was slow, and many and varied were the calculations as to when we should reach the pack-edge. On December 12th, 1915, one man wrote: 'We are now only 250 miles from Paulet Island, but too much to the east of it. We are approaching the latitudes in which we were at this time last year, on our way down. The ship left South Georgia just a year and a week ago, and reached this latitude four or five miles to the eastward of our present position on January 3rd, 1915.'

Thus, after a year's incessant battle with the ice, we had returned to almost identically the same latitude which we had left with such high hopes a year before. But under what conditions now! Our ship crushed and lost, and we drifting on a piece of ice at the mercy of the winds.

The loss of our ship meant more to us than we could ever put into words. After we had settled at Ocean Camp she still remained, nipped by the ice, only her stern showing and her bows overridden and broken by the relentless pack. The tangled mass of ropes, rigging and spars made the scene even more desolate and depressing.

It was almost a relief when the end came. On November 21st, 1915, one of the Expedition wrote in his diary: 'This evening, as we were lying in our tents, we heard the Boss call out: "She's going, boys!" . . . And, sure enough, there was our poor ship a mile and a half away, struggling in her death agony. She went down bows first, her stern raised in the air. She then gave one quick dive and the ice closed over her for ever. . . . Without her our destitution seemed more emphasised, our desolation more complete. The loss of the ship sent a slight wave of depression over the camp. . . . I doubt if there was one amongst us who did not feel some personal emotion when Sir Ernest, standing on the top of the look-out, said somewhat sadly and quietly: "She's gone, boys." It must, however, be said that we did not give way to depression for long.'

The continuance of southerly winds exceeded our best hopes, and by the middle of December I concluded that the ice around us was rotting and breaking up, and that the moment of deliverance was approaching.

After discussing the question with Wild, I, on December 20th, informed all hands that I meant to try and make a march to the west, so that we could reduce the distance between us and Paulet Island. A buzz of pleasurable anticipation went round the camp, and every one was anxious to get on the move.

I decided to keep December 22nd as Christmas Day, and then we consumed most of our small remaining stock of luxuries. For the last time for eight months we really had as much as we could eat. Anchovies in oil, baked beans, and jugged hare made a glorious mixture, such as we had not dreamed of since our school days. Everybody was working at high pressure, packing and repacking sledges and so forth; and as I looked round at the eager faces of the men I could not but hope that this time the fates would be kinder to us than they had been in our last attempt to march across the ice to safety.

THE MARCH BETWEEN

At 3 a.m. on December 23rd all hands were roused for the purpose of sledging the two boats, the *James Caird* and the *Dudley Docker*, over the dangerously cracked portion to the first of the young floes while the surface still held its night crust. Hot coffee was served, and we started off at half-past four.

Practically all hands had to be harnessed to each boat in succession, and after much labour and care, we got both boats over the danger-zone. We then returned to Ocean Camp for the tents and the rest of the sledges, and pitched camp by the boats, about one and quarter miles off. Everybody turned in at 2 p.m., for I intended to sleep by day and march by night, in order to take advantage of the slightly lower temperatures and consequent harder surfaces.

On December 25th, the third day of our march, we wished one another a 'Merry Christmas', and as we sat down to our 'lunch' of stale, thin bannock and a mug of thin cocoa, we also wondered what they were having at home.

Had it not been for these cumbrous boats we should have got along at a great rate, but on no account did we dare to abandon them. As it was we had left one boat, the *Stancomb Wills*, behind at Ocean Camp, and the remaining two would barely accommodate the whole party when we could leave the floe.

Still, however, we struggled on with fair success until the early morning of the 28th, when the surface was very soft and our progress, consequently, was slow and tiring. We camped at 5.30 a.m., and I climbed a small tilted berg and saw that the country immediately ahead of us was much broken up. Great open leads intersected the floes at all angles, and the outlook was most unpromising. The ice all around was too broken and soft to sledge over, and yet there was not enough open water to allow us to launch the boats with any degree of safety.

We had been on the march for seven days; rations were short and the men were weak. They were worn out with the hard pulling over soft surfaces, and our stock of sledging food was very small.

We had marched seven and a half miles in a direct line, and at this rate it would have taken us over 300 days to reach the land away to the west. As we only had food for forty-two days there was no alternative but to camp once more on the floe and to possess our souls in patience until conditions appeared more favourable for a renewal of the attempt to escape.

Our new home, which we were to occupy for nearly three and a half months, we called 'Patience Camp'.

PATIENCE CAMP

The ice between us and Ocean Camp was very broken, but I decided to send Macklin and Hurley back with their dogs to see if there was any more food which could be added to our scanty stock. I gave them written instructions to take no undue risk or cross any wide-open leads, and, although they both fell more than once through the thin ice up to their waists, they managed to reach the camp. It looked, they said, 'like a village that had been razed to the ground and deserted by its inhabitants'. They collected what food they could find and brought it back to the camp, and as their report seemed to show that the road was favourable, on February 2nd I sent back eighteen men under Wild to bring all the remainder of the food and the third boat, the *Stancomb Wills*. We were never again able to reach the abandoned camp, but there was very little there which would have been useful to us.

By the middle of February the blubber question was a serious one. Our meat supply was very low indeed. Fortunately, however, we caught two seals and four emperor penguins, and next day we captured forty adelies.

Our meals were now practically all seal meat, with the biscuit at midday; and I calculated that at this rate, allowing for a certain number of penguins and seals being caught, we could last for nearly six months. But we were all very weak, and as soon as it seemed likely that we should leave our floe and take to the boats I should have considerably to increase the ration.

One day a huge sea-leopard climbed on to the floe and attacked one of the men, and Wild, hearing the shouting, ran out and shot it. When it was cut up we found several undigested fish in its stomach. These we fried in some of its blubber, and so had our only 'fresh' fish meal during the whole of our drift on the ice.

On April 2nd the last two teams of dogs had to be shot, and the carcasses were dressed for food. We ate some of the cooked dog-meat, and it was not at all bad – just like beef, but, of course, very tough.

On January 18th we had a howling south-westerly gale, which increased next day to a regular blizzard with much drift. This lasted for six days, and then the drift subsided somewhat, although the southerly wind continued, and we were able to get a glimpse of the sun. This showed us to have drifted eighty-four miles north in six days, the longest drift we had made. By this amazing leap we had crossed the Antarctic Circle, and were now 146 miles from the nearest land to the west of us – Snow Hill – and 357 miles from the South Orkneys, the first land directly to the north of us.

On the 20th we experienced the worst blizzard we had met up to this time, though still worse were to come after we had landed on Elephant Island. For two or three days it was impossible to do anything but get inside one's frozen sleeping-bag and try to get warm.

By February 22nd we were still eighty miles from Paulet Island, which was now our objective. There was a hut there and some stores which had been taken there by the ship which went to the rescue of Nordenskjöld's Expedition in 1904, and whose fitting out and equipment I had been in charge of. We remarked how strange it would be if these very cases of provisions, which I had ordered and sent out so many years previously, were now to support us during the coming winter.

But this was not to be. By March 17th we were exactly on a level with Paulet Island, but sixty miles to the east. It might have been 600 miles for all the chance we had of reaching it by sledging across the broken ice in the condition in which it was at that time.

For the next few days we saw ourselves slowly drifting past the land which we could not reach, and towards the end of March we saw Mount Haddington fade away into the distance.

Our hopes were now centred on Elephant Island or Clarence Island, which lay 100 miles almost due north of us. If we failed to reach either of them we could try for South Georgia, but our chances of reaching it were very small.

EFFORTS TO ESCAPE FROM THE ICE

At daylight on April 7th the long-desired peak of Clarence Island came into view, but not until Worsley, Wild and Hurley had unanimously confirmed my observation was I satisfied that I was really looking at land. The island was still more than sixty miles away, but to our eyes it had something of the appearance of home. The longing to feel solid earth under our feet filled our hearts.

I wrote on this day: 'The swell is more marked today, and I feel sure we are at the verge of the floe-ice. One strong gale followed by a calm would scatter the pack, I think, and then we could push through. I have been thinking much of our prospects. . . . The island is the last outpost of the south and our final chance of a landing-place. Beyond it lies the broad Atlantic. Our little boats may be compelled any day now to sail unsheltered over the open sea, with a thousand leagues of ocean separating them from the land to the north and east. It seems vital that we should land on Clarence Island or its neighbour, Elephant Island.'

There were twenty-eight men on our floating cake of ice, which was steadily dwindling under the influence of wind, weather, charging floes and heavy swell. I confess that the burden of responsibility sat heavily on my shoulders, but, on the other hand, I was stimulated and cheered by the loyal attitude of the men.

At 6.30 p.m. a particularly heavy shock went through our floe. The watchman and other members of the party made an immediate inspection, and found a crack right under the *James Caird* and between the two other boats and the main camp. Within five minutes the boats were over the crack and close to the tents. We were now on a triangular raft of ice, the three sides measuring, roughly, 90, 100, and 120 yards. I felt that the time for launching the boats was approaching; indeed, it was obvious that, even if the conditions were unfavourable for a start during the coming day, we could not stay safely on the floe much longer, for the floe might split right under our camp.

The following day was Sunday, but it was no day of rest for us. In fact it saw both our forced departure from the floe on which we had lived for nearly six months and also the start of our journeyings in the boats.

'This,' I wrote, 'has been an eventful day for us. . . . At 7 a.m. the long swell from the north-west was coming in more freely than on the previous day and was driving the floes together in the utmost confusion. . . . Our own floe was suffering in the general disturbance, and after breakfast I ordered the tents to be struck and everything prepared for an immediate start when the boats could be launched.'

I had decided to take the *James Caird* myself, with Wild and eleven men. This was the largest of our boats, and she carried the major portion of our stores. Worsley had charge of the *Dudley*

Docker with nine men, and Hudson and Crean were the senior men in the *Stancomb Wills*.

Soon after breakfast the ice closed again, and we were standing by, with our preparations as complete as we could make them, when at 11 a.m. our floe suddenly split right across under the boats. We rushed our gear on to the larger of the two pieces, and watched anxiously for the next development. The crack had cut right through the site of my tent. Our home was being shattered under out feet, and we had a sense of loss and incompleteness hard to describe, for during all those months on the floe we had almost ceased to realise that it was but a sheet of ice floating on un-fathomed seas.

The call to action came at 1 p.m., after we had all eaten a good meal of seal meat. We could not take all our meat with us, so we regarded each pound eaten as a pound saved! The *Dudley Docker* and the *Stancomb Wills* were quickly launched. Stores were thrown in, and the two boats were pulled clear of the immediate floes towards a pool of open water three miles broad, in which floated a lone and mighty berg.

The *James Caird* was the last boat to leave, heavily loaded with stores and odds and ends of camp equipment. Many things regarded by us as essentials at that time were to be discarded later on. Man can sustain life with very scanty means, and the trappings of civilisation are soon cast aside in the face of stern realities.

For an hour we pulled hard to windward of the berg which lay in the open water. The swell was crashing on its perpendicular sides and throwing spray to a height of 60 feet. Under other conditions we might have paused to have admired the spectacle; but night was coming on fast, and we needed a camping-place. So we hastened forward in the twilight in search of a flat, old floe, and presently found a fairly large piece rocking in the swell. It was not by any means an ideal camping-place, but darkness had overtaken us. We hauled the boats up, and by 8 p.m. the tents were pitched and the blubber-stove was burning cheerily. Soon all hands were well fed and happy in their tents, and snatches of song came to me as I wrote up my log.

An intangible feeling of uneasiness made me leave my tent about 11 p.m. to glance round the quiet camp, and I had started to walk across the floe to warn the watchman to look carefully for cracks when the floe lifted on the crest of a swell and cracked under my feet as I was passing the men's tent.

The men were in one of the dome-shaped tents, and it began to stretch apart as the ice opened. A muffled sound, suggestive of suffocation, came from the stretching tent. I rushed forward, helped some men to come out from under the canvas, and called out, 'Are you all right?' 'There are two in the water,' someone answered.

The crack had widened to about 4 feet, and as I threw myself down at the edge I saw a whitish object floating in the water. It was a sleeping-bag with a man inside. I was able to grasp it, and, with a heave, lifted man and bag on to the floe. A few seconds later the ice-edges came together again with tremendous force. Fortunately, there had been but one man in the water, the rescued bag containing Holness, who was wet but otherwise unscathed.

Almost immediately the crack began again to open. The *James Caird* and my tent were on one side of the opening and the remaining two boats and the rest of the camp were on the other side. With help I struck my tent, and then all hands manned the painter and rushed the *James Caird* across the opening crack. We held on to the rope while, one by one, the men left on our side jumped the channel or scrambled over by means of the boat.

Finally I was left alone. The night had swallowed all the others, and the rapid movement of the ice forced me to let go the painter. For a moment I felt that my piece of rocking floe was the loneliest place in the world. But Wild's quick brain had immediately grasped the situation, and the boat was already being manned and hauled to the ice-edge. Two or three minutes later she reached me, and I was ferried across to the camp.

The first glimmerings of dawn came at 6 a.m., and two hours later the pack opened and we launched our boats. Immediately our boats began to make heavy weather. They shipped sprays which froze as they fell and covered men and gear with ice.

It was soon clear that we could not proceed safely, so I put the *James Caird* round and ran for the shelter of the pack again, the other boats following. By 3 p.m. we were back inside the outer line of ice where the sea was not breaking, but all hands were cold and tired. A big floeberg resting peacefully caught my eye, and half an hour later we had hauled up the boats and pitched camp for the night.

The hours dragged on. One of the anxieties in my mind was the chance that the current would drive us through the eighty-mile gap between Clarence Island and Prince George Island into the open Atlantic; but slowly the open water came nearer, and at noon it had almost reached us. A long lane, narrow but navigable, stretched out to the south-west horizon.

Our chance came a little later, and we rushed our boats over the edge of the reeling berg and swung them clear of the ice-foot as it rose beneath them. We flung stores and gear aboard and within a few minutes were away.

Constant rain and snow squalls blotted out the stars and soaked us through, and at times it was only by shouting to each other that we could keep the boats together. Nobody, owing to the severe cold, had any sleep, and since we could only see a few yards ahead we did not dare to pull fast enough to keep ourselves warm.

As noon approached I saw Worsley ready to take his observation, and after he had got it we waited eagerly for him to work out the sight. The result was a grievous disappointment. Instead of making a good run to the westward we had made a big drift to the south-east. After a whispered consultation with Worsley and Wild I announced that we had not made as much progress as we had hoped for, but I did not think it wise to inform the hands that we were actually thirty miles to the east of the position which we had occupied when leaving the floe on the 9th.

ESCAPE FROM THE ICE

The dawn of April 13th came clear and bright, but most of the men were now looking seriously worn and strained. Their lips were cracked, and the beards of even the younger men might have been those of patriarchs, for the frost and salt spray had made them white. Obviously it was imperative for us to land quickly, and I decided to run for Elephant Island.

At 6 a.m. we made a distribution of stores among the three boats, in view of the possibility that they might be separated. Hot breakfast was out of the question, but I gave orders that all hands might eat as much as they pleased, this concession being partly due to the fact that we should have to jettison some of our stores when we reached the open sea, and partly to the hope that a liberal meal would compensate to some extent for the lack of warm food and shelter. Unfortunately some of the men could not take advantage of the extra food owing to sea sickness, and it was hard indeed that this devastating sickness should have been added to the sufferings which they already had to bear.

We ran before the wind through the loose pack, a man in the bow of each boat trying to pole off with a broken oar the lumps of ice which could not be avoided. I regarded speed as essential. The *James Caird* was in the lead and bore the brunt of the encounters with the lurking fragments, then came the *Dudley Docker*, and the

Stancomb Wills followed. I gave orders that the boats should keep thirty to forty yards apart, so that the danger of a collision, if one boat was checked by the ice, should be reduced.

We made our way through the lanes until at noon we suddenly shot out of the pack into the open ocean. Sails were soon up, and, with the sun shining brightly, we enjoyed for a few hours a sense of the freedom and magic of the sea. At last we were free from the ice, in water which our ships could navigate; thoughts of home came to birth once more, and the difficulties ahead of us dwindled in fancy almost to nothing.

During the afternoon the wind freshened and the deeply-laden boats shipped much water, and steered badly in the rising sea. I had laid the course for Elephant Island, and we made such good progress that, had not the danger of the boats being separated been too great, I should have been tempted to carry on through the night. But it was imperative that the party should be kept together, and also I thought it possible that we might overrun our goal in the darkness and be unable to return.

So we made a sea-anchor of oars and hove to, and though we did what we could to make things comfortable during the hours of darkness there was really little that could be done. A terrible night followed, and I doubted if all of the men would survive it. The temperature was below zero and the wind penetrated our clothes and chilled us almost unbearably.

One of our troubles was lack of water, for we had emerged so suddenly from the pack into the open sea that we had not had time to take aboard ice for melting in the cookers, and without ice we could not have hot food. The condition of most of the men was pitiable. All of us had swollen mouths and could hardly touch the food. I longed intensely for the dawn, and at last daylight came; and a magnificent sunrise heralded in what we hoped would be our last day in the boats.

By this time we were all dreadfully thirsty, and although we could get momentary relief by chewing pieces of raw seal meat and swallowing the blood, our thirst was soon redoubled owing to the saltness of the flesh. I gave orders, therefore, that meat should only be served out at stated times during the day, or when thirst seemed to threaten the reason of any particular individual.

In the full daylight Elephant Island showed cold and severe. The island was on the bearings Worsley had laid down, and I congratulated him on the accuracy of his navigation under most difficult circumstances. The *Stancomb Wills* came up and McIlroy reported that Blackborrow's feet were severely frost-bitten, but, unfortunate as this was, nothing could be done. Most of the men were frostbitten to some extent, and it was interesting to notice that the 'old timers', Wild, Crean, Hurley and I, were all right. Apparently we were acclimatised to ordinary Antarctic temperature, though we discovered later that we were not immune.

Towards midnight the wind shifted, and this change enabled us to bear up closer to the island. A little later the *Dudley Docker* ran down to the *James Caird*, and Worsley shouted a suggestion that he should go ahead and search for a landing-place. I told him he could try, but that he must not lose sight of the *James Caird*. Just as he left a heavy snow-squall came down, and in the darkness the boats parted.

This separation made me anxious during the remaining hours of the night, for I could not be sure that all was well with the missing boat; but my anxiety was, as a matter of fact, groundless. I will quote extracts of Worsley's own account of what happened to the *Dudley Docker*.

'About midnight we lost sight of the *James Caird* with the *Stancomb Wills* in tow, but not long after saw the light of the *James Caird*'s compass-lamp, which Sir Ernest was flashing on their sail to guide us. We answered by lighting our candle under the tent and letting the light shine through. With this candle our poor fellows lit their pipes, their only solace, as our raging thirst prevented us from eating anything.

'I could not see or judge distance properly, and found myself falling asleep momentarily at the tiller. At 3 a.m. Greenstreet relieved me there. I was so cramped from long hours in the constrained position I was forced to assume at the tiller that the other men had to pull me amidships and straighten me out like a jack-knife, first rubbing my thighs, groin and stomach.

'At daylight we found ourselves close alongside the land, but the weather was so thick we could not see where to make for a landing. I had again taken the tiller after an hour's rest and I ran the *Dudley Docker* off before the gale, following the coast around to the north.

'All this time we had seen no possible landing-place, but at 9.30 a.m. we spied a narrow, rocky beach at the base of some very high crags and cliffs, and made for it. To our joy we sighted the *James Caird* and the *Stancomb Wills* sailing into the same haven just ahead of us. So delighted were we that we gave three cheers.'

Our experiences on the *James Caird* had been similar, although we had been unable to keep up to windward as well as the *Dudley Docker* had done. The weather was very thick in the morning, indeed at 7 a.m. we were right under the cliffs before we saw them.

The *Stancomb Wills* was the lighter and handier boat, and I called her alongside with the intention of taking her through the gap first to ascertain the possibilities of a landing. Just as I was climbing into the *Stancomb Wills* I saw the *Dudley Docker*, and the sight took a great load off my mind.

Rowing carefully we brought the *Stancomb Wills* towards the opening in the reef, then, with a few strong strokes, we shot through on the top of a swell and ran the boat on to a stony beach. The next swell lifted her a little farther. It was the first landing ever made on Elephant Island, and I thought the honour should belong to Blackborrow, the youngest member of the Expedition, but I had forgotten his frost-bitten feet would prevent him from appreciating the honour thrust upon him.

When I landed for the second time a curious spectacle met my eyes. Some of the men were reeling about the beach as if they were intoxicated. They were laughing uproariously, picking up stones and letting handfuls of pebbles trickle between their fingers, like misers gloating over hoarded gold. I remember that Wild came ashore as I was looking at the men, and stood beside me as easy and unconcerned as if he had stepped out of his car for a stroll in the Park.

The tents were pitched with oars for supports, and by 3 p.m. our camp was in order, and most of the men turned in early for a safe and glorious sleep.

Before getting into the tents, Wild, Worsley and Hurley accompanied me on an inspection of our beach, and we found the outlook to be anything but cheering. Obvious signs showed that at spring tides our little beach would be covered by the water right up to the foot of the cliffs. Clearly we should have to find some better resting-place, but I decided not to share this unwelcome news with the men until they had enjoyed the full sweetness of comparatively untroubled rest.

Early next morning all hands were astir. The sun shone brightly and we spread out our wet gear to dry and made the beach look like a particularly disreputable gipsy camp. I had decided to send Wild along the coast in the *Stancomb Wills* to look for a new camping-ground, on which I hoped the party would be able to live for weeks or even months in safety.

Wild, accompanied by Marston, Crean, Vincent and McCarthy, pushed off in the *Stancomb Wills* at 11 a.m. and proceeded westward along the coast.

The *Stancomb Wills* had not returned by nightfall, but at 8 p.m. we heard a hail in the distance and soon, like a pale ghost out of the darkness, the boat appeared. I was awaiting Wild's report most anxiously, and was greatly relieved when he told me that he had discovered a sandy spot, seven miles to the west, about 200 yards long, running out at right angles to the coast and terminating at the seaward end in a mass of rock.

Wild said that this place was the only possible camping-ground he had seen, and that, although in very heavy gales it might be spray-blown, he did not think that the seas would actually break over it. The boats could be run on a shelving beach, and, in any case, it would be a great improvement on our very narrow beach.

The move was absolutely necessary, and by 11 a.m. we were away, the *James Caird* leading.

We forged on slowly, and passed inside a great pillar of rock standing out to sea and towering to a height of about 2,400 feet. A line of reef stretched between the shore and this pillar, and at first I thought that we should have to face the raging sea outside, but a break in the white surf revealed a gap in the reef and we laboured through.

Rocks studded the shallow water round the spit, and the sea surged amongst them. I ordered the *Stancomb Wills* to run on to the beach at the place which looked smoothest, and in a few moments the boat was ashore, the men jumping out and holding her against the receding wave.

We were still labouring at the boats when I saw Rickenson turn white and stagger in the surf. His heart had been temporarily unequal to the strain placed upon it, and he needed prompt medical attention. He was one of those eager souls who do more than their share of work, and who will try to do more than they are physically capable of doing. Like many of the members of the Expedition he was suffering from bad salt-water boils.

The spit was by no means an ideal camping-ground; it was rough, bleak, and inhospitable, but some of the larger rocks sheltered us a little from the wind, and, as we clustered round the blubber-stove, we were quite a cheerful company. After all, another stage of the homeward journey was finished, and for an hour we could afford to forget the problems of the future.

Then all hands helped to pull the boats farther up the beach, and at this task we suffered a serious misfortune.

Two of our bags of clothing had been placed under the bilge of the *James Caird*, and, before we realised the danger, a wave had lifted the boat and carried the two bags into the surf. We had no chance to recover them. But this was not our only misfortune, for in the early morning our big eight-man tent was blown to pieces.

On the morning of April 19th the weather was still bad, and some of the men were showing signs of demoralisation and were disinclined to leave their tents when the hour came for turning out. It was apparent that they were thinking more of the discomforts of the moment than of the good fortune which had brought us to sound ground and comparative safety; and only by rather drastic methods were they induced to turn to.

Frankly, we needed all the comfort which hot food could give us. The icy fingers of the gale pushed relentlessly through our worn garments and tattered tents. The snow swathed us and our gear, and set traps for our stumbling feet. The rising sea beat against the rocks and shingle, and tossed fragments of floe-ice within a few feet of our boats. The consoling feature of the situation was that our camp was safe. We could endure the discomforts, and I felt that all of us would be benefited by this opportunity to rest and recuperate.

PREPARATIONS FOR THE BOAT JOURNEY

The increasing sea made it necessary for us to drag our boats farther up the beach, and when this was done I discussed with Wild and Worsley the chances of reaching South Georgia before the winter locked the sea against us. For every conceivable reason some effort to secure relief had got to be made. The health and mental condition of several men were causing me serious anxiety, and the food was also a vital consideration. I did not dare confidently to count upon supplies of meat and blubber, for animals seemed to have deserted the beach, and the winter was near.

The conclusion was forced upon me that a boat journey in search of relief was necessary and must not be delayed. The nearest port where assistance could certainly be secured was Port Stanley, in the Falkland Islands, 540 miles away; but we could scarcely hope to beat up against the prevailing north-westerly wind in a frail and weakened boat with a small sail area.

It was not difficult to decide that South Georgia, which was over 800 miles away but lay in the area of west winds, must be our objective. I could count upon finding whalers at any of the whaling-stations on the east coast, and, provided that the sea was clear of ice and that the boat survived the great seas, a boat party might make the voyage and be back with relief within a month.

The hazards of a boat journey across 800 miles of stormy sub-Antarctic ocean were obvious, but I calculated that at the worst this venture would add nothing to the risks of the men left on the island. The boat would not require to take more than one month's provisions for six men, for if we did not make South Georgia in that time we were sure to go under. A consideration which also influenced me was that there was no chance at all of any search being made for us on Elephant Island.

The perils of the proposed journey were extreme, and the risk was justified solely by our urgent need of assistance. The ocean south of Cape Horn in the middle of May is known to be the most tempestuous area of water in the world, and the gales are almost unceasing. We had to face these conditions in a small and weather-beaten boat, already strained by the work of the previous months. Worsley and Wild realised that the attempt must be made, and asked to be allowed to accompany me on the voyage.

I had at once to tell Wild that he must stay behind, for I relied upon him to hold the party together while I was away, and, should our attempt to bring help end in failure, to make the best of his way to Deception Island in the spring. I determined to take Worsley with me as I had a very high opinion of his accuracy and quickness as a navigator – an opinion that was only enhanced during our journey.

Four other men were required, and, although I thought of leaving Crean as a right-hand man for Wild, he begged so hard to come that, after consulting Wild, I promised to take him. Then I called the men together, explained my plan, and asked for volunteers. Many came forward at once, and I finally selected McNeish, McCarthy and Vincent, in addition to Worsley and Crean. McIlroy and Macklin were both anxious to go but realised that their duty lay on the island with the sick men. The crew seemed a strong one, and as I looked at the men I felt confidence increasing.

After the decision was made, I walked through the blizzard with Worsley and Wild to examine the *James Caird*. The 20-foot boat had never looked big, but when I viewed her in the light of our new undertaking she seemed in some mysterious way to have shrunk. She was an ordinary ship's whaler, fairly strong, but showing signs of the strain she had endured. Standing beside her, and looking at the fringe of the tumultuous sea, there was no doubt that our voyage would be a big adventure.

I called McCarthy, the carpenter, and asked him if he could do anything to make the ship more seaworthy. He asked at once if he was to go with me, and seemed quite pleased when I answered

'Yes'. He was over fifty years of age and not altogether fit, but he was very quick and had a good knowledge of sailing-boats. He told me that he could contrive some sort of covering for the *James Caird* if he was allowed to use the lids of the cases and the four sledge-runners, which we had lashed inside the boat for use in the event of a landing on Graham Land at Wihelmina Bay. He proposed to complete the covering with some of our canvas, and immediately began to make his plans.

During this day the cook, who had worked very well, suddenly collapsed, and to replace him I selected one of the men who had expressed a desire to lie down and die. The task of keeping the galley fire alight was both strenuous and difficult, and it took his thoughts away from the chances of immediate dissolution.

There was a lull in the bad weather on April 21st, and the carpenter was able to collect material for the decking of the *James Caird*. He fitted the mast of the *Stancomb* fore and aft inside the *James Caird* as a hogback, and thus strengthened the keel with the object of preventing our boat from buckling in heavy seas. He had not enough wood to provide a deck, but by using the sledge runners and box lids he made a framework extending from the forecastle aft to a well. It was a patched-up affair, but it provided a base for a canvas covering.

We had a bolt of canvas frozen stiff, and this material had to be thawed out foot by foot over the blubber-stove so that it might be sewn into the form of a cover. When it had been nailed and screwed into position it certainly gave an appearance of safety to the boat, though I had an uneasy feeling that it bore a strong likeness to stage scenery. But, as events proved, the covering served its purpose well, and without it we certainly could not have lived through the voyage.

When the *James Caird* was launched she nearly capsized, and Vincent and the carpenter, who were on deck, were thrown into the water – a piece of really bad luck as they would have small chance of drying their clothes after we started. Hurley, who had the eye of the professional photographer for 'incidents', secured a picture of the upset, and I firmly believed he would have liked the two men to remain in the water until he could 'snap' them at close quarters! But, regardless of his feelings, we hauled them out immediately.

The *James Caird* was soon clear of the breakers, and the *Stancomb Wills* come alongside, transferred her load, and went back to the shore for more. On this second journey the water-casks were towed behind the *Stancomb Wills*, and the swell, which was rapidly increasing, drove the boat on to the rocks, where one of the casks was slightly stove in. This accident proved later on to be serious, since sea water had entered the casks and made the contents brackish.

By midday the *James Caird* was ready for the voyage. Vincent and the carpenter had secured some dry clothes by exchange with members of the shore-party, and the boat's crew was standing by, waiting for the order to cast off.

Then, setting our jib, we cut the painter and moved away to the north-east. The men who were staying behind made a pathetic little group on the beach, but they waved to us and gave three hearty cheers. There was hope in their hearts, and they trusted us to bring the help which they so sorely needed.

THE BEGINNING OF THE BOAT JOURNEY

I had all sails set, and the *James Caird* quickly dipped the beach and its line of dark figures. The westerly wind took us rapidly to the line of pack, and as we entered it I stood up with my arm around the mast directing the steering. The pack thickened and we were forced to turn almost due east, running before the wind towards a gap which I had seen in the morning from the high ground.

The tale of the next sixteen days is one of supreme strife amid heaving waters, for the sub-Antarctic Ocean fully lived up to its evil winter reputation. I decided to run north for at least two days while the wind held, and thus get into warmer weather before turning to the east and laying a course for South Georgia.

We took two-hourly spells at the tiller. The men who were not on watch crawled into the sodden sleeping-bags and tried to forget their troubles for a period. But there was no comfort in the boat, indeed the first night aboard the boat was one of acute discomfort for us all, and we were heartily glad when dawn came and we could begin to prepare a hot breakfast.

Cramped in our narrow quarters and continually wet from the spray, we suffered severely from cold throughout the journey. We fought the seas and the winds, and at the same time had a daily struggle to keep ourselves alive. At times we were in dire peril. Generally we were encouraged by the knowledge that we were progressing towards the desired land, but there were days and nights when we lay hove to, drifting across the storm-whitened seas, and watching the uprearing masses of water, flung to and fro by Nature in the pride of her strength.

Nearly always there were gales. So small was our boat and so great were the seas that often our sail flapped idly in the calm between the crests of two waves. Then we would climb the next slope, and catch the full fury of the gale where the wool-like whiteness of the breaking water surged around us. But we had our moments of laughter – rare, it is true, but hearty enough.

The difficulty of movement in the boat would have had its humorous side if it had not caused so many aches and pains. In order to move along the boat we had to crawl under the thwarts, and our knees suffered considerably. When a watch turned out I had to direct each man by name when and where to move, for if all hands had crawled about at the same time the result would have been dire confusion and many bruises.

Then there was the trim of the boat to be considered. The order of the watch was four hours on and four hours off, three men to the watch. One man had the tiller ropes, the second man attended to the sail, and the third bailed for all he was worth.

While the new watch was shivering in the wind and spray, the men who had been relieved groped hurriedly among the soaking sleeping-bags, and tried to steal some of the warmth created by the last occupants; but it was not always possible to find even this comfort when we went off watch. At the time we thought that we never slept, but in fact we dozed off uncomfortably, to be roused quickly by some new ache or by another call to effort. My own share of the general discomfort was increased by a finely-developed bout of sciatica, which had begun on the floe several months earlier.

Our meals were regular in spite of the gales. Attention to this was essential, since the conditions of the voyage made ever-increasing calls upon our vitality. The meals, which consisted chiefly of Bovril sledging-ration, were the bright beacons in these cold and stormy days.

A severe south-westerly gale on the fourth day out forced us to heave to. The delay was vexatious, since up to that time we had been making up to seventy miles a day, good going with our limited sail area. A thousand times it seemed as if the *James Caird* must be engulfed; but the boat lived.

The gale had its birthplace above the Antarctic Continent, and its freezing breath lowered the temperature far towards zero. The spray froze upon the boat and gave bows, sides and decking a heavy coat of mail. We could not allow the load of ice to increase beyond a certain point, and in turn we crawled about the decking forward, chipping and picking at it with what tools we had.

When daylight came on the sixth day we saw and felt that the *James Caird* had lost her resiliency. She was not rising to the oncoming seas. The weight of the ice was having its effect, and she was becoming more like a log than a boat. The situation called for immediate action. First of all we broke away the spare oars, which were encased in ice and frozen to the sides of the boat, and threw them overboard. We kept two oars for use when we got inshore. Then two of the fur sleeping-bags went over the side, weighing probably 40 lb. each. We still had four bags, three in use and one in reserve should a member of the party permanently break down. The reduction of weight relieved the boat to some extent, and vigorous chipping and scraping, by which we got rid of a lot of ice, helped more. The *James Caird* lifted to the endless waves as though she lived again.

About 11 a.m. the boat suddenly fell off into the trough of the sea. The painter had parted and the sea-anchor had gone. This was serious. The boat went away to leeward, and we had no chance to recover the anchor and our valuable rope, which had been our only means of keeping the boat's head up to the sea without the risk of hoisting sail in a gale. Now we had to set the sail and trust to its holding.

Skin frost-bites were troubling us, and we had developed large blisters on our fingers and hands, but we held the boat up to the gale during the day, enduring as best we could discomforts amounting to pain.

When the morning of the seventh day dawned there was not much wind, and we shook the reef out of the sail and laid our course once more for South Georgia. The sun came out bright and clear, and presently Worsley got a snap for longitude. We hoped that the sky would remain clear until noon so that we could get the latitude, for we had been six days out without an observation, and our dead reckoning naturally was uncertain.

The boat on that morning must have presented a strange appearance. All hands basked in the sunshine. We hung our sleeping-bags to the mast, and our socks and other gear were spread all over the deck. Porpoises came blowing round the boat, and Cape pigeons wheeled and swooped within a few feet of us. These little black-and-white birds have an air of friendliness which is not possessed by the great circling albatross.

We revelled in the warmth of the sun during that day. Life, after all, was not so bad. Our gear was drying, and we could have a hot meal in more or less comfort. The swell was still heavy, but it was not breaking, and the boat rode easily. At noon Worsley balanced himself on the gunwale and clung with one hand to the stay of the mainmast while he got a snap of the sun. The result was more than encouraging. We had done over 380 miles and were getting on for half-way to South Georgia. It looked as if we were going to get through.

THE END OF THE BOAT JOURNEY

During the afternoon the wind freshened to a good stiff breeze, and the *James Caird* made satisfactory progress. I had not realised until the sunlight came how small our boat really was. So low in the water were we that each succeeding swell cut off our view of the skyline. At one moment the consciousness of the forces arrayed against us would be almost overwhelming, and then hope and confidence would rise again as our boat rose to a wave and tossed aside the crest in a sparkling shower. My gun and some cartridges were stowed aboard the boat as a precaution against a shortage of food, but we were not disposed to destroy our little neighbours, the Cape pigeons, even for the sake of fresh meat. We might have shot an albatross, but the wandering king of the ocean aroused in us something of the feeling that inspired, too late, the Ancient Mariner.

I found that it was now absolutely necessary to prepare hot milk for all hands during the night, in order to sustain life until dawn. This involved an increased drain upon our small supply of matches, and our supply was very small indeed. One of the memories which comes to me of those days is of Crean singing at the tiller. He always sang while he was steering, but nobody ever discovered what the song was.

On the tenth night Worsley could not straighten his body after his spell at the tiller. He was thoroughly cramped, and we had to drag him beneath the decking and massage him before he could unbend himself and get into a sleeping-bag.

A hard north-westerly gale came up on the eleventh day (May 5th), and in the late afternoon it shifted to the south-west. The sky was overcast and occasional snow-squalls added to the discomfort produced by a tremendous cross-sea – the worst, I thought, which we had encountered. At midnight I was at the tiller, and suddenly noticed a line of clear sky between the south and south-west. I called to the other men that the sky was clearing, and then, a moment later, realised that what I had seen was not a rift in the clouds but the white crest of an enormous wave.

During twenty-six years' experience of the ocean in all its moods I had never seen a wave so gigantic. It was a mighty upheaval of the ocean, a thing quite apart from the big white-capped seas which had been our tireless enemies for many days. I shouted, 'For God's sake, hold on! It's got us!' Then came a moment of suspense which seemed to last for hours. We felt our boat lifted and flung forward like a cork in breaking surf. We were in a seething chaos of tortured water; but somehow the boat lived through it, half-full of water, sagging to the dead weight and shuddering under the blow. We bailed with the energy of men fighting for life, flinging the water over the sides with every receptacle which came into our hands; and after ten minutes of uncertainty we felt the boat renew her life beneath us. She floated again, and ceased to lurch drunkenly as though dazed by the attack of the sea. Earnestly we hoped that never again should we encounter such a wave.

Not until 3 a.m., when we were all chilled to the limit of endurance, did we manage to get the stove alight and to make ourselves hot drinks. The carpenter was suffering particularly, but he showed grit and spirit. Vincent, however, had collapsed, and for the past week had ceased to be an active member of the crew.

Thirst took possession of us, but I dared not permit the allowance of water to be increased, because an unfavourable wind might have driven us away from the island and have lengthened our voyage by several days. Lack of water is always the most severe privation which men can be condemned to endure, and we found that the salt water in our clothing and the salt spray which lashed our faces made our thirst quickly grow to a burning pain. I had to be very firm in refusing to allow anyone to anticipate the morrow's allowance, which sometimes I was begged to do.

I had altered the course to the east so as to make sure of striking the island, which would have been impossible to regain if we had run past the northern end. The course was laid on our scrap of chart for a point some thirty miles down the coast. That day and the following day passed for us in a sort of nightmare. Our mouths were dry and our tongues were swollen. The wind was still strong and the heavy sea forced us to navigate carefully. But any thought of our peril from the waves was buried beneath the consciousness of our raging thirst. The bright moments were those when we each received our one mug of hot milk during the long, bitter watches of the night.

Things were bad for us in those days, but the end was

approaching. The morning of May 8th broke thick and stormy, with squalls from the north-west. We searched the waters ahead for a sign of land, and, although we searched in vain, we were cheered by a sense that the goal was near. About 10 a.m. we passed a bit of kelp, a glad signal of the proximity of land. An hour later we saw two shags sitting on a big mass of kelp, and we knew then that we must be within ten or fifteen miles of the shore. These birds are as sure an indication of the proximity of land as a lighthouse is, for they never venture far to sea.

We gazed ahead with increasing eagerness, and at 12.30 p.m., through a rift in the clouds, McCarthy caught a glimpse of the black cliffs of South Georgia, just fourteen days after our departure from Elephant Island. It was a glad moment. Thirst-ridden, chilled, and weak as we were, happiness irradiated us. The job was nearly done.

We stood in towards the shore to look for a landing-place, and presently we could see the green tussock-grass on the ledges above the surf-beaten rocks. Ahead of us, and to the south, blind rollers showed the presence of uncharted reefs along the coast. The rocky coast appeared to descend sheer to the sea. Our need of water and rest was almost desperate, but to have attempted a landing at that time would have been suicidal.

At 5 a.m. the wind shifted to the north-west, and quickly increased to one of the worst hurricanes any of us had ever experienced. A great cross-sea was running and the wind simply shrieked as it converted the whole seascape into a haze of driving spray. Down into the valleys, up to tossing heights, straining until her seams opened, swung our little boat, brave still but labouring heavily. We knew that the wind and set of the sea were driving us ashore, but we could do nothing.

The dawn revealed a storm-torn ocean, and the morning passed without bringing us a sight of the land; but at 1 p.m., through a rift in the flying mists, we got a glimpse of the huge crags of the island and realised that our position had become desperate. We were on a dead lee shore, and we could gauge our approach to the unseen cliffs by the roar of the breakers against the sheer walls of rock. I ordered the double-reefed mainsail to be set in the hope that we might claw off, and this attempt increased the strain upon the boat.

The chance of surviving the night seemed small, and I think most of us felt that the end was very near. Just after 6 p.m., as the boat was in the yeasty backwash from the seas flung from this iron-bound coast, just when things looked their worst, they changed for the best; so thin is the line which divides success from failure.

The wind suddenly shifted, and we were free once more to make an offing. Almost as soon as the gale eased the pin which locked the mast to the thwart fell out. Throughout the hurricane it must have been on the point of doing this, and if it had nothing could have saved us. The mast would have snapped like a carrot. Our backstays had carried away once before, when iced up, and were not too strongly fastened. We were thankful indeed for the mercy which had held the pin in its place during the hurricane.

We stood off shore again, tired almost to the point of apathy. Our water had long been finished. The last was about a pint of hairy liquid, which we strained through a bit of gauze from the medicine chest. The pangs of thirst attacked us with redoubled intensity, and I felt that at almost any risk we must make a landing on the following day.

About 8 a.m. the wind backed to the north-west and threatened another blow. In the meantime we had sighted a big indentation which I though must be King Haakon Bay, and I decided that we must land there. We set the bows of the boat towards the bay, and ran before the freshening gale. Soon we had angry reefs on either side. Great glaciers came down to the sea and offered no landing-place. The sea spouted on the reefs and thundered against the shore. About noon we sighted a line of jagged reef, like blackened teeth, which seemed to bar the entrance to the bay. Inside, fairly smooth water stretched eight or nine miles to the head of the bay.

A gap in the reef appeared, and we made for it, but the fates had another rebuff for us. The wind shifted and blew from the east right out of the bay. We could see the way through the reef, but we could not approach it directly. That afternoon we bore up, tacking five times in the strong wind. The last tack enabled us to get through, and at last we were in the wide mouth of the bay.

Dusk was approaching. A small cove, with a boulder-strewn beach guarded by a reef, made a break in the cliffs on the south side of the bay, and we turned in that direction. I stood in the bows, and directed the steering as we ran through the kelp and made the passage of the reef. The entrance was so narrow that we had to take in the oars, and the swell was piling itself right over the reef into the cove. But in a minute or two we were inside, and in the gathering darkness the *James Caird* ran in on a swell and touched the beach.

We heard a gurgling sound which was sweet music in our ears, and, peering round, we found a stream of fresh water almost at our feet. A moment later we were down on our knees drinking the pure ice-cold water which put new life into us. It was a splendid moment.

KING HAAKON BAY

Our next task was to get the stores and ballast out of the boat so that we might secure her for the night, and having taken out the stores and gear and ballast, we tried to pull the empty boat up the beach. By this effort we discovered how weak we were, for our united strength was not enough to get the *James Caird* clear of the water. Time after time we pulled together but without avail, and I saw that we must have food and rest before we beached the boat.

We made fast a line to a heavy boulder, and set a watch to fend the boat off the rocks of the beach. Then I sent Crean round to the left side of the cove, about thirty yards away, where I had noticed a little cave as we were running in. He could not see much in the darkness, but reported that the place certainly promised some shelter. We carried the sleeping-bags round and found a mere hollow in the rock-face, with a shingle floor sloping at a steep angle to the sea. There we prepared a hot meal, and when the food was finished I ordered the men to turn in. I took the first watch beside the *James Caird*, which was still afloat in the tossing water just off the beach.

The sea went down in the early hours of the morning (May 11th), and having braced ourselves with another meal, we again started to get the boat ashore. We waited for Byron's 'great ninth wave', and when it lifted the *James Caird* in we held her, and, by dint of great exertion, worked her round broadside to the sea. Inch by inch we dragged her up until we reached the fringe of the tussock-grass and knew that the boat was above high-water mark.

Our cove lay a little inside the southern headland of King Haakon Bay. A narrow break in the cliffs, which were about 100 feet high, formed the entrance to the cove. Our cave was a recess in the cliff on the left-hand of the beach.

Water had trickled down the face of the cliff and formed long icicles, which hung down in front of the cave to the length of about 15 feet. These icicles provided shelter, and when we had spread our sails below them, with the assistance of the oars, we had quarters which, under the circumstances, were reasonably comfortable. The camp at least was dry, and we moved our gear there with confidence. We also built a fireplace and arranged our sleeping-bags and blankets around it. The cave was about 8 feet deep and 12 feet wide at the entrance.

During the morning we started a fire in the cave with wood from the top sides of the boat, and, in spite of the dense smoke, we enjoyed the warmth and the splendid stew which Crean, who was cook for the day, provided for us. Four young albatrosses went into the pot, with a Bovril ration for thickening. The flesh was white and succulent, and the bones, not fully formed, almost melted in our mouths. That was a memorable meal.

The final stage of the journey was still before us. I realised that the condition of the party generally, and of McNeish and Vincent in particular, would prevent us putting to sea again except under pressure of absolute necessity. I also doubted if our boat in its weakened condition could weather the island. By sea we were still 150 miles away from Stromness Whaling Station.

The alternative was to attempt the crossing of the island. If we could not get over we must try to get food and fuel enough to keep us through the winter, but such a task was almost hopeless. On Elephant Island were twenty-two men whose plight was worse than ours, and who were waiting the relief which we alone could secure for them. Somehow or other we had got to push on, though several days must elapse before our strength would be sufficiently recovered for us to row or sail the last nine miles up to the head of the bay. In the meantime we could make what preparations were possible.

Our party spent a quiet day, attending to clothing and gear, checking stores, eating and resting. We had previously discovered that when we were landing from the boat on May 10th we had lost the rudder. The *James Caird* had been bumping heavily astern as we scrambled ashore, and evidently the rudder had then been knocked off. A careful search of the beach and rocks failed to reveal the missing rudder, and this was a serious loss, even if the voyage to the sound could be made in good weather.

The bay was still filled with ice on the morning of Saturday, May 13th, but the tide took it all away in the afternoon. Then a strange thing happened. The rudder, with all the broad Atlantic to sail in, came bobbing back into our cove. Nearer and nearer it came as we waited anxiously on the shore, oars in hand; and at last we were able to seize it. Surely a remarkable salvage!

The day was bright and clear; our clothes were drying and our strength was returning. In the afternoon we began to prepare the *James Caird* for the journey to the head of King Haakon Bay.

During the morning of this day (May 13th) Worsley and I tramped across the hills in a north-easterly direction for the purpose of getting a view of the sound, and possibly gathering useful information for the next stage of our journey. It was exhausting work, but after covering about two and a half miles in two hours we were able to look east up the bay. We, however, could not see very much of the country which we should have to cross in order to reach the whaling station on the other side of the island. Some gentoo penguins and a young sea-elephant which we found were killed by Worsley.

When we got back to the cave, tired and hungry, we found a splendid meal of stewed albatross chicken waiting for us. We had carried a quantity of blubber and the sea-elephant's liver in our blouses, and produced our treasures as a surprise for the men. Rough climbing on the way back had nearly persuaded us to throw the stuff away, but we held on and had our reward at the camp.

The long bay had been a magnificent sight, even to eyes which had dwelt long enough on grandeur and were hungry for the familiar things of every-day life. Its green-blue waters were being beaten to fury by the gale. The mountains peered through the mists, and between them huge glaciers poured down from the great ice-slopes which lay behind. We counted twelve glaciers, and every few minutes we heard the great roar caused by masses of ice calving from the parent streams.

May 15th was a great day. We made our hoosh at 7.30 p.m., and then loaded up the boat and gave her a flying launch down the steep beach into the surf. A gusty north-westerly wind was blowing, but the *James Caird* headed to the sea as if anxious to face the battle of the waves once more. As we sailed merrily up the bay the sun broke through the mists and made the tossing waters sparkle around us. We were a curious-looking party on that bright morning, but we were feeling happy.

The wind blew fresh and strong, and a small sea broke on the coast as we advanced. We had hoped to find sea-elephants on the upper beaches, and our expectations were realised. As we neared the head of the bay we heard the roar of the bulls, and soon afterwards we saw their great unwieldy forms lying on a shelving beach towards the bay-head.

We rounded a high, glacier-worn bluff on the north side, and soon after noon we ran the boat ashore on a low beach of sand and pebbles, with tussock-grass growing above high-water mark. Hundreds of sea-elephants were lying about, enough to provide food and blubber for years and years.

We soon converted the boat into a very comfortable cabin *à la* Peggotty, turfing it round with tussocks. One side of the *James Caird* rested on stones so as to afford a low entrance, and when we had finished she looked as if she had grown there. A sea-elephant provided us with fuel and meat, and that evening found a well-fed and fairly contented party in Peggotty Camp.

Our camp, as I have said, lay on the north side of King Haakon Bay near the head. The path towards the whaling stations led round the seaward end of the snouted glacier on the east side of the camp, and up a snow-slope which seemed to lead to a pass in the great Allardyce range, which forms the main backbone of South Georgia. The range dipped opposite the bay into a well-defined pass from east to west.

I planned to climb to the pass, and then be guided by the configuration of the country in the selection of a route eastward to Stromness Bay, where the whaling stations were established in the minor bays, Leith, Husvik and Stromness.

We overhauled our gear on Thursday, May 18th, and hauled our sledge to the lower edge of the snouted glacier. The sledge proved heavy and cumbrous, and I realised that three men would be unable to manage it amid the snow-plains, glaciers and peaks of the interior. Worsley and Crean were coming with me, and, after consultation, we decided to leave the sleeping-bags behind and make the journey in very light marching order.

We decided to take three days' provisions for each man in the form of sledging ration and biscuit, the Primus lamp filled with oil, the small cooker, the carpenter's adze (for use as an ice-axe), and the alpine rope, which made a total length of 50 feet when knotted, and would help us to lower ourselves down steep slopes or cross crevassed glaciers.

We had two boxes of matches left, one full and the other partially used. We decided to leave the full box at the camp and to take the second box, which contained forty-eight matches. I was unfortunate as regards footgear, as I had given away my heavy boots on the floe, and only had a lighter pair in poor condition. The carpenter helped me by putting several screws into the sole of each boot with the object of providing a grip on the ice. The screws came out of the *James Caird*.

We turned in early that night, but troubled thoughts kept me from sleeping. The task before the overland party would in all probability be heavy, and we were going to leave a weak party behind us in the camp. Vincent was still in the same condition and could not march. McNeish was pretty well broken up. These two men could not manage for themselves, and I had to leave McCarthy to look after them. Should we fail to reach the whaling station McCarthy might have a difficult task.

We had very scanty knowledge of the interior, for no man had ever penetrated from the coast of South Georgia at any point, and I knew that the whalers regarded the country as inaccessible.

At 2 a.m. on the Friday morning we turned out, and an hour later our hoosh was ready. The full moon was shining in a practically cloudless sky, and we made a start as soon as we had eaten our meal. Our first difficulty was to get round the edge of the snouted glacier, which had points like fingers projecting into the sea.

The snow-surface was disappointing, and as we sank over our ankles at each step our progress was slow. After two hours' steady climbing we were 2,500 feet above sea level, and the bright moonlight showed us that the interior was tremendously broken. High peaks, impassable cliffs, steep snow-slopes, and sharply descending glaciers could be seen in all directions, with stretches of snow-plain overlaying the ice-sheet of the interior. The slope which we were ascending mounted to a ridge, and our course lay direct to the top. The moon, which was a good friend to us, threw a long shadow at one point and told us that the surface was broken in our path. Thus warned we avoided a huge hole capable of swallowing an army. The bay was now about three miles away.

I had hoped to get a view of the country ahead of us from the top of this slope, but as the surface became more level a thick fog drifted down. Under these conditions we roped ourselves together as a precaution against holes, crevasses and precipices, and I broke trail through the soft snow. With almost the full length of rope between myself and the last man we could steer an approximately straight course, for if I veered to the right or left when marching into the blank wall of fog, the last man on the rope could shout a direction. So, like a ship with its 'port', 'starboard', 'steady', we tramped through the fog for the next two hours.

Then, as daylight came, the fog partially lifted, and, from a height of about 3,000 feet, we looked down on what seemed to be a huge frozen lake, with its farther shores still obscured by fog. We halted there to eat a bit of biscuit, and to discuss whether we would go down and cross the flat surface of the lake or keep on the ridge we had already reached. I decided to go down, as the lake lay on our course. After an hour's fairly easy travel through the snow we began to meet crevasses, which showed that we were on a glacier. Later on the fog lifted completely and then we saw that our lake stretched to the horizon, and suddenly we realised that we were looking down upon the open sea on the east coast of the island.

Evidently we were at the top of Possession Bay, and the island at that point could not be more than five miles across from the head of King Haakon Bay. Our rough chart was inaccurate, and there was nothing for it but to start up the glacier again. That was about seven o'clock, and in two hours we had more than recovered our lost ground.

We regained the ridge and then struck south-east, for the chart showed that two more bays indented the coast before Stromness. It was comforting to know that we should have the eastern water in sight during our journey, although we could see that there was no way around the shore-line owing to steep cliffs and glaciers.

Men lived in houses lit by electric light on the east coast. News of the outside world awaited us there, and, above all, the east coast meant for us the means of rescuing the twenty-two men left on Elephant Island.

ACROSS SOUTH GEORGIA

The slope became precipitous, and we had to cut steps as we advanced. For this purpose the adze proved an excellent instrument. At last I stood upon the razor-back, while the other men held the rope and waited for news. The outlook was disappointing. I looked down a sheer precipice to a chaos of crumpled ice 1,500 feet below. There was no way down for us.

Cutting steps with the adze we moved in a lateral direction round the base of a dolomite, but the same precipice confronted us. Away to the north-east there appeared to be a snow-slope which might give a path to the lower country, and so we retraced our steps down the long slope which had taken us three hours to climb. In an hour we were at the bottom, but we were beginning to feel the strain of unaccustomed marching.

Skirting the base of the mountain above us, we came to a gigantic gulley, a mile and a half long and 1,000 feet deep. This gully was semi-circular in form, and ended in a gentle incline. We passed through it, and at the far end we had another meal and short rest. This was at 12.30 p.m. Refreshed by our steaming Bovril ration we started once more for the crest, and after another weary climb we reached the top.

The ridge was studded with peaks, which prevented us from

getting a clear view either to the right or left, and I had to decide that our course lay back the way which we had come. It was of the utmost importance for us to get down into the next valley before dark. We were up 4,500 feet and the night temperature at that elevation would be very low. The afternoon was wearing on, and the fog was rolling up ominously from the west. We had neither tent nor sleeping-bags, and our clothes were terribly weather-worn.

Back we went, and presently reached the top of another ridge in the fading light. After a glance over the top I turned to the anxious faces of the men behind me and said: 'Come on, boys.' Within a minute they stood beside me on the ice-ridge, the surface of which fell away at a sharp incline before us but merged into a snow-slope.

We could not see the bottom, and the possibility of the slope ending in a sheer fall occurred to us, but the fog which was creeping up behind us allowed no time for hesitation. At first we descended slowly, cutting steps in the hard snow, then the surface became softer, indicating that the gradient was less severe. There could be no turning back now, so we unroped and slid in the fashion of youthful days. When we stopped on a snow-bank at the foot of the slope we found that we had descended at least 900 feet in two or three minutes. We looked back and saw the grey fingers of the fog appearing on the ridge. But we had escaped.

From the top we had seen that our course lay between two huge masses of crevasses, and we thought that the road ahead was clear. This belief and the increasing cold made us abandon the idea of camping. At 6 p.m. we had another meal, and then we started up the long, gentle ascent. Night was upon us, and for an hour we plodded on in almost complete darkness, watching warily for signs of crevasses. But about 8 p.m. the full moon rose ahead of us and made a silver pathway for our feet.

We had been on the march for over twenty hours, only halting for occasional meals. After 1 a.m. we cut a pit in the snow, piled up loose snow around it, and again started the Primus. Worsley and Crean sang their old songs when the Primus was going merrily. Laughter was in our hearts, though not on our parched and cracked lips.

Within half an hour we were away again, still downward to the coast. We now felt almost sure that we were above Stromness Bay, and joyfully pointed out various landmarks revealed by the light of the moon, whose friendly face was by this time cloud-swept. Our high hopes were soon shattered. Crevasses warned us that we were on another glacier, and presently we looked down almost to the seaward edge of the great riven ice-mass. I knew that there was no glacier in Stromness and realised that this must be Fortuna Glacier. The disappointment was severe. Back we turned and tramped up the glacier again, working at a tangent to the south-east. We were very tired.

At 5 a.m. we were at the foot of the rocky spurs of the range. The wind blowing down from the heights was chilling us, and we decided to get under the lee of a rock and rest. We put our sticks and the adze on the snow, sat down on them as close to one another as possible, and put our arms round each other. I thought that in this way we might keep warm and have half-an-hour's rest. Within a minute my two companions were fast asleep, and I realised how disastrous it would be if we all slumbered together, for sleep under such conditons merges into death. So after five minutes I awoke them and gave the word for a fresh start. So stiff were we that for the first 300 yards or so we marched with our knees bent.

A jagged line of peaks with a gap like a broken tooth con-fronted us. This was the ridge which runs in a southerly direction from Fortuna Bay, and our course to Stromness lay across it. A very steep slope led up to the ridge and an icy wind burst through the gap. With anxious hearts as well as with weary bodies we went through the gap at 6 a.m. Had the farther slope proved impassable our situation would have been almost desperate; but the worst was turning to the best for us.

The twisted, wave-like rock formations of Husvik Harbour appeared right ahead of us in the opening of dawn. Without a word we shook hands with one another. While breakfast was being prepared, I climbed the ridge above us to secure an extended view of the country below; and at 6.30 a.m. I thought I heard the sound of a steam-whistle. I dared not be certain, but I knew that the men at the whaling stations would be called from their beds about that time.

Descending again to the camp I told the others, and in intense excitement we watched the chronometer for seven o'clock, when the whalers would be summoned to work. Right to the minute the steam-whistle came clearly to us, and never had any one of us heard sweeter music. It was the first sound created by outside human agency which had come to our ears since December, 1914. That whistle told us that men were near, that ships were ready, and that very soon we should be on our way back to Elephant Island to rescue the men waiting there. It was a moment hard to describe. Pain and aches, boat journeys, marches, hunger and fatigue, were forgotten, only the perfect contentment which comes from work accomplished remained.

My examination of the country before us had not provided definite information, so I put the situation before Worsley and Crean. Our obvious course lay down a snow-slope in the direction of Husvik. 'Boys,' I said, 'this snow-slope seems to end in a precipice, but perhaps there is no precipice. If we don't go down we shall have to make a detour of at least five miles before we reach level going. What shall it be?' They both replied at once, 'Try the slope.' So again we started downwards.

A steep gradient of blue ice was the next obstacle. Worsley and Crean got a firm footing in a hole excavated with the adze, and then lowered me as I cut steps until the full 50 feet of our alpine rope was out. Then I made a hole big enough for the three of us, and the other two men came down the steps. In this laborious fashion we spent two hours descending about 500 feet. Half-way down we had to strike away diagonally to the left, for we noticed that the fragments of ice loosened by the adze were taking a leap into space at the bottom of the slope. At last, and very thankfully, we got off the steep ice at a point where some rocks protruded, and then we could see that there was a perilous precipice directly below the point where we had started to cut the steps.

At 1.30 p.m. we climbed round a final ridge and saw a little steamer, a whaling boat, entering the bay, 2,500 feet below. A few moments later the masts of a sailing ship lying at a wharf came in sight. Minute figures moving to and fro caught our gaze, and then we saw the sheds and factory of Stromness Whaling Station. Once more we paused and shook one another warmly by the hand.

Cautiously we started down the slope which led to warmth and comfort, but the last lap of the journey was extraordinarily diffi-cult. Vainly we sought a safe, or reasonably safe, way down the steep ice-clad mountain side. The sole possible pathway seemed to be a channel cut by water running from the upland. Down through icy water we followed the course of this stream. We were wet to the waist, shivering, cold and tired.

Presently our ears detected an unwelcome sound which might under other conditions have been musical. It was the splashing of a waterfall, and we were at the wrong end. When we reached the top of this fall we peered over cautiously and discovered that there was a drop of 25 or 30 feet, with impassable ice-cliffs on both sides. To go up again was, in out utterly wearied condition, scarcely thinkable. The way down was through the waterfall itself.

With some difficulty we made fast one end of our rope to a boulder, and then Worsley and I lowered Crean, who was the heaviest man. He disappeared altogether in the falling water and came out gasping at the bottom. I went next, sliding down the rope, and Worsley, who was the lightest and nimblest of us, followed. At the bottom of the fall we again stood on dry land.

The rope could not be recovered. We had flung down the adze from the top of the fall, and also the log-book wrapped in one of our blouses. That was all we brought, except our wet clothes, from the Antarctic, which a year and a half before we had entered with well-found ship, full equipment and high hopes. That was all of tangible things; but in memories we were rich. We had pierced the veneer of outside things. We had seen God in His splendours, we had heard the text that Nature renders. We had reached the naked soul of man.

Shivering with cold, yet with hearts light and happy, we set off towards the whaling station, now not more than a mile and a half distant. The difficulties of the journey lay behind us. The thought that there might be women at the station made us painfully conscious of our uncivilised appearance, and we tried to straighten ourselves out a bit. Our beards were long and our hair was matted. We were unwashed, and the garments which we had worn for nearly a year without a change were tattered and stained. Three more unpleasant-looking ruffians could scarcely be imagined. Worsley produced several safety-pins from some corner of his garments, and made some temporary repairs which really emphasised his disrepair.

Down we hurried, and when quite close to the station we met two small boys ten or twelve years old. I asked them where the manager's house was, and they did not answer. They gave us one most informing look and then they ran from us as fast as their legs would carry them.

We reached the outskirts of the station and passed through the 'digesting house', which was dark inside. Emerging at the other end we met an old man who gave us no time to ask any question. He hurried away. This greeting was not friendly. Then we came to the wharf, where the man in charge stuck to his station. I asked him if Mr Sorlle (the manager) was in the house.

'Yes,' he said as he stared at us.

'We would like to see him,' said I.

'Who are you?' he asked.

'We have lost our ship and come over the island,' I replied.

'You have come over the island?' he said, in a tone of entire disbelief.

Then he went towards the manager's house and we followed him. I learned afterwards that he said to Mr Sorlle: 'There are three funny-looking men outside, who say they have come over the island and they know you. I have left them outside.' A very necessary precaution from his point of view.

Mr Sorlle came out to the door and said: 'Well?'

'Don't you know me?' I said.

'I know your voice,' he replied doubtfully. 'You're the mate of the *Daisy*.'

'My name is Shackleton,' I said.

Immediately he put out his hand and said, 'Come in. Come in.'

'Tell me, when was the war over?' I asked.

'The war is not over,' he answered. 'Millions are being killed. Europe is mad. The world is mad.'

Mr Sorlle's hospitality had no bounds. He would scarcely let us wait to remove our freezing boots before he took us into his house, and gave us seats in a warm and comfortable room. We were not fit to sit in any one's house until we had washed and put on clean clothes, but the kindness of the station manager was proof even against the unpleasantness of being in a room with us. He gave us coffee and cakes in the Norwegian fashion, and then showed us upstairs to the bathroom, where we shed our rags and scrubbed ourselves luxuriously.

Mr Sorlle's kindness did not end with his personal care to us. While we were washing he gave orders for one of the whaling vessels to be prepared at once, so that it might leave that night to pick up the other three men on the other side of the island. Soon we were clean again, and then we put on delightful new clothes supplied from the station stores and got rid of our superfluous hair. Then came a splendid meal, while Mr Sorlle told us the arrangements he had made, and we discussed plans for the rescue of the main party on Elephant Island.

I arranged that Worsley should go with the relief ship to show the exact spot where the carpenter and his two companions were camped, while I began to prepare for the relief of the party on Elephant Island. The whaling vessel that was going round to King Haakon Bay was expected back on the Monday morning, and was to call at Grytviken Harbour, the port from which we had sailed in December, 1914, in order that the magistrate resident there might be informed of the fate of the *Endurance*. It was also possible that letters were awaiting us there.

Worsley went aboard the whaler at ten o'clock that night; and on the next day the relief ship entered King Haakon Bay and Worsley reached Peggotty Camp in a boat. The three men were delighted beyond measure to be relieved, but they did not recognise Worsley, who had left them a hairy, dirty ruffian and had returned spruce and shaven.

Within a few minutes the whalers had moved our bits of gear into their boat. They towed off the *James Caird*, and, having hoisted her to the deck of their ship, they started on the return voyage. They entered Stromness Bay at dusk on Monday afternoon, and the men of the whaling station mustered on the beach to receive the rescued party, and also to examine the boat which we had navigated across 800 miles of the stormy ocean they knew so well.

When I look back at those days I do not doubt that Providence guided us, not only across those snowfields, but also across the stormy white sea which separated Elephant Island from our landing place on South Georgia. I know that during that long march of thirty-six hours over the unnamed mountains and glaciers of South Georgia it often seemed to me that we were four, not three. And Worsley and Crean had the same idea. One feels 'the dearth of human words, the roughness of mortal speech,' in trying to describe intangible things, but a record of our journeys would be incomplete without reference to a subject very near to our hearts.

THE RESCUE

Our first night at the whaling station was blissful. Crean and I shared a beautiful bedroom in Mr Sorlle's house, and we were so comfortable that we could not sleep. Outside a dense snow-storm, which started two hours after our arrival and lasted until the following day, was swirling about the mountain-slopes. It would have gone hard with us had we still been on the mountains, and we were thankful indeed to be in a place of safety. Deep snow lay everywhere on the following morning.

After breakfast Mr Sorlle took us round to Husvik in a motor launch. Avidly we listened to his account of the war. We were like men arisen from the dead to a world gone mad, and it took our minds some time to accustom themselves to the tales of nations in arms, of deathless courage and unimagined slaughter. The reader may not realise quite how difficult it was for us to envisage nearly two years of the most stupendous war of history. I suppose our experience was unique. No other civilised men could have been as blankly ignorant of world-shaking events as we were when we reached Stromness Whaling Station.

When we reached Husvik on that Sunday morning we were warmly greeted by the magistrate (Mr Bernsten), who was an old friend of mine, and by the other members of the little community. Moored in the harbour was one of the largest of the whalers, the *Southern Sky*, owned by an English company, but now laid up for the winter. I had no means of communicating immediately with the owners, but, on my accepting all responsibility, Mr Bernsten made arrangements for me to take this ship down to Elephant Island. I wrote out an agreement with Lloyd's for the insurance of the ship. There was no difficulty in getting a crew, for the whalers were eager to assist in the rescue of the men in distress. There is a brotherhood of the sea. The men who go down to the sea in ships, serving and suffering, bring into their own horizons the perils of their brother sailormen.

At 9 a.m. on Tuesday morning the *Southern Sky* steamed out of the bay, while the whistles of the whaling station sounded a friendly farewell.

On the third night out the sea seemed to grow silent. The sea was freezing around us, and presently lumps of old pack began to appear among the new ice. I realised that an advance through pack-ice was out of the question. The *Southern Sky* was a steel-built steamer and could not endure the blows of masses of ice.

To admit failure at this stage was hard, but facts had to be faced. The *Southern Sky* could not enter ice of even moderate thickness, the season was late, and we could not be sure that the ice would open for many months. The *Southern Sky* could only carry coal for ten days, and we had been out six days. We were 500 miles from the Falkland Islands and about 600 miles from South Georgia. So I determined that I would go to the Falklands, get a more suitable vessel either locally or from England, and make a second attempt to reach Elephant Island from that point.

We reached Port Stanley on August 8th, and I learned that the ship *Discovery* was to leave England at once, and would reach the Falkland Islands about the middle of September. My good friend the Governor said that I could settle down at Port Stanley, and take things easily for a few weeks. But I could not be content to wait for six or seven weeks, knowing that 600 miles away my comrades were in desperate need. So I asked the Chilean Government to send the *Yelcho* to take the schooner across to Punta Arenas, and they consented promptly, as they had to all my requests. So in a north-west gale we went across, narrowly escaping disaster on the way, and reached Punta Arenas on August 14th.

No suitable ship could be obtained, but the weather was improving, and I begged the Chilean Government to let me have the *Yelcho* for a last attempt to reach the island. A small steel-built steamer, she was quite unsuitable for work in the pack, but I promised not to touch the ice. The Government gave me another chance, and on August 25th I started south for the fourth attempt at relief.

This time Providence favoured us. I found as we neared Elephant Island that the ice was open. A southerly gale had sent it northward temporarily, and the *Yelcho* had her chance to slip through. We approached the island in a thick fog, but I did not dare to wait for this to clear. At 10 a.m. on August 30th we passed some stranded bergs, then we saw the sea breaking on a reef, and I knew that we were just outside the island.

It was an anxious moment, for we had still to locate the camp and the pack could not be trusted to allow time for a prolonged search; but presently the fog lifted and revealed the cliffs and glaciers of Elephant Island. I proceeded to the east, and at 11.40 a.m. Worsley's keen eyes detected the camp, almost invisible under its covering of snow. The men ashore saw us at the same time, and we saw tiny black figures hurry to the beach and wave signals to us. We were about a mile and a half away from the camp.

I turned the *Yelcho* in, and within half an hour reached the beach with Crean and some of the Chilean sailors. I saw a little figure on a surf-beaten rock and recognised Wild. As I came nearer I called out, 'Are you all well?' and he answered, 'We are all well, Boss,' and then I heard three cheers.

As I drew close to the rock I flung packs of cigarettes ashore; they fell on them like hungry tigers, for well I knew that for months tobacco had been dreamed and talked about. Some of the hands were in a rather bad way, but Wild had kept hope alive in their hearts. There was no time then to exchange news or congratulations. I did not even go up the beach to see the camp, which Wild assured me had been much improved.

A heavy sea was running, and a change of wind might bring the ice back at any time. I hurried the party aboard with all possible speed, taking also the records of the Expedition and the essential portions of equipment. Everybody was aboard within an hour, and we steamed north at the *Yelcho*'s best speed. The ice was still open, and nothing worse than an expanse of stormy ocean separated us from the South American coast.

We entered the Straits of Magellan on September 3rd and

reached Rio Secco at 8 p.m. Two or three hours later we were at Punta Arenas, where we were given a welcome which we shall never forget. The Chilean people were no less enthusiastic than the British residents. The whole populace appeared to be in the streets. It was a great reception, and after the long, anxious months of strain we were in a mood to enjoy it.

During the next few weeks I received congratulations and messages of friendship from all over the world, and my heart went out to the good people who had remembered us in the press of terrible events on the battlefields.

ELEPHANT ISLAND

I have obtained an account of the experiences of the twenty-two men left behind on Elephant Island from their various diaries, supplemented by details obtained in conversation on the voyage back to civilisation.

The first consideration, even more important than that of food, was to provide shelter, for several of the men were suffering severely from the ordeals through which they had passed. Rickenson, who bore up gamely to the last, collapsed from heart failure; Blackborrow and Hudson could not move. All were frost-bitten in varying degrees.

The blizzard which sprang up on the day we landed at Cape Wild lasted for a fortnight; the tents, with the exception of the square tent occupied by Hurley, James and Hudson, were torn to ribbons. Sleeping bags and clothes were wringing wet, and the physical discomforts tended to produce acute mental depression. The two remaining boats had been turned upside down with one gunwale resting on the snow, and the other raised about two feet on rocks and cases, and under these the sailors, the invalids and some of the scientists at least found head-cover.

Shelter and warmth to dry their clothes was imperative, so Wild, who was left in command and in whom I had absolute confidence, hastened the excavation of the ice-cave in the slope, which had been started before I had left.

The high temperature, however, caused a continuous stream of water to drip from the roof and sides of the ice-cave, so Wild directed that big flat stones should be collected, and with these, two substantial walls, 4 feet high and 19 feet apart, were made.

'We are all ridiculously weak. Stones that we could easily have lifted at other times we found quite beyond our capacity, and it needed two or three of us to carry some that would otherwise have been one man's load.

'The site chosen for the hut was where the stove had been erected on the night of our arrival. It lay between two large boulders, which at least provided valuable protection from the wind, and further protection was provided to the north by Penguin Hill. As soon as the walls were completed and squared off, the two boats were laid upside down on them side by side. Their exact adjustment took some time, but was of paramount importance if our structure was to be the permanent affair we hoped it would be. Once in place they were securely chocked up and lashed down to the rocks. The few pieces of wood that we had were laid across from keel to keel, and over this the material of one of the torn tents was spread and secured with guys to the rocks. The walls were ingeniously contrived and fixed up by Marston.

'At last all was completed and we were invited to bring in our sodden bags, which had been lying out in the drizzling rain for hours; for the tents and boats that had previously sheltered them had all been requisitioned to form our new residence. We took our places under Wild's direction. There was no squabbling for best places, but it was noticeable that there was rather a rush for the billets up on the thwarts of the boat. Rickenson, who was still very weak and ill, but very cheery, obtained a place in the boat directly above the stove.'

The floor was at first covered with snow and ice, frozen in among the pebbles, but this was cleared out, and the remainder of the tents spread out over the stones. Within the shelter of these cramped, but comparatively palatial, quarters, cheerfulness once more reigned among the party. Subsequently, when fine drift-snow forced its way through the crevices between the stones forming the end walls, Jaeger sleeping-bags and coats were spread over the outside of these walls, packed over with snow and securely frozen up, and they effectively kept out the drift.

At first all the cooking was done outside under the lee of some rocks, further protection being provided by a wall of provision cases. There were two blubber-stoves made from old oil-drums, and one day, when the blizzard was unusually severe, an attempt was made to cook inside the hut. Pungent blubber-smoke, however, was the result of the first attempt, but a chimney, made by Kerr out of the tin lining of one of the biscuit cases, was soon fitted, and the smoke nuisance inside the hut was a thing of the past.

The cook and his assistant, which latter job was taken by each man in turn, were called about 7 a.m., and breakfast was generally ready about 10 a.m. Provision cases were then arranged in a wide circle round the stove, and those fortunate enough to be next it could dry their gear. So that all should benefit equally each man occupied his place at meal times for one day only, and moved up one on the succeeding day.

The great trouble in the hut was the absence of light. The canvas walls were covered with blubber-soot, and, with the snow-drifts accumulating round the hut, its inhabitants lived in a state of perpetual night. Wild was the first to overcome this difficulty by sewing the glass lid of a chronometer box into the canvas wall. Later on three other windows were added, and this enabled those men who were near enough to them to read and sew, which considerably relieved the monotony of the situation.

'Our reading material at this time consisted of two books of poetry, one book of *Nordenskjöld's Expedition*, one or two torn volumes of the *Encyclopaedia Britannica*, and a penny cookery book, owned by Marston. Our clothes . . . had to be continually patched to keep them together.'

The floor of the hut, having been raised by the addition of loads of clean pebbles, kept fairly dry during the cold weather, but when the temperature rose to just above freezing point the hut became the drainage-pool of all the surrounding hills. Wild noticed it first, when he found one morning that his sleeping-bag was practically afloat. Other men examined theirs with a like result, so bailing operations began forthwith. Hundreds of gallons of water had to be bailed out from the large hole which was dug in the floor. Eventually this watery problem was completely solved by removing a portion of one wall and digging a long channel nearly down to the sea.

A huge glacier across the bay behind the hut nearly put an end to the party. Enormous blocks of ice would break off and fall into the sea, the disturbance giving rise to great waves. One day Marston was outside the hut when a noise 'like an artillery barrage' startled him. Looking up, he saw a tremendous wave, over 30 feet high, advancing rapidly across the bay, and threatening to sweep both the hut and its inhabitants into the sea. Fortunately, however, the loose ice which filled the bay damped the wave down so much that, though it flowed right under the hut, nothing was carried away. But it was a narrow escape, as nothing could have saved the men had they been washed into the sea.

Although they themselves gradually became accustomed to the darkness and dirt, extracts from their diaries show that they could still realise the conditions under which they were living.

'The hut grows more grimy every day. Everything is sooty black. It is at least comforting to feel that we can become no filthier. Our shingle floor will scarcely bear examination by strong light without causing even us to shudder and express our disapprobation at its state. Such is our Home, Sweet Home.'

'All joints are aching through being compelled to lie on the hard, rubbly floor which forms our bedsteads.'

'Thank heaven man is an adaptable brute! If we dwell sufficiently long in this hut we are likely to alter our method of walking, for our ceiling, which is but 4 feet 6 inches high at its highest part, compels us to walk bent double or on all fours.'

'We are as regardless of our grime and dirt as is the Esquimau. We have been unable to wash since we left the ship, nearly ten months ago. For one thing we have no soap or towels; and, again, had we possessed these articles, our supply of fuel would only permit us to melt enough ice for drinking purposes. Had one washed, half a dozen others would have to go without a drink all day. One cannot suck ice to relieve the thirst, as it cracks the lips and blisters the tongue. Still, we are all very cheerful.'

During the whole of their stay on Elephant Island the weather was described by Wild as 'simple appalling'. On most days the air was full of snow-drift blown from the adjacent heights. On April 25th, the day after I left for South Georgia, the island was beset by heavy pack-ice, with snow and a wet mist. April ended with a terrific wind-storm which nearly destroyed the hut. This lasted well into May, and a typical May day is thus described: 'A day of terrific winds, threatening to dislodge our shelter. The wind is a succession of hurricane gusts that sweep down the glacier. Each gust heralds its approach by a low rumbling which increases to a thunderous roar. Snow, stones and gravel are flying about, and any gear left unweighted by very heavy stones is carried away to sea.'

Heavy bales of sennegrass and boxes of cooking-gear were lifted bodily in the air and carried away out of sight. These gusts often came without any warning, and on one occasion Hussey, who was outside digging up the day's meat, which had frozen to the ground, was very nearly blown into the sea. On rare occasions there were fine, calm, clear days, when the glow of the dying sun on the mountains and glaciers was incomparably beautiful.

About the middle of May a terrific blizzard sprang up, and Wild entertained grave fears for their hut. In this blizzard huge ice-sheets, as big as window-panes and about a quarter of an inch thick, were hurled about by the wind, making it as dangerous to walk about outside as if one were in an avalanche of splintered glass. Still, these winds from the south and south-west, though invariably accompanied by snow and low temperatures, were welcome, because they drove the pack-ice from the island, and so on each occasion gave rise to hopes of relief. North-east winds, on the other hand, filled the bay with ice, and made it impossible for any ship to approach the island.

Thus the weather continued, alternating between the south-west blizzards, when all hands were confined to the hut, and north-east winds which brought cold, damp, misty weather. Towards the end of July and beginning of August there were a few fine, calm days. Occasional glimpses of the sun were seen after the south-west winds had blown all the ice away, and the party, their spirits raised by Wild's unfailing optimism, again began to look eagerly for the rescue ship.

Unfortunately, however, the first three attempts to relieve the party coincided with the times when the island was beset by ice. From August 16th to August 27th the island was surrounded by pack-ice, but on the latter day a strong south-west wind drove all this ice from the bay, and, except for some stranded bergs, left a clear ice-free sea through which we finally made our way to Elephant Island.

Midwinter's Day, the great Polar festival, was duly observed. A 'magnificent breakfast' of sledging ration hoosh, full strength, and well boiled to thicken it, with hot milk, was served. Luncheon consisted of a wonderful pudding, invented by Wild, and made of powdered biscuit boiled with twelve pieces of mouldy nut-food. Supper was a very finely-cut seal hoosh flavoured with sugar. After supper they had a concert, accompanied by Hussey on his 'indispensable banjo'. The banjo was the last thing saved from the ship before she sank, and it was landed on Elephant Island practically unharmed, and did much to cheer the men. Nearly every Saturday night a concert was held.

The cook, who had carried on so well and for so long, was given a rest on August 9th, and as the cook and his 'mate' had the privilege of scraping out the saucepans there was anxiety to secure the job. Food was getting terribly short, for the penguins and seals, which had migrated at the beginning of winter, had not yet returned, and old seal bones, which had been once used for a meal and thrown away, were dug up and stewed down with sea-water. Penguin carcasses were likewise treated. One man wrote in his diary: 'We had a sumptuous meal today – nearly five ounces of solid food each'. No wonder, under the circumstances, that the thoughts and conversation of the party should turn to food.

It was largely due to Wild, and to his energy and resource, that the party kept cheerful all along, and, indeed, came out alive and so well. Assisted by the two surgeons, Drs McIlroy and Macklin, he kept a watchful eye on the health of each man. His cheery optimism never failed, and each man in his diary speaks with admiration of him. I think without doubt that all the stranded party owe their lives to him. He more than justified the absolute confidence which I placed in him. Hussey, with his cheeriness and banjo, was another vital factor in chasing away symptoms of depression.

Once settled in the hut, the health of the party was, under the conditions, quite good. Every one, of course, was rather weak, some were light-headed, all were frost-bitten, and others, later, had attacks of heart failure. Blackborrow, whose toes were so badly frost-bitten in the boats, had to have all five amputated while on the island. That this operation, under the most difficult conditions, was very successful, speaks volumes for the skill and initiative of the surgeons. Hudson, who developed bronchitis and hip disease, was practially well when relief came. All the men were naturally weak when rescued, but all, thanks to Frank Wild, were alive and very cheerful.

August 30th, 1916, is described in their diaries as a 'day of wonders'. Food was very short, only two days' seal and penguin meat being left, and there was no prospect of any more. The whole party had been collecting limpets and seaweed to eat with the stewed seal bones. Lunch was being served by Wild; Hurley and Marston were waiting outside to take a last look at the direction from which they expected the ship to come.

From a fortnight after I had left, Wild had rolled up his sleeping-bag each day with the remark: 'Get your things ready, boys, the Boss may come today.' And sure enough, one day, the mist opened and revealed the ship for which they had been waiting and longing for over four months.

'Marston was the first to notice it, and immediately yelled out "Ship O!" Those in the hut mistook it for a call of "Lunch O!" so took no notice at first. Soon, however, we heard him pattering along the snow as fast as he could run, and, in a gasping voice, hoarse with excitement, he shouted: "Wild, there's a ship! Hadn't we better light a flare?" We all made one dive for our narrow door. Those who could not get through tore down the canvas walls in their hurry and excitement. The hoosh-pot, with our precious limpets and seaweed, was kicked out in the rush. There, just rounding the island which had previously hidden her from our sight, we saw a little ship flying the Chilean flag.

'We tried to cheer, but excitement had gripped our vocal cords. Macklin had made a rush for the flagstaff, previously placed in the most conspicuous position on the ice-slope. The running-gear would not work, and the flag was frozen into a sold mass, so he tied his jersey to the top of the pole for a signal.

'Wild put a pick through our last remaining tin of petrol, and, soaking coats, mitts and socks with it, carried them to the top of Penguin Hill, and soon they were ablaze.

'Meanwhile, most of us were on the foreshore watching anxiously for any signs that the ship had seen us, or for any answering signals. As we stood and gazed she seemed to turn away as if she had not seen us. Again and again we cheered, though our feeble cries could certainly not have carried so far. Suddenly she stopped, a boat was lowered, and we could recognise Sir Ernest's figure as he climbed down the ladder. Simultaneously we burst into a cheer, and then one said to the other, "Thank God, the Boss is safe". For I think that his safety was of more concern to us than our own.

'Soon the boat was near enough for the Boss, who was standing up in the bows, to shout to Wild: "Are you all well?" To which he replied: "All safe, all well," and we could see a smile light up the Boss's face as he said, "Thank God".

'Before he could land he threw ashore handfuls of cigarettes and tobacco, and these the smokers, who for two months had been trying to find solace in such substitutes as seaweed, finely chopped pipe-bowls, seal meat, and sennegrass, grasped greedily.

'Blackborrow, who could not walk, had been carried to a high rock and propped up in his sleeping-bag, so that he could view the wonderful scene.

'Soon we were tumbling into the boat, and the Chilean sailors, laughing up at us, seemed as pleased at our rescue as we were. Twice more the boat returned, and within an hour of our first having sighted the boat we were heading northwards to the outer world, from which we had had no news for over twenty-two months.

'We were like men awakened from a long sleep. We are trying to acquire suddenly the perspective which the rest of the world has acquired gradually through two years of war.

'Our first meal, owing to our weakness, proved disastrous to many of us, but we soon recovered. Our beds were shake-downs on cushions and settees, but I think we got very little sleep. It was just heavenly to lie and listen to the throb of the engines, instead of to the crack of the breaking floe, or the howling of the blizzard.

'We intend to keep August 30th as a festival for the rest of our lives.'

You can imagine my feelings, as I stood in the little cabin watching my rescued comrades eating the first good meal which had been offered to them for many, many months.

THE FINAL PHASE

The foregoing chapters of this book represent the general narrative of our Expedition. That we failed to accomplish the object we set out for was due, I consider, not to any neglect or lack of organisation, but to the overwhelming natural obstacles, especially the unprecedented severe summer conditions on the Weddell Sea side. But, though the Expedition failed in one respect, it was, I think, successful in many others. A large amount of important scientific work was carried out; the meteorological observations in particular have an economic bearing. The hydrographical work in the Weddell Sea has done much to clear up the mystery of this, the least known of all the seas.

To the credit side of the Expedition one can safely say that the comradeship and resource of the members of the Expedition was worthy of the highest traditions of Polar service; and it was a privilege to me to have under my command men who, through dark days and the stress and strain of continuous danger, kept up their spirits and carried out their work regardless of themselves and heedless of the limelight.

The same energy and endurance which they showed in the Antarctic they brought to the Greater War in the Old World. And having followed our fortunes in the South it may interest you to know that practically every member of the Expedition was employed in one or other branches of the active fighting forces during the war. Of the fifty-three men who returned out of the fifty-six who left for the South, three have since been killed and five wounded. McCarthy, the best and most efficient of the sailors, always cheerful under the most trying circumstances, and who for these reasons I chose to accompany me on the boat journey to South Georgia, was killed at his gun in the Channel. Cheetham, the veteran of the Antarctic, who had been more often south of the Antarctic Circle than any man, was drowned when the vessel in which he was serving was torpedoed a few weeks before the Armistice.

Ernest Wild, Frank Wild's brother, was killed while mine-sweeping in the Mediterranean. Manger, the carpenter on the *Aurora*, was badly wounded while serving with the New Zealand Infantry. The two surgeons, Macklin and McIlroy, served in France and Italy, McIlroy being badly wounded at Ypres. Frank Wild, in view of his unique experience of ice and ice conditions, was at once sent to the North Russian front, where his zeal and ability won him the highest praise. Macklin served first with the Yorks and later transferred as medical officer to the Tanks, where he did much good work. Going to the Italian front with his battalion, he won the Military Cross for bravery in tending wounded under fire.

James joined the Royal Engineers, Sound-Ranging Section, and after much front-line work was given charge of a Sound-Ranging School to teach other officers this latest and most scientific addition to the art of war. Wordie went to France with the Royal Field Artillery and was badly wounded at Armentières.

Hussey was in France for eighteen months with the Royal Garrison Artillery, serving in every big battle from Dixmude to Saint-Quentin. Worsley, known to his intimates as Depth-Charge Bill, owing to his success with that particular method of destroying German submarines, has the D.S.O. and three submarines to his credit.

Stenhouse was with Worsley as his second in command when one of the German submarines was rammed and sunk, and received the D.S.C. for his share in the fight. He was afterwards given command of a Mystery Ship, and fought several actions with enemy submarines.

Clark served on a mine-sweeper. Greenstreet was employed with the barges on the Tigris. Rickenson was commissioned as Engineer-Lieutenant, R.N. Kerr returned to the Merchant Service as an engineer.

Most of the crew of the *Endurance* served on mine-sweepers.

Of the Ross Sea Party, Mackintosh, Hayward and Spencer-Smith died for their country as surely as those who gave up their lives in France or Flanders. Hooke, the wireless operator, became navigator of an airship.

Nearly all the crew of the *Aurora* joined the New Zealand Field Forces and saw active service in one of the many theatres of war.

Four decorations have been won, and several members of the

Expedition have been mentioned in dispatches.

On my return, after the rescue of the survivors of the Ross Sea Party, I offered my services to the Government, and was sent on a mission to South America. When this was concluded I was commissioned as Major and went to North Russia in charge of Arctic Equipment and Transport, having with me Worsley, Stenhouse, Hussey, Macklin and Brocklehurst, who was to have come South with us, but who, as a regular officer, rejoined his unit on the outbreak of war.

Worsley was sent across to the Archangel front, where he did excellent work, and the others served with me on the Murmansk front. The mobile columns there had exactly the same clothing, equipment and sledging food as we had on the Expedition. No expense was spared to get the best of everything for them, and consequently not a single case of avoidable frost-bite was reported.

Taking the Expedition as a unit, out of fifty-six men, three died in the Antarctic, three were killed in action and five have been wounded, so that our casualties have been fairly high.

Though some have gone, there are enough left to rally round and form a nucleus for the next Expedition; when troublous times are over and scientific exploration can once more be legitimately undertaken.

AFTERWORD

by Christopher Ralling

Concern for his men was always Shackleton's guiding principle; and it must have touched him deeply that three of those not under his immediate command should have lost their lives in the Ross Sea area. But no one knew better than he how close they had been to a much greater disaster.

When he and his two companions had stood on that lonely ridge in South Georgia and decided to launch themselves into the unknown depths beneath on a coil of rope, they still held the key to the whereabouts of all the men who were then widely scattered throughout the Antarctic region. If that coil of rope had taken them over a precipice or straight into the waiting jaws of a crevasse, it is just possible that the other survivors of the boat journey, McNeish, Vincent and McCarthy, even in their weakened state, might have launched the *James Caird* once more and groped their way round the coast of the island to a whaling station. But if they had failed, the situation of the men on Elephant Island would have been almost hopeless. No one would have come looking for them because no one would have had the slightest reason to believe they were there.

It is true Shackleton had left instructions that if he did not return, another boat crew was to try and reach Deception Island to the West where there were thought to be stores for shipwrecked sailors trying to round the Horn. But such a journey would have been against the prevailing wind and current, and undertaken in a boat even less suitable for the task than the *James Caird*.

If that attempt had failed, the remaining men would have had no choice but to live out their lives among those bleak and inhospitable islands, totally cut off from a world which would, long since, have presumed them dead. The fate of Shackleton and his men would have remained as great a mystery as that of Sir John Franklin, who disappeared with his entire ship's crew while trying to solve the mysteries of the North West Passage.

Proud though he was of rescuing his men, Shackleton was realistic enough to grasp that in terms of what he set out to achieve, the *Endurance* expedition had been a total failure. He had seen a possible landing place just once on his journey South through the Weddell Sea, and failed to take the chance which was offered. As a result he did not even start on the primary purpose of the expedition, which was to make the first crossing of the Antarctic continent.

In the light of this, the overwhelming reception he received in Chile after he had rescued his men seems to have taken him by surprise. As he put it in a letter to his wife it was 'as if I had made a triumph instead of the Expedition having failed'. The truth was that, in spite of his fame, he still felt a nagging sense of unfulfilment; and would do so for the rest of his life.

There was to be one more grand attempt at polar exploration in the five years that remained to him. But before another such venture could even be contemplated, there was the all-pervading prospect of the War. For two years the nations had been locked in appalling struggle; which Shackleton and his men had known nothing about. They were determined to make up for their absence now.

To men who had endured the trenches of Flanders and the beaches of Gallipoli, Shackleton's somewhat naive and un-tempered patriotism may have rung a little false. But he was not to be stopped. In March 1917, on his way back from relieving the Ross Sea party, he paused in Sydney long enough to deliver a rousing speech to the Australian nation:

To you men and women of Australia I have something to say. I come from a land where there are no politics and no clashing of personal interest. For nearly two years I heard nothing and knew nothing of what was happening in the civilised lands. Then I came back to a world darkened by desperate strife, and as people told me of what had happened during those two years I realised one great thing, and that was this:

To take your part in this war is not a matter merely of patriotism, not a matter merely of duty or of expediency; it is a matter of the saving of a man's soul and of a man's own opinion of himself.

We lived long dark days in the South. The danger of the moment is a thing easy to meet, and the courage of the moment is in every man at some time. But I want to say to you that we lived through slow dead days of toil, of struggle, dark striving and anxiety; days that called not for heroism in the bright light of day, but simply for dogged persistent endeavour to do what the soul said was right. It is in that same spirit that we men of the British race have to face this war. What does the war mean to Australia? Everything. It means as much to you as though the enemy was actually beating down your gate. This summons to fight is a call imperative to the manhood within you.

Death is a very little thing – the smallest thing in the world. I can tell you that, for I have been face to face with death during long months. I know that death scarcely weighs in the scale against a man's appointed task. Perhaps in the quiet hours of night, when you think over what I have said, you will feel the little snakes of doubt twisting in your heart. I have known them. Put them aside. If we have to die, we will die in the pride of manhood, our eyes on the goal and our hearts beating time to the instinct within us.

For this call to fight means to men more than ease, more than money, more than love of women, more even than duty; it means the chance to prove ourselves the captains of our own souls.

Sensing that he might have more to offer the allied cause as a propagandist than a naval officer, the Government decided to send Shackleton back to South America, where he had already demonstrated his popularity, with a loose brief to assist the British Information services. It can hardly have been the sort of job he would have chosen, but he carried it out conscientiously and well, doing what he could to counteract German influence in the area.

But his final wartime job must have been considerably more congenial. In August 1918, he was given the task of taking charge of all the winter equipment for the North Russian expedition. The work was not so very different from planning a polar expedition, and it would take him to the sort of latitudes in which he thrived. The main base for the operation was Murmansk.

Lenin had overthrown Kerensky's Government nine months before, but there is nothing in Shackleton's letters to suggest, either that he was interested in, or had any real understanding of the momentous events that were taking place in Russia at that time. Before long he had surrounded himself with old chums, Macklin, Hussey and Worsley among them; and the thoughts and plans that they had for the future were all to do with developing the resources of that bleak region, and thus making those elusive fortunes that they had so endlessly discussed during the long days and nights marooned in the pack-ice of the Weddell Sea.

In the end it all came to nothing, but not before Shackleton had tried very hard to set up his own company and secure concessions from the Russian Government to explore the area with a view to commercial exploitation. With hindsight, it would be hard to think of a scheme less calculated to appeal to the men who were forging the Russian Revolution.

With the war over, all his old restlessness returned. In a letter to Emily he wrote:

> Sometimes I think I am no good at anything but being away in the wilds just with men and sometimes I grow restless and feel any part of youth is slipping away from me and that nothing matters. I want to upset everybody's calm and peace of mind when I meet calm and contented people. I feel I am no use to anyone unless I am outfacing the storm in wild lands. I think you are a wonderful girl and woman to have stood my erratic ways all these years; I think you understand me more than all the people I know put together.

If she had been hoping that, at last, he might be ready for a settled domestic life, she must have known then that it was never to be.

Now Shackleton stood on the brink of his last adventure. If the coast of Russia was closed to him, there still remained the great archipelago to the north of the Canadian mainland, and to the west of it, the Beaufort Sea. In that vast region there were plenty of geographical mysteries still to be solved; perhaps even tribes of eskimos untouched by contact with the rest of the world.

He first put his plan to the Royal Geographical Society in Feburary 1920. Within weeks he had a wealthy backer, an old school friend named John Quiller Rowett, and a ship in mind called the *Goshawk*, for which Emily suggested a new name; the *Quest*. Better still, many of his most tried and trusted old shipmates began flocking to the colours. Worsley, Wild, McIlroy, Macklin, even Green the cook, were all ready to sign on once more, and follow wherever Shackleton led them, even to another Elephant Island. There could hardly have been a better demonstration of the depths of loyalty he inspired in those who truly knew and understood him.

The destination seemed almost secondary. Indeed it proved to be when an incoming Canadian government had second thoughts about contributing funds to the expedition. Shackleton simply transferred his gaze to the South. A new set of objectives was somewhat hastily drawn up. John Rowett was persuaded to put up additional funds; and for the fourth time in his life, Shackleton found himself bound for his spiritual home, 'the birthplace of the clouds and the nesting place of the four winds'; the Antarctic.

The *Quest* sailed from London on September 17th, 1921. Shackleton was forty-seven years old, with just a few more months to live. If he had any inkling of how ill he was, there is no hint of it in his diary which is full of the familiar mixture of romance and practicality:

> At last we are off. The last of the cheering crowded boats have turned, the syrens of shore and sea are still, and in the calm hazy gathering dusk on a glassy sea we move on the long Quest. Providence is with us even now. At this time of Equinoctial gales not a catspaw of wind is apparent. I turn from the glooming mystic immensity of the sea, and looking at the decks of the *Quest*, am roused from dreams of what may be in the future to the needs of the moment, for in no way are we shipshape, or fitted to ignore even the mildest storm. Deep in the water; decks littered with stores; our very lifeboats receptacles for sliced bacon and green vegetables . . . ; steel ropes and hempen brothers jostle each other; mysterious gadgets connected with the wireless on which the Admiralty officials were working up to the sailing hour are scattered about. But our willing twenty one hands will soon snug her down.

Much more time would be spent aboard ship than on his previous expeditions. The detailed plans included the charting of the Antarctic coastline, a search for economic commodities like tungsten, wolfram and even deposits of guano, a survey of possible sites for future meteorological or whaling stations, and even contacts with the inhabitants of the South Pacific Islands with a view to mutual trade. There was no single objective like the South Pole or the crossing of the Continent. It was more a case of anything and everything which came into Shackleton's head.

It was all the more alarming therefore, when the *Quest* began to show signs of failing to live up to her promise. On the journey to Rio, she had failed to average the eight knots she was supposed to be capable of. As Shackleton wrote in his diary:

> She evidently must be treated as a five-knot vessel dependent mainly on fair winds, and all this is giving me much food for thought.

Before continuing to South Georgia the engines were completely stripped down. But even so their condition remained far from satisfactory. In truth, she was not in a fit state to enter the most dangerous waters in the world; and neither was Shackleton. In letters to his wife he admitted:

> I am not very well but I think in a couple of days will be my old self.

And a few days later:

> This cannot be a long letter for I am just tired and hot. I have been in a whirl and strain ever since we came in. Everything seemed to go wrong. Twice the engines had to be altered; then I had trouble with some of the new men, and altogether it has been hell. Now it is 110° in the shade and the blasted mosquitoes are biting me.

A few days later, overcome by the heat on board, he had to be taken ashore. Shortly afterwards he collapsed. A heart attack was suspected and Macklin was immediately summoned. But Shackleton insisted it had merely been a fainting fit, brought on by the heat. Not only did he refuse to be examined but also made Macklin promise to play down the episode in front of the rest of the crew. It was December 17th, 1921. Next day the *Quest* set sail for South Georgia.

Almost at once they were struck by violent storms which lasted right through Christmas up to the New Year. Shackleton's cabin was flooded out, one of the fresh water tanks was found to have leaked dry, and most serious of all, a crack had been found in the furnace. There was nothing for it but to reduce speed drastically all the way to South Georgia.

Then with the coming of the New Year the storm abated. As the ship moved into calmer waters, so did Shackleton's mind. That evening in his diary, he quoted some lines from Browning:

> There are two points in the adventures of the diver . . .
>   one when a beggar he prepares to plunge
>   one when a prince he rises with his pearl.

Next morning, guarding the approaches to South Georgia, they sighted their first iceberg, Shackleton had come home.

It is difficult not to recall the image of the dying Arthur, surrounded by his faithful knights:

> The sequel of today unsolders all
> The goodliest fellowship of famous knights
> Whereof this world holds record. Such a sleep
> They sleep – the men I loved. I think that we
> Shall never more, at any future time,
> Delight our souls with talk of knightly deeds,
> Walking about the gardens and the halls
> Of Camelot, as in the days that were.
> I perish by this people which I made –
> Tho' Merlin swore that I should come again
> To rule once more – but let what will be, be;
> I am so deeply smitten thro' the helm
> That without help I cannot last till morn.

As the *Quest* passed along the coast, Shackleton stood on deck in the sunshine, recalling the scene of his past exploits. In the evening he played a few hands of cards; then retired to his bunk to write his diary before turning in:

At last after sixteen days of turmoil and anxiety, on a peaceful sunshiny day we came to anchor in Grytviken. How familiar the coast seemed as we passed down. We saw with full interest the places we struggled over after the boat journey. The old smell of dead whale permeates everything. It is a strange and curious place. A wonderful evening. 'In the darkening twilight I saw a lone star hover, gem-like above the bay.'

In the night he was woken by the onset of severe pain. He called for Macklin to give him some medicine to relieve it. While taking it, he suffered a very severe paroxysm during which he died. Macklin gave the cause of death as angina pectoris, or heart failure.

Shackleton's body was first taken to Uruguay, in preparation for a return to England. But Emily decided that his last resting place should be South Georgia. Perhaps she felt that, in some mysterious and instinctive way, he had gone there to die.

PICTURE CREDITS